KIN

JEAN RACINE: FOUR GREEK PLAYS

JEAN RACINE
FOUR GREEK PLAYS

**ANDROMACHE – IPHIGENIA
PHAEDRA – ATHALIAH**

Translated, with introduction and notes by

R.C. KNIGHT
Emeritus Professor of French
University College of Swansea

CAMBRIDGE UNIVERSITY PRESS

Cambridge

London   New York   New Rochelle

Melbourne   Sydney

Published by the Press Syndicate of the University of
Cambridge
The Pitt Building, Trumpington Street, Cambridge CB2 1RP
32 East 57th Street, New York, NY 10022, USA
296 Beaconsfield Parade, Middle Park, Melbourne 3206,
Australia

First published 1982

Printed in Great Britain
at the University Press, Cambridge

Library of Congress catalogue card number: 81–15537

British Library Cataloguing in Publication Data

Racine, Jean
Four Greek plays.
I. Title II. Knight, R.C.
842′.4   PQ1888.E5

ISBN 0 521 24415 3
ISBN 0 521 28676 X Pbk

CONTENTS

GENERAL INTRODUCTION

These four plays are among the greatest examples of what the French call (or have called) classical tragedy. Three have Greek backgrounds and (in varying measure) Greek sources; and the fourth, biblical in origin, has an affinity with Greek tragedy which, though a little less obvious, is the closest of all. While my choice of title was designed to suggest that this Greekness constitutes a sort of common ground between them, not shared with plays by Racine's contemporaries nor with the rest of his own, it must be admitted that they are not all Greek in the same way. Nor do I insist that their Greekness explains their greatness. It does however, I hope, offer a useful viewpoint for looking at the poet's art and its development, and at his unique position among playwrights of his time.

While Racine was writing, an old and influential literary tradition was at its last gasp — that part of Renaissance doctrine which had taught that all the arts could find themselves, and rise again, only by imitating the works and methods of classical antiquity; with freedom and originality, but in the spirit of admirers and learners. Instead, a new spirit was growing, of self-confidence and self-congratulation before the evidence of recent advances in scientific knowledge, technology, and also literature and art; a complacency far from groundless, but aided by a fading awareness of what had been the greatness of Greece and Rome. The 'Quarrel of the Ancients and Moderns' was a long succession of petty cavils and critical skirmishes: of the two pitched battles, in which the Ancients were defeated by their own pedantry and the ignorance of their opponents, one came late in Racine's life and the other after his death. He took his place among the Ancients, but inconspicuously, and no doubt never realised how much of a Modern he was in the nature of things.

For the drama in which he excelled (born of Renaissance imitations of the Latin tragedies of Seneca, with an admixture of the drama of love and adventure, inspired by the modern novel, and in France called tragi-comedy) is modern, and has few of the features or the beauties of Attic tragedy. It has great merits of its own, which redeem what the English reader tends to see as considerable constraints. Thus, rigid (but not quite complete) unity of tone forbad comic relief or colloquial language (though not simplicity and directness) to intrude into a fairly sustained nobility of tragic vocabulary and expression. An exalted sense of decorum, which would have seemed exaggerated in any less hierarchical society, excluded the sight of bloodshed, violence and crowd scenes, but led back at the same time to the realisation that drama resides much less in pageantry or any other visual appeal, than in great crises of emotion, shifts of emotion, clashes of wills (or ideas), crucial dilemmas and decisions. The cramping effect of the famous Unities of Time, Place and Action has often been over-stressed. The first two were born of a misconceived devotion to 'verisimilitude', taken to mean a hundred per cent illusion of reality in performance instead of the credibility of the story-line; their effect was to eliminate all plots but those which could be played out in a single place and a single burst of activity, based on a situation which had to be explained by, often, a great deal of reference to the past. But they were powerful aids to concentration and intensity; so, even more, was the strict Unity of Action, under which sub-plots were not excluded, but had to be very closely integrated. At the same time a new awareness of 'plot' developed the arts of climax and suspense.

Such was the dramatic form into which Racine infused a poetry and a sense of tragedy (we are still struggling to define those terms) which made his dozen years of writing the apogee of this utterly French genre. (He wrote nine tragedies for the Paris stage, 1664–77, then two in retirement, 1689 and 1691.) Meanwhile in his prefaces, which contain all the ideas he ever expressed on the art of tragedy, he wrote from the beginning as if all the merits of his plays had been due to a return to the examples of Sophocles and Euripides, and the lessons of Aristotle.

True, he had received an exceptionally good grounding in Greek. Yet once he escaped from the rather oppressive atmos-phere of his early years, he made every effort, as his letters and his first verse compositions make clear, to turn himself into a fashionable wit. His first play (1664), produced by Molière when Racine was twenty-four, looked as though he had decided this time to exploit his scholarly vein – it was called *La Thébaïde*; it portrayed the quarrel and the deaths of the two sons of Oedipus; it dwelt in several passages on the in-justice of the Gods and the inherited curse:

See the high justice of these mighty Gods –
They lead us to the very brink of crime,
Make us commit it, and will not forgive. (608ff.)

Yet the Greek appearance is partly illusory. There is a very human love-interest. The brothers think only of their human passions and interests. And Creon is a cynical traitor who stokes up their hatred for his own ends. The literary influences are more French than Latin, and more Latin than Greek.

No doubt if a modern theatre public is to be interested in a mythological subject, it is almost necessary to interpret it in modern terms, or to overlay it with some action having modern appeal. In seventeenth-century practice this meant the superimposition of a love-plot in the contemporary mode, and of a conflict of what can broadly be called political interests. It has been done clumsily here, but Racine, like his contemporaries, always does it, with increasing subtlety; the join is visible to us, because we can see the manners and thought of two periods, neither of which is our own. In *Phèdre* alone of his 'Greek' plays the political conflict is hardly noticeable, but it exists.

The next play — a success as *La Thébaïde* was not — was *Alexandre le Grand* (1665), quite unmythological and only partly historical. The next was *Andromaque* (1667).

It would be wrong to belittle the Greek element in *Andromaque*, for it certainly does as much as any other element to give the play the atmosphere it has. But what we find is a set of characters connected with the Trojan war, put into a modern situation which is worked out according to modern patterns of sentiment and plot. The ideas of Destiny, the will of the Gods, the divine curse incurred by wickedness, are all expressed, but what determines the fate of the characters is their own passions. This is a tragedy of love, with all its consequences of hate, treachery, irresolution and moral degradation, and a play of mirrors or echoes as each of three characters passes through similar phases of emotion and treats the others with similar indifference or cruelty. This major Racinian theme would never be more central or more thoroughly treated in any of his works.

He next wrote four tragedies, three (*Britannicus* 1669, *Bérénice* 1670, *Mithridate* 1673) on themes from ancient Roman history (a very popular setting at the time), and one drawn from a recent event in Constantinople (*Bajazet* 1672). Then, for reasons not clearly known, he turned to Greek tragedy with more serious attention than ever before. It looks as though some of the study we know he devoted to the three Attic tragedians (in their own language) dated from this period. Certainly in the preface to *Iphigénie* (1674, published 1675) he shows himself more conscious even than before of the prestige to be gained by playing on this indebtedness, which none of his rivals could claim.

This tragedy and *Phèdre*, which followed it (1677), used not merely Greek legend, but the situations and plots of two actual Greek plays (though with necessary modifications and the intermingling of other influences). The author of both was Euripides: Racine never used Aeschylus, who was out of favour, and never directly imitated Sophocles, who had the highest reputation of the three. Euripides draws character with more profundity, more complexity and more pathetic effect, which may be what attracted the French playwright. He also has an ironic, irreverent, questioning mind; his attitude to his people's Gods is not simple rejection, but it can be corrosive and devastating. The plays Racine chose to use show Diana demanding a human sacrifice, and Venus drawing Phaedra into sin by irresistible temptation. The first of these situations Euripides tried to save by a last-minute happy ending (discussed adversely in Racine's preface) — in the version that has come down to us, at all events, though this is possibly a recasting. But the second, if we take the mythology seriously, sets us in a horrifying world of divine injustice and oppression.

It had in any case become very hard for a tragic playwright in France to take the Greek Gods seriously (or the Roman Gods: the seventeenth century sees no difference between them and uses the Latin names as 'translations' of the Greek). No modern, of course, believed in them. As traditional ornaments of poetry, they might be referred to allegorically or symbolically; otherwise they stood for the justice or the providence of the God of Christian belief — and it is remarkable how the monotheistically minded French writer tends to allude collectively to 'Heaven' or 'the Gods' *en bloc*, rather than, even in *Iphigénie* or *Phèdre*, to Diana or Venus. But here arose the problem. For if a divinity took an active part in a tragedy (unseen of course: tragedy, unlike opera, never brought them on the stage), it had to be either by helping or by harming a mortal hero. The first solution would create a happy ending, for which the hero, moreover, lost the credit; and this was precisely the *deus ex machina* that Aristotle had condemned. But, according to another principle in the *Poetics* to which Racine appeals in three of the five prefaces translated in this volume, a hero who falls into misfortune must not be so entirely wicked as to forfeit our sympathy; so a God who causes that downfall must be to some extent an unjust God.

In fact Racine directs as much attention as he can on his human actors. When he introduces a supernatural intervention, we shall see that as often as possible he leaves his audience or readers free to reject it if they prefer. Phaedra, in particular,

falls into an incestuous love by whatever fatality it is that does
sometimes cause such things to happen, as we all know: *she*
sees in it the personal hatred of Venus, but even the other
characters are not aware of this, and we do not have to accept
her word. Whatever explanation we choose, her consciousness
of helpless guilt and her aspiration towards innocence – in
which she stands alone among Racinian characters – make her
the richest and most poetic figure of them all.

No further approximation to Attic tragedy was possible to
a poet writing for the Paris stage. But this Racine ceased to do
precisely at this point; and in a new life as a staid married man
and a protégé of the King he must have thought his playwright's career was closed. He may indeed have mused at times
on ways in which, by a return to Greek models, his art could
have been purged of the worldly features that had brought it
into disfavour in strict religious circles (cf. the ending of the
preface to *Phèdre*, written while he was contemplating the
break). Sophocles and Euripides had known nothing of the
love-interest his century would not do without, or the conventions under which it was forced to operate; they could and
did express moral and religious ideas; they had a completer art-
form, in which poetry joined with music and dance – a form
of which the opera, adapted for Paris from its Italian origins
by Lully, was giving a notion (in the Académie royale de
Musique from 1672), though Racine cannot have approved of
its moral tone or its frivolous use of classical mythology.

Then a commission which must have been quite unexpected
gave him the opportunity to put some of these aspirations into
practice, and compose two tragedies with singing choruses
(*Esther* 1689, *Athalie* 1691 – the first may be considered little
more than a trial shot) which were Greek by their inner spirit
but biblical in subject, and where the God of the Jews and
Christians directed the action for his own ends, upheld the
virtuous characters and punished the wicked.

In his use of divinities in dramatic action, Racine therefore
passed through three stages, with *Phèdre* occupying the turning-
point between the tragedies of human passion and the
tragedies of divine vengeance and salvation.

The poetic style of the writer appears to follow a similar
course, with *Phèdre* still in the midway position. The 'poetic
diction' of the early group relies, since the taste of the age
rejected archaism, on the same fairly restricted gamut of
images used by all his contemporaries – laurels or trophies
(for military glory), blood (with perpetual play between the
two connotations of 'slaughter' and 'dynasty'); in the domain

of love-making, the post-Petrarchan metaphors of flames, wounds and bonds; and the preference for metonymies (heart, arm, hand, eyes) over personal nouns or pronouns. Clichés all, or in the process of becoming clichés — only we must beware when we speak of clichés, for these were simply the successful turns of expression favoured, because of their known power to communicate the sense of poetry, until the moment when over-familiarity caused distaste; but while they were as widely current as they were in Racine's day, that moment had clearly not come. In *Athalie*, at the other end of the poet's career, the lovers' language is necessarily absent, and the new elements are a little of the directness, even brutality, of the Old Testament narrative, and a poetry relying on unfamiliar and stronger images drawn from the psalmists and the prophets — a reflection of Hebrew poetry which Racine was alone among the French poets of his day to love or even recognise, even though here he had to use translations. Among the thematic images of the play are those of growth and withering (from the same source); and the often rather stiff dialogue is relieved with the lyricism of the choruses.

In this also, *Phèdre* comes between the two groups, in that the lovers' language has a new depth and reality — love's fires and wounds are real torment, its bondage, real humiliation. The tone is often moral, almost religious. Here too the evocative use of legendary names and mythological allusions becomes, more than in *Andromaque* or even *Iphigénie*, a conscious poetic resource; and it is perhaps to Euripides' figure of Hippolytus, hunting in the thickets or driving his chariot along the seashore, that Racine owes a powerful recurrent imagery, or symbolism, of light and shadow.

If even now I have not mentioned the principal beauty of Racine — the sheer music of his verse, equalled in his own century only at rare moments by Malherbe and sometimes by La Fontaine, and never in the next — it is because a translator does better not to dwell on it. It depends on vowels and consonants, speech rhythms, metrical and intonation patterns, which are French and not English. Here has always been the barrier to recognition of Racine in English-speaking countries. Perhaps the barrier is insurmountable. Each translator does what he can to find some sort of equivalents. Here I will explain what I have tried to do, rather than why I could not do better.

The metrical form itself cannot be reproduced; French and English are too different in their ways of applying stress and therefore creating rhythm. Only by the number of syllables (twelve) does Shelley's alexandrine in the *Skylark* ode, or Byron's in *Childe Harold*, resemble the French alexandrine. So, like most or all other English translators, I take our traditional English line for serious verse, the decasyllable; but I do not attempt rhyme, for one thing because English is poor in rhymes and it would be too difficult to reconcile rhyme with tolerable fidelity to sense, but also because the couplets of Dryden, Racine's contemporary, to say nothing of those of Pope, are not perhaps more often endstopt or more neatly balanced than Racine's, but being shorter they are more evidently so. But my blank verse is less irregular than much of Shakespeare's, is never mixed with prose, and has no incomplete lines. For all specific effects — pauses, phrasing, climax, *accelerando* and *rallentando* — I try to find equivalents.

In one place I have thrown over these principles and aimed at reproducing Racine's own rhythms exactly: in the choral songs of *Athalie*, which — I say this with confidence thanks to the expert checking of my friend Mrs Allison Walker-Morecroft, LRAM, LTCL, LGSM — can be sung to the original score composed for the play by J.-B. Moreau, and reproduced in the music album attached to the eight-volume edition of Racine's complete works in the Grands Ecrivains series.[1] The composer took delight in emphasising the rhythmical variety to be found in his text; my renderings therefore may appear exceedingly irregular by English metrical conventions. The alexandrines I could only make to look like verse at all by cutting each of them into two hexasyllables.

The vocabulary of Racine's tragedies is restricted to some 2,000 words, some of which, because of the relative scarcity of available synonyms, have taken on great richness of meaning. In a more copious language I could not imitate this, though I have respected his use of theme-words as much as I could, together with his avoidance of low or inelegant turns of speech, and some of the dead metaphors of lovers' language which I have described as clichés — but not those too obviously dead; by trying to find how we today might express the same concepts I hoped to recover some of the freshness that they must have had once.

I have respected some of Racine's linguistic conventions — for instance that by which all high-born characters address each other normally as *Seigneur* or *Madame*, or occasionally, for a little more familiarity (strange as it may seem) as *Prince* or *Princesse*. Other such conventions were hard to reproduce — those adjectives (used as nouns) of hyperbolical denunciation which English no longer possesses, *cruel*, *inhumain*, *barbare*, *perfide*, *infidèle*, *ingrat* (in either gender); and that supremely useful resource which our language has long lost, of dropping from the civil *vous* to the *tu* of superiority or over-powering emotion.

Two particular details in these translations may need comment.

Unity of Place in Racine's time means that the whole of each tragedy is played in the same set, representing the same location: so, within an act, there cannot be changes of scene in the English sense. But French publishers have retained a convention according to which any entrance or exit, with few exceptions, gives rise to a new 'scene'. I have kept such scene-numbers out of my text (as Dryden did in *All for Love*, which keeps Unity of Place), but noted them in the pageheadings for the convenience of those who may wish to consult a French text, or find a reference.

The proper names appear, in the first three plays, in the English forms corresponding to Racine's, which often go back to Latin, not Greek. These English forms came to us through French, but subsequently developed within the normal development of English sound-values. They were universally accepted by English speakers until (I think) about 1920, when the 'restored' pronunciation of Latin, quite rightly introduced into schools for the study of that language, created a confusion from which we have not recovered. My translations retain in all cases the older traditional forms we still use in such names as Jesus, Plato, Euripides, Caesar, as against Crayon, Fydra, I-neigh-ass. Vowels matter so much in verse — and even mcre, of course, the proper placing of stress — that I have added a glossary of proper names, which I beg and pray everyone to consult before reading aloud, and especially before acting, these translations.

To that glossary I have added the less familiar Old Testament names of *Athaliah*, which have the forms and pronunciations used in English-speaking churches, based on the Author-ised Version ('King James Bible'). Two exceptions made for special reasons (Trozen, Josabeth) are explained in notes to the plays in which they appear.

The translation of *Phèdre* published here dates from 1945, and was published in 1971 by the Edinburgh University Press, by whose kind permission it is reprinted, with very slight revisions. The others are new, and I would express my warmest gratitude to the friends who have helped me with their comments, especially to Miss Margaret Tillett, Mrs Dilys Jenkins and Mr Neville Masterman, who have read every line critically, and Mrs Allison Walker-Morecroft, whose work on the music of *Athalie* I have already mentioned.

Geoffrey Brereton, *Racine: a Critical Biography* (Cassell, 1951; 2nd edn, Methuen, 1973)

Eugène Vinaver, *Racine et la poésie tragique* (1951; 2nd edn, 1963), translated by P.M. Jones as *Racine and Poetic Tragedy* (Manchester University Press, 1955)

J.C. Lapp, *Aspects of Racinian Tragedy* (University of Toronto Press, 1955; 2nd edn, 1964)

Katherine E. Wheatley, *Racine and English Classicism* (University of Texas Press, 1956)

Odette de Mourgues, *Racine: or, The Triumph of Relevance* (Cambridge University Press, 1967)

R.C. Knight (ed.), *Racine* (Modern Judgements) (Macmillan, 1969). Fourteen critical essays in English.

Martin Turnell, *Jean Racine Dramatist* (Hamish Hamilton, 1972)

Geoffrey Brereton, *French Tragic Drama in the Sixteenth and Seventeenth Centuries* (Methuen, 1973)

Philip Butler, *Racine: a Study* (Heinemann, 1974)

P.J. Yarrow, *Racine* (Plays and Playwrights) (Oxford: Basil Blackwell, 1978)

John Lough, *Seventeenth-Century French Drama: the Background* (Oxford: Clarendon Press, 1979)

For recent French studies, including what has become known as 'la nouvelle critique', see R.C. Knight, *Racine* (above), pp. 11—14 and bibliography. Of these, only Lucien Goldmann has appeared in English: *Le dieu caché* (1955), translated by Philip Thody as *The Hidden God* (Routledge & Kegan Paul, 1964); and *Racine* (1966), translated by Alastair Hamilton (Cambridge: Rivers Press, 1972).

ANDROMACHE
(1667)

INTRODUCTION

Andromache is, as I tried to show earlier, a clear case of a
dramatic situation and action inspired by modern taste and
modern sources (very likely a single source, *Pertharite* (1652)
by Corneille), but using characters whose names and repu-
tations belong to the story of the Trojan war, or its immediate
sequel, bringing with them an atmosphere and constant
reminiscences going back to Greek and Latin writers, including
Homer, whom Racine's original preface omits to mention.
Racine takes over the mourning widow of Hector, in captivity
under Pyrrhus, but without recalling that she was quite unable
in her position to resist his advances, and bore him a son: he
never thought of marrying her, but did marry Hermione,
which was the reason why Orestes killed him. Classical writers
all made Astyanax perish before the Greeks left Troy; but a
late tradition, as the second of Racine's prefaces mentions,
does allow him to survive and become the ancestor of the first
dynasty of kings of France. But the chain-gang of lovers, each
loving one and loved by another, the blackmail exerted on the
mother by threats against her son's life, the revenge of the
jilted rival which she instantly disavows, are commonplace in
seventeenth-century tragedy; none of them appears in any
Greek or Latin source.

One of these lovers purports to be Orestes, the figure who
recurs more often than any other in the Greek tragedies that
remain to us; known there principally as the killer of his
mother Clytemnestra in vengeance for her murder of her husband Agamemnon (these two appear in Racine's *Iphigenia*);
the Furies persecuted him in punishment of his matricide. Has
he killed her yet when he appears in *Andromache*? Racine
never breathes a word of her — he must want to keep some
sympathy for his character until he commits a different crime,
and catches a glimpse of the Furies in his last delirious speech.
Orestes speaks much of the injustice of Heaven in our play,
but with nothing to justify it objectively beyond his melancholy and a hopeless love; indeed his earliest speeches accuse
in turn Fortune, the Gods and Destiny — strictly three inde-
pendent supernatural agencies — and finally Love. At the same

time we must not deny that he brings into the tragedy much
of the poetry of ancient legend in which it is bathed.

Not only is the play a compound of ancient and modern in
plot and characters; it has a wide range of emotion and tone,
elegiac, passionate, and often full of elegant but sometimes
bitter irony — irony consciously employed by the speakers, or
betrayed in the contrast between their professions and actions,
even more than the 'tragic irony' unknowingly conveyed by
their words; so that Racine's friend Boileau condemned one
scene (II 5) as fit only for comedy (but Racine was safely dead
when he said this). There are scenes of threat and struggle, and
gleams of illusory hope; scenes of what Eugène Vinaver has
called tragic error followed by tragic recognition of the truth;
scenes of calm despair. *Phèdre* and *Athalie* are both more
homogeneous in texture, and yield in a sense a purer tone; but
it is wise to accept these contrasts and variations with gratitude, and become as sensitive as we can to the acute obser-
vation, subtle wit and cutting sarcasm which are also elements
in Racine's style.

No later play of his has been so thoroughly revised. He
pruned weak lines, and removed obscurities, incoherent metaphors and excesses of lovers' jargon, particularly the figurative
use of 'hearts' and of 'eyes' (signifying feminine beauty). He
also deprived his titular heroine of an appearance in the
denouement (see note on line 1532). But in its uncorrected
form it was the work that first made the poet's name.

VIRGIL
IN THE THIRD BOOK
OF THE AENEID

Aeneas speaks:
We skimm'd along Epirus' flying shores.
On the Chaonian port at length we fall;
Thence we ascend to high Buthrotos' wall. . . .
By chance, Andromache that moment paid
The mournful offerings to her Hector's shade.
A tomb, an empty tomb, her hands compose
Of living turf, and two fair altars rose.
Sad scene! that still provok'd the tears she shed. . . .
To this, with lowly voice, the fair replies,
While on the ground she fix'd her streaming eyes:
Thrice blest Polyxena! condemn'd to fall
By vengeful Greece beneath the Trojan wall;
Stabb'd at Pelides' tomb the victim bled,
To death deliver'd from the victor's bed.
Nor lots disgrac'd her with a chain, like me,
A wretched captive, drag'd from sea to sea!
Doom'd to that hero's haughty heir, I gave
A son to Pyrrhus, more than half a slave.
From me, to fair Hermione he fled
Of Leda's race, and sought a Spartan bed; . . .
But fierce Orestes, by the Furies tost
And mad with vengeance for the bride he lost,
Swift on the monarch from his ambush flew,
And at Apollo's hallow'd altar slew.

Here, in a few lines, is the whole story of this tragedy. Here are
the scene of the play, the action that takes place there, the
four main actors, and even their characters — except that of
Hermione, whose raging jealousy is sufficiently shown in the
Andromache of Euripides.

But in truth my personages are so famous in antiquity that
anyone who knows it at all will see quite clearly that I have
rendered them as the old poets have shown them. Nor have I
felt free to change anything in their dispositions. The sole
liberty I have taken is to soften slightly the fierceness of Pyrrhus, which Seneca in his *Troad* and Virgil in Book II of the
Aeneid have carried much further than I thought it right to do.

Even so there have been some who complained that he showed
anger to Andromache, and endeavoured to marry his captive at
all costs. I admit that he is not sufficiently resigned to his mistress's will, and that Celadon understood perfect love better
than he does. But what could I do? Pyrrhus had not read our
romances. He was violent by nature. And not every hero is cut
out to be a Celadon.

However this may be, I have been too well treated by the
public to be concerned at the personal ill-humour of two or
three people who would like to see all the heroes of antiquity
reformed into faultless heroes. I am sure their intention is
excellent, to have none but impeccable characters shown on
the stage. But I beg them to remember that it is not for me to
change the rules of drama. Horace tells us to depict Achilles
wild, inexorable, violent, as he was in life, and as his son is
depicted. And Aristotle, far from calling for perfect heroes,
desires on the contrary that tragic characters, that is, those
whose misfortune constitutes the catastrophe of the tragedy,
should be neither entirely good nor entirely bad. He does not
want them extremely good, because the punishment of a good
man would arouse the audience's indignation rather than its
pity; nor excessively wicked, because no one pities a villain.
Therefore they should have an intermediate kind of goodness,
that is, a virtue liable to weakness, and should fall into misfortune through some fault that makes us pity but not detest
them.

[PREFACE OF 1676]

[Racine's new preface for his first collective edition in 1676 begins with the same quotation from Virgil, and goes on:]

Here, in a few lines, is the whole story of this tragedy. Here are the scene of the play, the action that takes place there, the four main actors, and even their characters — except that of Hermione, whose raging jealousy is sufficiently shown in the *Andromache* of Euripides.

That is about the only thing I borrow from this author here. For, although my tragedy bears the same name, its subject is nevertheless quite different. Andromache in Euripides fears for the life of Molossus, a son of hers by Pyrrhus, whom Hermione wishes to put to death with its mother. But here there is no question of Molossus. Andromache knows no husband but Hector and no son but Astyanax. I felt that by this I was conforming to the idea we have of the princess today. Most of those who have heard of Andromache probably know her only as the widow of Hector and the mother of Astyanax. It is not felt that she should love either another husband or another son. And I doubt if Andromache's tears would have affected my audiences as they have, had they flowed for another son than Hector's.

It is true I have had to let Astyanax live a little longer than he did. But I am writing in a country where this freedom could hardly be taken amiss. For, not to mention Ronsard who took this same Astyanax as the hero of his *Franciade*, who is unaware that our early kings are held to descend from this son of Hector, and that our old chronicles save his life after the devastation of his country, to make him the founder of our monarchy?

How much bolder was Euripides in his tragedy, *Helen*! He goes openly against the common belief of all Greece. In his play Helen never set foot in Troy, and after the city has been burnt Menelaus finds his wife in Egypt where she had been all the time. All this, following a belief accepted only by the Egyptians, as may be read in Herodotus.

I do not think I should need this precedent from Euripides to justify the slight liberty I have taken. For there is a great difference between destroying the principal basis of a legend and altering a few incidents, which change almost entirely in every hand that uses them. Thus Achilles, according to most poets, can only be wounded in the heel, though Homer shows him wounded in the arm, and does not consider him invulnerable in any part of his body. Thus too Sophocles makes Clytemnestra die immediately Oedipus discovers his true identity, far from living, as she does in Euripides, to see the duel and death of her two sons. And it is on some conflict of this nature that an ancient commentator of Sophocles* quite rightly says 'that we should not waste our time cavilling at poets for any changes they may have made in legend, but pause to consider the excellent use they have made of those changes, and their cleverness in adapting legend to their subject'.

*Sophocles, *Electra*. [Racine's note]

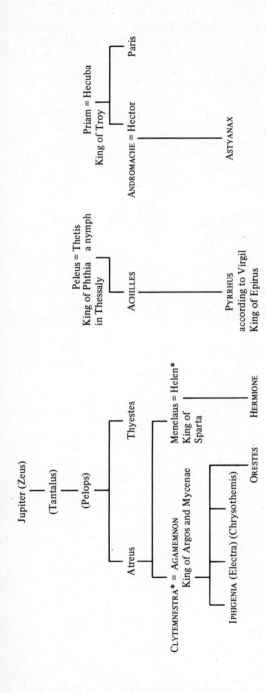

Jupiter (Zeus)
|
(Tantalus)
|
(Pelops)

Atreus — Thyestes

CLYTEMNESTRA* = AGAMEMNON
King of Argos and Mycenae

Menelaus = Helen*
King of Sparta

IPHIGENIA (Electra) (Chrysothemis) ORESTES

HERMIONE

Peleus = Thetis
King of Phthia   a nymph
in Thessaly

ACHILLES

PYRRHUS
according to Virgil
King of Epirus

Priam = Hecuba
King of Troy

Hector   Paris

ANDROMACHE = Hector

ASTYANAX

* Helen and Clytemnestra were half-sisters, both being born to Leda
(Names in parenthesis for characters not named in the plays)

Genealogical table for *Andromache* and *Iphigenia*

DRAMATIS PERSONAE

Andrŏmachē	widow of Hector, captive of Pyrrhus
Pyrrhus	son of Achilles, king of Epirus
Oréstes	son of Agamemnon, in love with Hermione
Hermíonē	daughter of Helen and Menelaus, betrothed to Pyrrhus
Pýladēs	friend of Orestes
Cleónē	confidant of Hermione
Cephíssa	confidant of Andromache
Phŏënix	formerly governor of Achilles, then of Pyrrhus

Soldiers of Orestes

The scene is in Buthrotum, a city of Epirus;
a room in the palace of Pyrrhus.

ACT I

ORESTES, PYLADES

Orestes   Yes, with the truest of my friends to greet me,
I must believe my Fortune is relenting;
For surely her displeasure must be past
Now she has brought the two of us together.
How should I guess that on a shore I dreaded
Pylades would be waiting for Orestes,
And here, in Pyrrhus' court, would be the man
I'd lost to sight for six long months and more?
Pylades   Thanks be to the Gods, that never ceased to
      thwart me,
And held me off a hundred times from Greece   10
Since the disastrous day that wind and wave
Scattered our ships so near Epirus' shore.
How I feared for you in our separation,
And wept for all the things I feared you suffered!
Things that my helpless friendship could not share,
And most of all, that cloud of melancholy
That overshadowed you so long before;
I feared the cruel kindness of some God
Would give you the death to which your soul aspired.
But you are here, my lord, and to all seeming   20
You come to Epirus under luckier omens;
For the brilliant retinue that follows you
Does not attend a wretch in search of death.
Orestes   Ah, but who knows what Fate has brought me
      here?
Love leads me, Love for one who still rejects me.
And who can prophesy what is to come?
Is life my goal, or death in spite of all?
Pylades   What, still, like an abject slave, are you
      prepared
To take your sentence or reprieve from Love?
What magic, after all your former woes,   30
Has brought you back into your cast-off chains —
As if Hermione, so cold in Sparta,
Would welcome you with kindness in Epirus?
You were ashamed to plead in vain; you loathed her:

At least, you spoke no more of her. I was
Deceived, my lord.
Orestes   I was the one deceived.
Friend, have some pity on a helpless friend:
You cannot say I ever hid my heart,
You watched this flame, you knew my earliest sighs;
Then, after Menelaus gave his daughter   40
To the avenger of his house, to Pyrrhus,
You saw me in despair; and you have seen
Me drag my dreary chain and drag my grief
From shore to shore. I found you always near me,
Patiently following me unbidden always
To calm my rage as often as it rose
And daily save Orestes from himself.
Then — for I told myself that while I languished
Hermione was flinging all her beauty
At Pyrrhus' feet — you know I swore revenge,   50
Swore to forget if I had been forgotten;
I said — I thought — that I had won my battle;
I smarted, but I thought the smart was hatred,
Cursing her coldness, crying down her charms,
Daring her eyes to break my peace again.
And so I thought my passion safely dead,
And travelled back to Greece in seeming calm.
But I found the princes of the land had met,
Just then, in council on some pressing danger.
I rushed to join them. I hoped that war and glory   60
Would fill my thoughts with other, weightier business,
And if my mind grew strong and keen again
The last of love would vanish from my heart.
But look how like a wily hunter fate
Drove me into the very toils I dreaded:
These fears, this indignation, was for Pyrrhus,
Who, as I heard, reckless of faith and blood,
Had sheltered Hector's orphan at his court,
Astyanax, the enemy of Greece,
The last descendant of so many Kings   70
Buried beneath Troy towers. Andromache,
Cheating the shrewd Ulysses of his blood,
Had clutched a borrowed infant to her breast,
A counterfeit that took his master's name
And, dying, saved her son. — I learnt there too
That, tiring of Hermione, my rival
Is offering his heart and crown elsewhere.
Her father, unbelieving, yet offended,

Protests to see her wedding still delayed.
His disappointment is my secret joy;   80
At first my exultation seemed to me
Sheer satisfaction at a just revenge;
But soon her image took its former place,
I felt again where the old fire had burned,
I knew that soon my hatred would be dead —
No: I knew I loved her and I always shall.
I canvassed every vote, and I was sent
Envoy to Pyrrhus. I sailed; and I am here
Empowered to snatch the infant from his hands
Whose life is such a menace to our people,   90
But thinking of my love, and longing only
To lose Astyanax and win my lady.
For do not suppose that, doubled by delay,
My ardour can be cooled by any danger;
Since all my strength resisted unavailing
I close my eyes and drift with the Fate that drives me.
I love; I come to bid Hermione
Pity me, follow me, or see me die.
You know this Pyrrhus: what do you think he'll do?
What's happening in his palace, in his heart?   100
Is he still true, my Pylades, or shall I
Win back the treasure that was mine before?
Pylades   I dare not promise you so much, my lord;
Not that he holds it in such high esteem —
He makes no mystery of the new passion
For the dead Hector's wife, his prisoner.
He loves her. She has not responded yet
Except to pay his proffered love with hate.
Day after day he uses all his art
To stir his captive's pity, or her fear.   110
He parts her from her son, threatens his life;
Then tries to dry the tears he makes her shed.
A hundred times she has seen him storm away
With fury in his heart disguised as love,
In doubtful tribute, to Hermione.
So do not think that I can safely judge
Of one who cannot answer for himself;
For easily he might, yes easily,
Marry the one for vengeance on the other.
Orestes   And my Hermione? How does she endure   120
Her marriage broken, and her slighted charms?
Pylades   Hermione, at least before the world,
Makes light of his inconstancy, and waits

Till Pyrrhus, contrite, fearful of refusal
Returns and begs her to accept his heart.
But I know, for I have been her confidant,
What tears she weeps in her humiliation;
Ever in mind to leave, but never going,
Sometimes she calls Orestes to her aid.

Orestes   If I thought that, my Pylades, there's nothing   130
Could hold me back . . .

Pylades   First play your mission out.
The King will see you. Speak, and show him plainly
All Greece arrayed against the Trojan princeling —
He will not let them have her son: their hate
Will only serve to make his passion blaze.
Attempt to part them, you will bring them closer.
Press hard, ask much, for fear he should consent.
— He is coming now.

Orestes   You go then and prepare
My faithless love to greet a faithful lover
Whose only mission is to her alone.   140

                              Exit Pylades
                              Enter Pyrrhus

Orestes   Before you hear me as spokesman of my
              country
Let me express my pleasure in this mission
Through which, my lord, I taste the privilege
To see Achilles' son, Troy's conqueror —
For we revere your exploits as his own —
Troy fell to you, as Hector fell to him;
His toils, his triumphs have no other equal,
And only Achilles' son could fill his place.
But Greece laments — what he would not have
              shown —
Your dangerous pity to our fallen foes   150
Or what is left of foes so hardly conquered
In all the years and all the trials of war.
Is Hector's name so weak a word to you,
My lord? Not so in our enfeebled lands:
In every home a mother, maid or wife
Flinches at Hector's name; each family
Calls out for reckoning from Hector's child
For father, son or husband Hector killed.
This child, consider what he may become:
Who knows, but we shall see him in our ports,   160
Fire in his hand, as once his father fired
Our ships, and harried them across the waves?

Dare I say all I think? Beware yourself,
My lord, the gratitude that pity earns
After the full-grown snake you fostered turns
To punish what preserved it. In a word,
Content the wishes of your fellow princes,
Complete their vengeance, and protect yourself.
Destroy the common enemy of Greece,
Dangerous to all, most dangerous to you   170
Who stand the nearest to his novice sword.

Pyrrhus   Greece is too kind and too solicitous.
. I own, my lord, I thought her busied with
Some weightier care, and, seeing whom she sent,
I guessed a vaster scope in her intentions.
For it is hard to see why such an errand
Needed the voice of Agamemnon's son,
Or all these lands, with all their foes defeated,
Should care to plot a wretched infant's death.
But who requires his sacrifice? Has Greece   180
The right, as things stand now? May I, alone
Of all the Greeks, not rule my captives' fate?
Listen, my lord: under those reeking ruins
We bloodstained victors shared the Trojan spoils
By casting lots, and I obtained by lot
Andromache, this infant at her breast.
Hecuba found her fate under Ulysses;
Cassandra went with your father back to Argos;
Did I contest their prize, deny their right,
Or claim the just fruit of their victories?   190
— You fear a new Troy and a second Hector,
You fear for my life unless I kill this boy:
My lord, to search for evils out of sight
Needs too much caution, too much skill for me.
I see that citadel as once I knew it,
Sublime in battlements, mother of many a hero,
Mistress of Asia — that was Troy of late;
Then I remember what is Troy today,
Nothing but bastions buried in their ashes,
A river red with blood, a country ravaged,   200
A child in chains; and it is hard to think
That such a Troy is fretting for revenge.
Why, if the son of Hector had to die,
Why wait a year? Why could we not have left him,
Another corpse under the piles of corpses,
In Priam's arms, under the fallen towers?
Then, all was fair: not infancy, not age,

Found any safety in their helplessness;
Victory, darkness, fiercer than our hate,
Hounded us on, confused and veiled our strokes.   210
I was stern, too stern, to those that met me then
While passion was at heat. But now, at leisure,
Now passion's gone and pity fills its place,
Now, coldly, shed an infant's blood? Ah no,
Let the Greeks go and find another prey,
Some Trojan remnant in some other land:
My enmity, my lord, has run its course —
What Troy allowed to live, Epirus shelters.

Orestes   Surely you know, my lord, the trick that sent
A false Astyanax to meet the fate   220
Ordained for Hector's son. For it is Hector,
Not Troy, the Greeks would persecute: and the boy
Only because he is the child of one
Who earned such hate from Greece for blood he shed
That all his blood is forfeit. And for that
They'll come, perhaps, to Epirus. But, my lord,
Act first.

Pyrrhus   Not I. No, let them come with pleasure
And make a Trojan war here in Epirus,
Change loves and hates, and pay the same reward
To those who won, and those they overcame.   230
It would be nothing new if Greece acknowledged
Achilles' benefits with injuries.
Hector was gainer once, and it may be
The child he leaves will profit in his turn.

Orestes   So Greece has reared a disobedient son?

Pyrrhus   Was it to be her vassal that I conquered?

Orestes   The fair Hermione will mediate,
My lord, between her father and your anger.

Pyrrhus   My lord, I trust that it is possible
To love Hermione and not to be   240
Her father's slave. I hope to reconcile
Some day the claims of state and of affection.
Now you will wish to see the child of Helen:
I know the ties of blood are strong between you.
That done, my lord, I'll not detain you longer,
And you may tell the Greeks that I refuse.

                                        Exit Orestes

Phoenix   And so you send him to his lady's feet?

Pyrrhus   They say he has been a very faithful suitor.

Phoenix   And if that flame burnt up again, my lord,
And if they both . . .

Pyrrhus   Ah, Phoenix, if they would!   250
   Let her go back, let him escort her home,
   Let them adore each other, back in Sparta!
   All ports are open to them, if they would
   Free me from this constraint and misery.
Phoenix   But, my lord . . .
Pyrrhus   You shall probe my inmost
        thoughts
   Another time. Andromache is here.

                           Exit Phoenix
                 Enter Andromache *and* Cephissa
Pyrrhus   Was it to look for me you came, my lady?
   May I take comfort from that flattering thought?
Andromache   I was passing through to where they keep
       my boy.
   Since once a day you suffer me to visit   260
   All I have left of Hector and of Troy,
   I meant to go and weep a moment with him:
   He has not had his kiss today.
Pyrrhus   My lady,
   If Greek anxiety should end in action
   You have other tears to shed.
Andromache   Anxiety,
   My lord? and what is there that should alarm them?
   Is there some Trojan that has slipped your hands?
Pyrrhus   Hatred still burns for Hector's memory;
   They dread his son.
Andromache   Fit object for their terror!
   An infant, and unhappy, and too young   270
   To know that Hector was his father's name,
   Pyrrhus his master's.
Pyrrhus   Be he what he may,
   They want him dead, and Agamemnon's son
   Is here to press his instant execution.
Andromache   And you? Have you confirmed that cruel
       sentence?
   Is it because of me that he is guilty?
   You do not fear he will avenge his father,
   You fear he might console a mother's tears,
   And be a father and a husband to me:
   But I must lose all I have, and now as ever   280
   Lose it through you.
Pyrrhus   You need not grieve, my lady;
   I have refused the claims of Greece already,
   And now, if they launch a thousand ships again

To win your child with ten more years of war
And make blood flow as then it flowed for Helen;
If I must see my castle sink in ashes;
I do not care how much his safety costs,
I stake my life for his. But when my country
Hates me and seeks my death, among the dangers
Which I shall gladly face to do you pleasure,   290
Can you consent to think of me less harshly?
I offer you my sword; may I not hope
One day this heart of mine that worships you
Will be accepted too, and I your soldier
Find you no more among my enemies?

Andromache   Do you mean this, my lord? Are noble
    natures
Prone to such weakness? Shall your resolution,
That generous resolution, seem to be
Merely the whim of an infatuate mind,
For Greece to laugh at? How could Andromache,   300
The prisoner, the inconsolable,
Inspire in you the wish that she should love you?
How could those eyes allure, those haunted eyes
That you have doomed to weep eternally?
No, no; but if you wished to manifest
Chivalry for an enemy in despair,
And face the cruelty of confederate kings
To give a mother back her son again —
Not barter him for my consent, but save him
Against my will, if need be — those attentions,   310
My lord, would not disgrace Achilles' son.

Pyrrhus   Come, must there be no limit to your anger,
No end to hatred and to punishment?
I too, I know, have made unfortunates;
I reddened Phrygian earth a thousand times,
And with your blood. But your victorious eyes
Have made me pay, how many times, the drops
I made them shed, and rue how many times
The sufferings I wrought at Troy — no greater
Than the long suffering I now endure,   320
Bowed in bondage, wasting in remorse,
Burnt with fires fiercer than all I kindled,
And all these tears, these ardours, these entreaties . . .
If mine was cruelty, tell me, what is yours?
But now, we have hurt each other long enough,
And common enemies should make us friends.
Say but a word to tell me I may hope,

Your son is yours again; I name him heir;
He learns from me how to avenge his country,
And Greece shall expiate his wrongs and mine   330
Together. With one glance to hearten me
I can do anything. Your Ilium
New-born, can spring up from its ashes yet,
And I, more quickly than the Greeks destroyed it,
Will rear those walls and crown your son their king.
Andromache   Those high ambitions are for us no more,
    My lord. I used to cherish them for him,
    Before his father fell. Ah no, those towers,
    Those holy towers my Hector could not save,
    Do not look to see us come again.   340
    The dispossessed have humbler dreams. My prayer
    Is exile, refuge somewhere far away
    From all the Greeks, and even far from you,
    To keep my son concealed, and mourn my husband.
    Think, think what enmity your love awakens
    Against us both. Go back to Helen's daughter.
Pyrrhus   Can I go back? Oh, you are merciless.
    Can I give back a heart that's not my own?
    I know that it was pledged to her; I know
    She landed in my kingdom to be Queen,   350
    Under a fate the opposite of yours —
    She to enjoy, and you to suffer, conquest.
    Yet have I sought a single way to woo her?
    Would it not seem to any that considered
    How potent is your beauty, hers so weak,
    That she was prisoner here and you supreme?
    Ah, could she snare the faintest of those sighs
    You wring from me, what ecstasy for her!
Andromache   Why should she not accept? Will she
            forget
    The deeds that earned her hand? Has Troy, has Hector   360
    A voice to rally all her soul against you?
    Has she a husband's urn to claim her heart?
    And what a husband! Oh, must I remember?
    Only his death immortalised your father,
    Only that blood gave lustre to his arms,
    And both of you trace your glory to my tears.
Pyrrhus   So be it, you shall be obeyed; so be it.
    I shall forget you, or rather I shall hate you.
    Yes, for this heart has gone too far in passion
    To cool hereafter to indifference.   370
    Consider well: there is no middle way,

Either I wildly love or blindly hate.
Nothing shall stand before my just resentment.
The son shall answer for the mother's coldness;
Greece calls for him, and honour does not ask
That always I should serve ingratitude.

Andromache   Then he must die; for he has no defenders
Except his mother's tears, his innocence.
And so perhaps I may attain at last
Deliverance from life and weariness   380
That I endured for him alone; but now
My son shall lead to where his father waits.
There reunited, three again, by you
At last . . .

Pyrrhus   Go in, go in and see your son,
My lady. For it may be at his side
A mother's love will find a better counsel,
Less proud than anger. I will come once more
To know your will. I pray you, when you kiss him,
Say to yourself that you could save his life.

ACT II

HERMIONE, CLEONE

Hermione   I did as you wished. I said that he could see
     me.   390
Let him enjoy that satisfaction also.
Pylades said that he would bring him in;
Not that I would have seen him, but for you.

Cleone   Why are you so afraid of him, my lady?
It is Orestes, still the same Orestes
That many a time you hoped to see again,
And praised his passion and his constancy.

Hermione   If he had loved me less, or moved me more,
It would be easier to endure his presence.
Now that my lot's as bitter as his own,   400
Think what revenge, and what humiliation!
'So then, Hermione,' I can hear him say,
'She that was not for me, has found at last
That she was not for *him*, and had to learn
How to be less than nothing in her turn?'
Ah, Gods!

Cleone   Come, these are unjust fears; forget them.
He is too firmly tangled in your meshes.

Will he exult? He brings you back a heart
He tried to tear away, but tried in vain.
— But you say nothing of a father's message?   410
Hermione   My father writes, if Pyrrhus dallies longer
And will not let us have the Trojan child,
I must leave the country with the other Greeks.
Cleone   Come then, my lady. Accept Orestes' escort,
And go with him. Pyrrhus has shown the way,
Do but the little that remains. It is better
You should disown him first. Have you not told me
You hated him?
Hermione   I hated him, Cleone?
I must, or what becomes of my slighted name?
After such condescensions, all forgotten,   420
Such tenderness — tenderness cast aside —
What can I do but hate, since I have loved?
Cleone   Then leave him now, my lady, and since the
          other . . .
Hermione   No, give me time, more bitterly to loathe
          him;
Give me more time, more to prepare my mind;
Then be our parting, when we come to part,
Wild, horrible, Cleone. I can trust him
At least to help me there.
Cleone   With worse rebuffs?
When he loves a prisoner, loves her in your sight,
And this is not enough? What more can he do?   430
If you could ever hate him, surely you
Would hate him now.
Hermione   Why are you so persistent
To goad my grief, to make me recognise
That in myself I shudder to acknowledge?
Try not to credit all you see and hear;
Believe love's dead, applaud my victory,
Believe my heart is hardened in its rage —
And oh! make me believe it if you can!
— Leave him, you say. Well, what is there to wait for?
I will. Why should I grudge his shameful conquest?   440
Let him go grovel slave-like to a slave.
I will. — Yet, if he turned again to his duty,
If some faint memory of vows forsworn
Brought him a suppliant to my feet for pardon,
If love's sweet power could persuade him some day
Back to fidelity; if only he
Would . . . All he wants is to insult me.

And yet I'll stay, to spoil their happiness
And find some pleasure in destroying theirs;
Or, if I can drive him to take back his word,   450
Brand him before all Greece a perjurer.
I caused the Greeks to clamour for her infant;
Now I'll inspire them to demand the mother,
And he shall die, unless he lets her die.
Cleone   Do you imagine eyes that overflow
With endless tears, find pleasure in the hope
Of rivalling your own? and such a heart,
In such adversity, aspires to charm
Its own tormentor? Or have you perceived
Any alleviation in her grief?   460
Why should she mourn? If she desires his love
Why does she still inflexibly resist?
Hermione   I let him move me — that was my undoing.
I never sought the mystery of silence,
I never saw the folly of my frankness,
Never tried him with a moment's coldness;
I only spoke the language of my heart.
And who would not have yielded, as I yielded,
To protestations of such urgency,
To looks of love I have not seen again?   470
You can remember: everything was for him —
Our honour vindicated, Greece exulting,
Our vessels loaded with the Trojan plunder,
His father's exploits dimmed by his renown,
His love that seemed more ardent than my own,
This heart of mine — you, dazzled by his glory —
All these betrayed me: he never betrayed me,
All of you had done it. But enough;
Pyrrhus and his misdeeds are past; Hermione
Has eyes to see, Orestes has his virtues —   480
He can love at least, and unrewarded;
And love, it may be, can awaken love.
So be it then. Let him come.
Cleone   He is here.
Hermione   Oh! but I never thought he was so close.
                               Enter Orestes
Hermione   May I suppose some memory of affection
Brings you to wait on an unhappy lady?
Or is it just a pleasant courtesy
I have to thank?
Orestes   A love like mine is blindfold;
You know that well, my lady, as you know

Orestes has a destiny that drives him   490
Time after time to seek you and adore,
And swear each time never to come again.
I know that here my wounds will be reopened,
That each step towards you is an oath forsworn —
I know, and blush. Yet witness, all ye Gods
That watched the fury of my last leave-taking,
How far I wandered and how long I sought
For certainty of death to loose my vows
And end my tortures. Like a suppliant
I begged for slaughter from those pitiless tribes   500
Whose Gods are moved only by blood of men:
They barred their temple to me; savages
Were niggard of my freely proffered blood.
So I return; and from your eyes at last
I must obtain the death I never found.
Let faithful love read its rejection there,
Let them but tell the hopeless to despair,
Let them but once, that death at last may claim me,
Tell me again what they have always told me.
These twelve months I have lived for this alone.   510
The sacrifice awaits your hand, my lady;
Consummate what already would be done
Were Scythians as pitiless as you.
Hermione   My lord, you have talked enough of fate
               and folly.
Greece sent you here on more important business.
Forget your savage Scythians, and think
Of all the kingdoms that you represent.
Is their just vengeance to depend upon
A lover's whim? and is Orestes' blood
The blood they call for? Discharge the offices   520
You undertook.
Orestes   They were discharged, my lady,
When Pyrrhus gave his answer. I am dismissed.
He assumes the championship of Hector's heir
For motives of his own.
Hermione   Oh, faithless, faithless!
Orestes   So then, before I take my leave of him,
I come to consult you on my destiny. —
You need not answer: I can read unspoken
The predetermined answer of your hate.
Hermione   What, bitter as ever and unjust as ever,
Are you still railing at my enmity?   530
What is this unkindness that you make so much of?

I came here to Epirus? I was sent here,
My father made me. How do you know, since then,
I never shared privately in your grief?
Do you think you alone have had to suffer,
And I was never wretched in Epirus?
What makes you think, in spite of all my duty,
I did not sometimes wish to see you here?

Orestes   To see me here? My Princess! Oh my Goddess!   540
But are these words addressed to me, I beg you?
This is Orestes here: open your eyes —
Orestes, on whom they never smiled before.

Hermione   Yes, you, who loved me in my earliest
          beauty,
And taught me first the power of its charms;
You that I valued for so many virtues;
You that I pitied; you I could wish to love; . . .

Orestes   I understand. That is my destined lot —
Your heart to Pyrrhus, and a wish for me.

Hermione   Ah, never wish to stand in Pyrrhus' place,
Or I should loathe you.

Orestes   And love me all the more.   550
Would I had the happiness of Pyrrhus!
You try to love, and cannot even like me;
But then — such power has Love if Love once reigns —
Then you would love me while you tried to hate.
Great Gods! such long, such infinite devotion,
How much could plead for me, if you could listen!
Only you favour Pyrrhus, though perhaps
You wish you did not. Surely, so does he.
You know you are hateful to him: his desires
Are —

Hermione   Where did you hear that he despised me?   560
Did he say so? Did you read it in his eyes?
Is mine a face that men despise, do you think?
And hearts I set on fire are cold so soon?
Other judges may be more indulgent.

Orestes   Go on, go on, and triumph over me,
Hard heart! So it is I despise you here?
Are you not yet assured of my submission?
Am I the proof your charms are soon forgotten?
Have I belittled them? What would you give
If he could prize them half as much as I?   570

Hermione   What do I care whether he loves or hates
          me?
Go back, range all the Greeks against the rebel,

Bring him a rebel's recompense, and make
Another Troy out of Epirus. Go.
Now will you say I love him?
Orestes   One thing more,
My lady; come yourself. Don't stay to be
A hostage. Come, your bright eyes will inspire us.
Come, fight our common enemy with me.
Hermione   But what if then he marries Andromache,
My lord?
Orestes   You see!
Hermione   Consider our dishonour   580
If he were husband to a Phrygian slave!
Orestes   Is that your hate? My lady, come, admit it;
Love is a flame you cannot hide away.
A voice betrays it, or silence, or a glance;
The fiercest fires are those we try to hide.
Hermione   I see, my lord, how strong is the obsession
That poisons anything that I can say;
You doubt each motive, even hate you twist
Until it makes another proof of love.
Here's my last word, and you may act upon it: 590
You know I came here for my duty's sake —
My duty keeps me here; I cannot go
Till Pyrrhus or my father set me free.
You may explain on my behalf to Pyrrhus
That only a friend of Greece can have his daughter.
Make him release the Trojan boy, or me;
Let him decide which he prefers to keep,
And settle for the one or for the other.
Goodbye. If he agrees, I go with you.

                                        Exit Hermione
Orestes   You'll come, you'll come, I'll take my oath on
          that.   600
My life upon it, Pyrrhus will agree.
Why should he keep her, when he has no eyes
For any other than his Trojan mistress,
Impatient of all else, and very likely
Looking for nothing but a fair excuse
To let her go? A word, and it is done,
And mine the joy to carry from Epirus
This priceless plunder. All that is left of Troy,
All Hector left on earth, his wife, his child,
Keep them, Epirus, on condition she   610
Never sets eyes on you and your King again!
— Why, here he is, led by a lucky fate.

Now to it. Love, still blind his careless eyes
To so much beauty that he has disdained!
                              Enter Pyrrhus *and* Phoenix
Pyrrhus   Ah, here you are. Just now I may have seemed
   Impatient with your reasoned arguments,
   I do admit. But since I spoke, my lord,
   Their force has struck me, and their equity.
   You have made me see my action was at odds
   With Greece, Achilles, and, therefore, myself.   620
   I might have raised up Ilium and undone
   All my great father's exploits, and my own.
   I cannot blame a just severity,
   And you shall have your victim.
Orestes   Thus, my lord,
   Your wise decision — prudent but severe —
   Will purchase peace with a helpless infant's life.
Pyrrhus   Yes; but I mean to found it more securely —
   Hermione will make the bond enduring,
   So I shall marry her. And I am pleased
   That you are here to see the happy day;   630
   For none more fittingly can represent
   All Greece, and also represent her father,
   Being the son of Menelaus' brother.
   Go, find her then, and tell her that tomorrow
   You will give away the bride, and with her, peace.
Orestes   Immortal Gods!   *Exit* Orestes
Pyrrhus   Is Love the master now?
   Do you still say you cannot recognise me?
Phoenix   You are yourself, my lord. This welcome
     harshness
   Makes you a Greek, and your own man again;
   No sport of a degrading love, but Pyrrhus,   640
   The son of great Achilles, and his equal,
   Once more responsive to the call of honour.
   You have fought Troy again, and won again.
Pyrrhus   Put it that I had never won till now,
   And only now enjoy the sweets of conquest.
   You saw how low I sank; but, conquering Love,
   I win the greatest fight I ever fought.
   Only think, Phoenix, what I have escaped —
   The turmoil, the innumerable evils
   That come with Love; the friends, the obligations,   650
   I was betraying, and the dangers that . . .
   One single glance could have outweighed them all.
   The kingdoms of the Greeks were at my throat,

And I was glad to perish for her sake!
Phoenix   Yes, there are times, my lord, when cruelty
   Is right.
Pyrrhus   You saw the way she treated me.
   I thought a mother's fears would have disarmed her
   Once she had seen that cherished boy and kissed him.
   But no, I met a storm of tears and passion;
   Suffering makes her wilder; all her speech   660
   Dwelt upon Hector, time and time again.
   To all my promises to save her son
   She answered, between kisses, 'He's my Hector —
   His very eyes, his lips, his spirit even,
   Are his: my husband, it is you I enfold.'
   — And does she really think that I shall let
   Her keep a son to feed a widow's love?
Phoenix   What other gratitude did you expect?
   Forget her, my lord.
Pyrrhus   I see what gives her hope.
   She thinks her beauty is invincible,   670
   And she will see me soon, for all my rancour,
   Flinging myself before her feet again.
   Why, she could fall at mine for all I care:
   She's Hector's widow, I'm Achilles' son.
   A war divides Andromache and Pyrrhus.
Phoenix   If so, my lord, find something else to talk of.
   Go to Hermione and play the suitor
   And let even this anger be forgotten.
   It lies with you to move her thoughts to marriage:
   Why delegate a Prince who is your rival   680
   And mad with love?
Pyrrhus   Do you think Andromache
   Can fail to feel some pangs if I forsake her?
Phoenix   Andromache, always Andromache!
   What matter what she feels or what she hopes?
   Why think of her? You speak like one bewitched.
Pyrrhus   No, there are a hundred things I have not said
   To make her feel how she has angered me,
   How deep is my resentment. Come with me,
   I'll flout her to her face, give full career
   To all my hate. You shall see me humble   690
   That haughty beauty. Come.
Phoenix   Go back, my lord,
   And grovel at her feet protesting love,
   And teach her once again how to despise you.
Pyrrhus   I see how it is. You think I could forgive

And hanker after reconciliation.

Phoenix   You love her. There is nothing more to say.

Pyrrhus   Love her? She hates me, she disdains me more
The more she takes advantage of my love.
Friendless, bereaved and helpless but for me —
I can destroy her son, perhaps I should —   700
An alien, nay a slave, in my Epirus,
I give him back, I give myself, my kingdom,
And never earn from that deceitful heart
A kinder name than that of her tormentor?
Never again! I've sworn to be revenged.
The time has come to justify her hate.
Her son shall die . . . What floods of tears will fall,
What desperate reproaches on my head!
How will she bear to face the dreadful sight?
She too will die, Phoenix, and die through me,   710
No less than if I stabbed her with this hand.

Phoenix   Then why did you announce that you would
            do it?
Why did you not foresee your weakness then?

Pyrrhus   You are right. Forgive if fondness dies so
            slowly.
Did you think my anger was too weak to quench
These final flickerings of expiring love?
Come, Phoenix, I will do as you advise.
Am I to yield the boy? see the Princess?

Phoenix   See her, my lord, renew your protestations,
Tell her . . .

Pyrrhus   I will go through with all I said.   720

ACT III

ORESTES, PYLADES

Pylades   My lord, I beg you, moderate this passion;
You are not yourself. I have never seen you so.
Let me . . .

Orestes   Your words are useless, Pylades.
I have had enough of listening to reason.
I cannot drag my burden any further;
I'll kidnap her, or die in the attempt.
That much is settled, and I'll do it too.
Yes, I will.

Pylades   Very well, then, so we will.

But till we can, consider where you are.
What will they think, to see you act like this?   730
Try to dissemble, moderate your rage,
Control your eyes and make them keep your secret:
The guard, the court, even the air you breathe,
Depend on Pyrrhus. So, most of all, does she,
Hermione. She less than anyone
Must see you in this fury. What possessed you
To try to see her in a mood like this?

Orestes   How should I know? I was beside myself,
Blinded with grief, and ready, I suppose,
To threaten and abuse the two of them.   740

Pylades   Much good would that have done!

Orestes   But who, I ask you,
Could take a blow like this and keep his reason?
He says he weds Hermione tomorrow,
And begs that I will give away his bride.
I know what I should like to give the scoundrel!

Pylades   You blame this unexpected blow on him;
But he has torments, and perhaps deserves
As much compassion as I give to you.

Orestes   Not he; I know him. He enjoys my anguish.
Hermione, her beauty, left him cold;   750
He takes her for the sake of spiting me.
Ah Gods! And I had won her, I had triumphed,
She never would have seen his face again.
Half in, half out of love, she only needed
One last rejection to be in my arms;
Her eyes were opening, she was listening, speaking
With kindness to Orestes. One more word
And it was done.

Pylades   You think?

Orestes   What, all that raging
At his betrayal . . .

Pylades   She never loved him more.
Suppose he let her go, do you imagine   760
She'd not have found one of a hundred reasons
To stay behind? Listen, I beg: forget
Her treacherous charms, forget your plan, and fly.
Why let your passion bind you to a Fury
Who'll loathe you as an enemy all your life
And dwell on nothing but that other wedding
So nearly . . .

Orestes   That is why I mean to take her.
Shall she get all she wants, and send me out

Frustrated, empty-handed, mocked, to see
If this time I can manage to forget her?   770
Oh no, if I must suffer, so must she.
I've whimpered for her pity till I'm tired;
Now I intend for once that she shall fear me.
There shall be tears at last in those cold eyes,
And she shall call me all I ever called her.

Pylades   So then Orestes the ambassador
      Ends up a kidnapper?

Orestes   Why not, Pylades?
      Why should our princes gloat over their vengeance
      If she is gloating over my distress?
      And what is it to me that Greece acclaims me,   780
      If I become the byword of Epirus?
      Can you blame me? But to tell the truth,
      Innocence comes to be a burden to me;
      Some power unjust, I know not what, has always
      Left sin alone and punished innocence.
      Look as I may upon my life, I see
      Nothing but sufferings that dishonour Heaven.
      So why not do the deeds that earn its hatred?
      Enjoy at least the sins that I shall pay for?
      But you, my Pylades, I will not have you   790
      Draw to yourself an anger aimed at me.
      Leave me my doom, my guilt, leave me alone.
      I tell you, you are mad to pity me.
      Leave me my danger, since the prize is mine;
      Take back the boy that Pyrrhus has surrendered,
      And go.

Pylades   Come on, my lord. Danger will show
      What men we are. Hermione shall be ours.
      What can resist a lover and a friend?
      We will rouse up your Greeks. Our ships are ready.
      The wind invites us. I know Pyrrhus' palace   800
      And all its secrets. The sea laps at its walls,
      And easily tonight a hidden passage
      Will see your captive hurried to your ship.

Orestes   I never ought to use your friendship thus,
      But for these sorrows, which no other man
      Pities or knows. Forgive me, dearest friend,
      Forgive the wretch with nothing more to lose
      Of all he ever loved, hateful to others,
      And hateful to himself. If only I
      Could in my turn . . .

Pylades   Keep calm, I ask no more,   810

My lord; dissimulate your true intent,
Let nothing show until the moment strikes.
Till then forget all your frustrated passion.
— I see her coming.

Orestes   Leave us alone together,
And count on me, if I can count on her.   *Exit* Pylades
                    Enter Hermione *and* Cleone

Orestes   Well, I have brought your conquest back, my
    lady.
I talked to Pyrrhus; and your wedding's near.

Hermione   So I have heard; and I believe that you
Came to me simply to convey the news.

Orestes   And you will take him back without reluctance?   820

Hermione   Who would have thought Pyrrhus was not
    unfaithful?
Thought that so late he would declare his love,
And turn at last, the moment I was leaving?
As you will say, he surely fears the Greeks,
Consults his interest more than his heart —
Less humble and submissive far than you.

Orestes   Not so, my lady; not a doubt he loves you.
Those bright eyes never failed to gain their ends;
And it was not your purpose to repel him.

Hermione   What else can I do? My heart's not in my gift.   830
Can I revoke the pledge another made?
Love does not rule the lot of a Princess;
We have no glory but obedience.
Even so, I had nearly left; and you can witness
How near I came to failing in my duty.

Orestes   How can you say such callous . . . ? But, my
    lady,
Each heart has freedom to bestow its love:
Your choice was yours. I hoped. But I confess
I had no right to talk of robbery.
Nor is it you, but Fortune, I accuse;   840
So why afflict you with my lamentations?
You follow duty; and my duty now
Is to cut short a tedious dialogue.   *Exit* Orestes

Hermione   Did you expect so much restraint, Cleone?

Cleone   It may be dangerous. I pity him,
Caught as he is in his own stratagem.
You know how long this wedding hung in doubt;
Orestes speaks, Pyrrhus makes up his mind.

Hermione   You think Pyrrhus could fear? What would
    he fear?

A rabble Hector hunted ten years long,   850
Who cowered in their ships ablaze above them
A hundred times, whenever great Achilles
Was absent from the field; who even now,
But for the presence of Achilles' son
Would still be fighting Troy to rescue Helen?
No, no, Cleone, no man makes him do
More than he wants to: if he marries me
He loves me. If Orestes wants to blame me,
Let him. Am I obliged to mourn with him?
Pyrrhus is mine again. Ah, dear Cleone,   860
Can you conceive the wildness of my rapture?
Do you know Pyrrhus? Have you listened to
The record of his deeds? But who can tell them?
Dauntless, and waited on by Victory,
Courtly and gracious, yes and faithful too,
What hero could be more . . . ?
Cleone   We are not alone.
Your rival comes in tears to implore your pity.
Hermione   Not even a moment to indulge my joy?
Come; there is nothing I can say to her.

                        Enter Andromache *and* Cephissa
Andromache   Why do you fear to let me speak, my
        lady?   870
Is it not pleasant to behold the sight
Of Hector's widow weeping at your feet?
I have not come with tears of jealousy
To appeal against the conquest you have made.
The only heart I ever sought to rule
Was pierced in battle by an enemy steel;
My only love was lit by Hector's flame,
And lies for ever buried in his tomb.
But still a son remains. You'll learn one day,
My lady, what a mother's love can be;   880
But never will you know, I hope at least,
The mortal pangs a son can make us suffer
When, out of all we treasured, this alone
Is left, and this they seek to take away.
Ah, when the Trojans, after ten long years
Of weary war, threatened your mother's life,
I spoke for her to Hector, and he saved her;
Your word with Pyrrhus has as great a power.
What danger's in a child whose life is done
While still he lives? I only ask to hide him   890
In some unpeopled isle, where I shall teach him —

Can you not take his mother's word for this? —
Only to live as I live, and to weep.
Hermione   I see your sorrow. But a sacred duty
Forbids me to speak out against my father;
For it was he demanded this of Pyrrhus.
If another influence can sway him,
Whose better than your own? We know how long
Your charms have ruled his heart. Make him relent:
I shall be happy to endorse the judgement.   900

                                        Exit Hermione
Andromache   How slightingly she let fall her refusal!
Cleone   But why not plead with Pyrrhus, as she said?
You could defeat her, you could rout the Greeks
With one glance, even now. — Why, here he is,
Looking for you.

                              Enter Pyrrhus *and* Phoenix
Pyrrhus (*to* Phoenix)   Where is Hermione?
Wasn't the Princess here?
Phoenix   So I was told.
Andromache (*to* Cephissa)   So much for what a glance
        of mine can do!
Pyrrhus   What did she say, Phoenix?
Andromache   There is no hope.
Phoenix   This way, my lord; Hermione went here.
Cephissa   Speak, snatch the moment. Force yourself
        to speak.   910
Andromache   He's given his word.
Cephissa   But not performed it yet.
Andromache   What is the use of pleas? They're going
        to kill him.
Pyrrhus   She will not condescend to look this way.
The arrogance!
Andromache   I only anger him
More deeply. Let us go.
Pyrrhus   Fetch Hector's son,
We'll take him to the Greeks.
Andromache   No, my lord! Stop,
You cannot mean it. If you do intend
To give the son, give them the mother too!
After the kindness that you swore me once
Can I not find even a grain of pity?   920
Is he condemned, can there be no reprieve?
Pyrrhus   Phoenix will tell you: I have given my word.
Andromache   And all those dangers you would brave
        for me?

Pyrrhus   Then I was blind, my eyes are open now.
　　　He could have had his pardon for a word:
　　　You never even brought yourself to speak it.
　　　Now, is too late.
Andromache   My lord, you understood
　　　The language of unspoken pleas that feared
　　　To find themselves rejected. Will you not
　　　Forgive, as memories from a brighter past,   930
　　　Those last remains of pride, that cannot bear
　　　To beg for favours? For you know, too well,
　　　That never but for you Andromache
　　　Had clasped a master's feet.
Pyrrhus   No no, you hate me.
　　　Within your heart of hearts you would be sorry
　　　If you owed anything to my devotion —
　　　Even your son, that son you love so much,
　　　If I had saved him, would be less to you.
　　　You've shown me nothing but disdain and loathing;
　　　You hate me more than all the Greeks together.   940
　　　Go on, and feed on this sublime resentment!
　　　Come away, Phoenix.
Andromache (*to* Cephissa)   Come to my husband's grave.
Cephissa   My lady . . .
Andromache   What is there left for me to tell him?
　　　He knows it all — did he not cause it all?
　　　— My lord, see what you have reduced me to:
　　　I have seen a father slain, our ramparts fired,
　　　My family cut off, my husband's body
　　　Covered with gore, and dragged along the dust.
　　　Only his son remains, and I, in bondage.
　　　But, for a son, one may endure. I live,   950
　　　I live a servant. And even more than this —
　　　Sometimes I have felt comfort in the thought
　　　That here, not elsewhere, I have found my exile,
　　　And the sad scion of so many Kings,
　　　Happy at least in this, if serve he must,
　　　Should be your servant. I have felt a hope
　　　That, in his prison, he would have a home.
　　　The suppliant Priam found Achilles gentle:
　　　I looked for greater kindness in his son . . .
　　　Forgive me, Hector, my credulity!   960
　　　I never thought this of your enemy;
　　　I thought he must possess, for all his showing,
　　　Some generosity; enough at least
　　　To let us join you in the grave I made you,

Ending his hatred and our misery
In that reunion with my cherished dead.
Pyrrhus   Wait for me there, Phoenix.   *Exit* Phoenix
                                          — My lady, stay.
You still could have the son you mourn. I know,
I know too well, each tear I made you shed
Is a new weapon I have given you.   970
I thought my hate was stronger than it is . . .
But look at me at least, my lady; see
Whether I bear the aspect of a judge,
A torturer that seeks to do you harm.
Why do you force me to betray your interests?
For your son's sake, can we not cease to hate?
Must *I* beg *you* for pity? Must I weep,
Am I to clasp your knees on his behalf?
For the last time, save him and save yourself.
I know what solemn oaths I have to break,   980
What furious hates will burst upon my head:
I jilt Hermione, and on her brow
Leave, not a crown, but an undying slight;
I lead you to the temple decked for her,
And with her diadem I crown you Queen.
But this time ponder well upon the offer.
Either you reign, believe me, or he dies.
I've borne a year of passion disappointed;
So now, no more uncertainty; I've feared,
I've threatened, I've entreated long enough.   990
I die if I lose you; but to wait like this
Is also death. Therefore, make up your mind:
I leave you now, but when I come again
I take you to the temple, where your child
Will wait for us; and I, your ardent lover
Or else, my lady, your relentless judge,
Will crown your head, or kill him in your sight.
                                          Exit Pyrrhus
Cephissa   Have I not told you that in spite of Greece
You could be mistress of your fate again?
Andromache   Can you not see the harm you did in
          speaking?   1000
Now I myself pass sentence on my son.
Cephissa   This constancy, my lady, to the dead,
Fine as it is, may make you criminal.
Hector himself would counsel milder thoughts.
Andromache   What, shall I fill his empty place with
          Pyrrhus?

Cephissa   You must, if you would keep his son alive.
Do you believe his spirit would be shamed,
Would scorn, my lady, a victorious King
Who means to give you back your former state,
Who tramples on your furious conquerors,   1010
Forgets that great Achilles was his father,
And makes his mighty deeds of none effect?
Andromache   He may forget, but I must still remember.
Shall I forget the unburied corpse of Hector
Dragged in dishonour round our city walls?
Forget his father dashed before my feet,
Clutching the altar where his own blood flowed?
Think of that night of horror, think, Cephissa —
A night without a dawn for all our race;
Imagine Pyrrhus, with his flashing eyes   1020
Bright in the blazing of our royal halls,
Hacking his way over my brothers' bodies,
Bloody himself, cheering the bloodshed on;
Imagine all the clamour — victors' cries
And cries of those that died, by flame, by sword;
And, cowering in the midst, Andromache.
That was how Pyrrhus came before my eyes,
These were the exploits where he gained his glory;
This is the man you want to see me marry!
How could I be a party to his guilt?   1030
Let him take us, the last of all his victims,
Before I lose the right to curse his name!
Cephissa   Then let us go and watch them kill your son;
They wait for you. — That makes you flinch, my lady.
Andromache   Ah, what a memory you have awoken,
Cephissa! Must I watch another death,
That of my son, my only happiness,
The image of my Hector, and the pledge
He left me of his love? I see him now,
As on that day he ventured forth to face   1040
Mighty Achilles, and to meet his doom:
He made me bring his babe, he took him up,
And wiped my tears, and spoke: 'My dearest wife,
I cannot tell how I shall end this day.
Receive my son, the token of my love;
If I should perish, fill his father's place;
In memory of all our happiness
Spend on the child the love you bore his father.'
And can I let that legacy be destroyed,
And with that blood, the blood of all his line?   1050

Merciless King, is he to die for me?
Because I hate you, must he pay the price?
Has he called you the murderer of his kin?
Has he blamed you for ills he cannot feel?
Yet you must die, my child, unless I stay
The savage sword almost upraised to fall.
I can stop him; and shall I let you die?
Never, you shall not. I will not endure it.
We must find Pyrrhus. No, but, sweet Cephissa,
Go to him for me.

Cephissa   And what shall I say?   1060
Andromache   Tell him, such is the love I bear my
          son . . .
But do you think he really means to kill him?
Could any lover ever stoop so low?
Cephissa   This moment he may reappear in fury.
Andromache   Well then, go take him . . .
Cephissa   Take him . . . ? your solemn word?
Andromache   Is it still mine, to promise it again?
O ashes of my husband! O my country!
O child, how dearly must I buy your life!
Come.
Cephissa   Where, my lady? What is your resolve?
Andromache   To go and talk to Hector on his grave.   1070

ACT IV

ANDROMACHE, CEPHISSA

Cephissa   Beyond all doubt, my lady, it is Hector,
Your lord, that works this marvel in your mind.
It is his will that Troy should rise again
Under this happy son he has made you save;
For you have Pyrrhus' promise; and you have seen
How joyfully he gave it, and how freely.
His father and his sceptre and his allies
He sacrifices, simply for your love,
Proclaiming you the Queen of all his subjects.
Is this the conqueror that you have hated?   1080
Look how defiantly he braves the Greeks
And shields your son against their violence
As if he were his own; he has given him
His guard, and left himself in jeopardy.

— But now the temple waits; and you have
    promised . . .
Andromache   I shall be there; but first we'll see my son.
Cephissa   Why now, my lady? Henceforward there is
    nothing
    To stop you seeing him and showering on him
    All the caresses that your heart desires.
    Oh think, what joy, that you can bring him up,   1090
    Not as a slave who learns to please a master
    But to perpetuate the noble line
    Of all the Kings that ruled in Troy before!
Andromache   Let us go now and visit him, Cephissa,
    For the last time.
Cephissa   The last! What do you mean?
Andromache   Ah, sweet Cephissa, why should I conceal
    My thought from you, you who in all my sorrows
    Have never failed me? But I hoped that also
    You understood me better. Did you think
    Andromache could break faith, and betray   1100
    The trust a husband left her to fulfil;
    And, waking the pain of all those honoured dead,
    Secure my peace at the expense of theirs?
    Was that the devotion promised to his ashes?
    But I was forced to act to save my son.
    Marrying Pyrrhus, I buy his protection
    And I'm content. I trust him, for I know him —
    Violent, but honest. He will do, Cephissa,
    More even than he said. The Greeks will make him;
    Their rage gives Hector's son a second father.   1110
    So then, I shall surrender, since I must,
    To Pyrrhus the remainder of my days;
    Who, as he makes his vows before the altar,
    Will bind himself by everlasting bonds
    To serve my son. But at the self-same moment
    I, with a stroke hurtful to me alone,
    Will cut the course of this disloyal life,
    Redeem my oaths, and render what is due
    To him, to my son, to my husband, to myself.
    Such is the innocent stratagem of love   1120
    My husband's spirit whispered in my ear;
    I go alone to Hector and my forebears,
    And you, Cephissa, will close up my eyes.
Cephissa   Not I. You must not think I could outlive . . .
Andromache   No, no. You have to stay here. Hector's
    son

Is left to you, my last and dearest treasure.
You lived for me, live now for him. Remember
The hopes of Troy lie in your hands alone.
Think of the Kings that cannot reign without you.
Watch over Pyrrhus. See that he is faithful;   1130
Make mention, if you have to, of my name;
Remind him of the marriage I accepted.
Tell him, I put myself in his dependence
Before I died; tell him his anger must
Be now assuaged; that leaving him my son
Is proof of my esteem. Speak to my son
About the heroes of his line, and lead him,
As far as lies in you, to follow them.
Talk of the deeds for which their names were
          known:
The things they did, and not the place they held.   1140
Speak to him daily of his father's virtues,
And also sometimes tell him of his mother.
But let him never think of vengeance now.
We have left him a master to be humoured.
Let him remember his great ancestors,
Though not with pride — he is the blood of Hector,
But he is all that's left; and for that all
I have myself in sacrifice, in one day,
Offered my blood, my hatred, and my love.

Cephissa   Alas!
Andromache   Do not come with me, if you think
                                        your heart   1150
Cannot control its trouble and its tears.
— Someone approaches. Dry your eyes, Cephissa;
Remember that Andromache confides
The secret of her destiny to you.
It is Hermione. Quick, come away.
I cannot face her now.   *Exeunt*
                    Enter Hermione *and* Cleone
Cleone   I am amazed:
What, not a word, my lady? Such an outrage
Leaves you serene, wordless and unprotesting?
You stand unmoved in face of this rebuff,
You, who could not endure Andromache   1160
So much as named; you who were in despair
If Pyrrhus even cast a glance at her?
And now he marries her. She gets his crown,
She hears the vows you heard, only today,
Of everlasting love, made now to her;

And with such grounds of jealousy and grief
You have not deigned to show that you are hurt?
But such a silence is too menacing;
Much rather would I . . .
Hermione   Is Orestes coming?
Cleone   Yes, he is sent for, yes. You may be sure   1170
    You w uld have found him swiftly at your feet,
    Ready to serve without reward for ever,
    The helpless prisoner of your bright eyes . . .
    He is here.
                                        Enter Orestes

Orestes   Ah, my lady, is it true
    For once Orestes is a welcome guest?
    Have I been flattered by a false report
    Or did you truly wish to see my face?
    Can I believe that after long aversion
    Your eyes . . .
Hermione   I wish to ask you if you love me.
Orestes   Love you, O Gods! The oaths I swore and
        broke,   1180
    My escape and my return, revolts, surrenders,
    My agonies and my unceasing tears —
    If these are not enough, how can I prove it?
Hermione   Revenge me: I believe.
Orestes   Willingly. Come.
    Let us away and set all Greece in flames,
    Win glory for my prowess and your name,
    A second Helen, a new Agamemnon;
    Bring back the horrors of the Trojan siege
    And live in men's memory as do our fathers.
    Come, I am ready.
Hermione   No, my lord. We stay: 1190
    I will not leave with such a slight upon me.
    Do you suppose that I would quit the field
    Before the insults of my enemies
    And sit to await the fortunes of a war
    That after all might give me no revenge?
    I'll leave, when all Epirus weeps behind me.
    But if you will be my avenger, do it
    Within the hour. To talk to me of waiting
    Is to refuse. Away, into the temple
    And slaughter . . .
Orestes   Who?
Hermione   Pyrrhus!
Orestes   Pyrrhus, my lady!   1200

Hermione   Ah, so your hate has cooled, has it? Make
          haste,
     Away, and hope I do not call you back!
     It is not for you to plead in his defence
     Or talk to me of rights that I reject.
Orestes   What, I defend him? After your favours, which
     Are proofs of his wickedness? I will revenge you —
     No greater privilege: but not like that.
     We can be enemies, not murderers,
     Compass his ruin by a just defeat.
     Am I to bear for answer back to Greece   1210
     A bloody head? And is the charge Greece gave me
     To be fulfilled by an assassination?
     In the Gods' name, let Greece decide the case,
     And let the people's hate pronounce his death.
     He is a King; and round the heads of kings . . .
Hermione   What, is it not enough that I condemn him?
     Is it not enough that my good name
     Requires a victim killed for me alone?
     That for a tyrant brought to his account
     The due reward will be Hermione?   1220
     That I hate him? nay more, that I did love him?
     It's true: unworthy as he was, I loved him.
     Which was to blame, my father or my heart,
     No matter now. This is enough for you —
     For all the shamefulness of his betrayal,
     For all the horror that I feel for him,
     Beware: as long as Pyrrhus is alive
     I may forgive him. I'll not answer for it
     Until he's dead. Either he dies today,
     Or else perhaps tomorrow I shall love him.   1230
Orestes   So, he must fall before he can be pardoned;
     That is enough. — But how am I to do it?
     How shall I execute your doom so quickly?
     How can I find a ready way to strike him?
     Almost before I land, you order me
     To overthrow a state. You want to see
     A monarch die, and for his death you give me
     One day, one hour, one moment. Must I kill him
     In the sight of all his subjects? How can I
     Devise a means to coax the sacrifice   1240
     Up to the altar? Trust me, I will do it;
     All that I ask is time to see the place
     And plan the deed. This night I strike. This night
     I carry out your will.

Hermione   Yes, but this day
He weds Andromache. The throne's decked now,
His crime's fulfilled, my shame is consummated.
What do you need? How could he make it easier?
He goes to celebrate his happiness
Unguarded, unattended. All his men
Are round the son of Hector — anyone   1250
Who cares to claim revenge for me may take it.
Will you protect a life he throws away?
Speak to your friends, and marshal all your men;
Take mine — they're all against him. He has broken
His word to me and you, humbled us all.
They hate him as the husband of a Trojan,
And rage no less than I do for revenge.
With them you cannot fail. Let them but work,
They'll do it for you. You can lead them on
Or merely follow. And if you return   1260
Bathed in the lifeblood of the perjurer,
You may be sure that you have won my heart.
Orestes   My lady, but consider . . .
Hermione   That will do!
Your quibbles are an insult to my rage.
I thought to give you means to find my favour,
To make Orestes happier. Now I see
That he is happier to keep a grievance
That win rewards. — Goodbye; go somewhere else
To boast your constancy. Leave revenge to me.
I blush for all the kindness I have shown you.   1270
Today, I cannot stomach more rebuffs.
So I shall go, and I shall go alone,
Up to the temple where the bridal waits
And you are too afraid to earn my thanks.
I shall find means to reach my enemy.
I'll pierce that heart that I could never touch,
Then pierce my own, and the one bloodstained knife
Will join in death what nothing else could join;
And I shall die, for all his cruelty,
More willingly with him than live with you!   1280
Orestes   You shall not have that grisly satisfaction,
My lady. None but I shall strike him down.
You shall have the victim that you call for,
And afterwards reward me, if you will.
Hermione   Away, then, quickly. Leave the rest to me,
And put our ships in instant readiness.

                                              Exit Orestes

Cleone   My lady, this is madness. Think at least . . .
Hermione   Madness or not, I think of my revenge.
   If only I were sure, for all his promises,
   That I do well to leave it to another.   1290
   I have more reasons for condemning Pyrrhus,
   And I could do it better far than he.
   What would I give to take my own revenge,
   To see my own hands reddened with his blood,
   And, for his torment and my greater pleasure,
   Conceal my rival from his dying eyes!
   If I were sure at least that, as he kills him,
   Orestes tells him that he dies for me!
   Go after him. Make sure he tells the traitor
   That I condemned him — not the Greeks, but I.   1300
   Quickly, Cleone. It is not a vengeance
   Unless he knows in dying that I killed him.
Cleone   It shall be done. — But in the name of Heaven!
   How can it be? My lady, here's the King.
Hermione   Oh, find Orestes. Tell him, my Cleone,
   To hold his hand till we have met again.   *Exit* Cleone
                                     Enter Pyrrhus *and* Phoenix
Pyrrhus   I know that you were not expecting me,
   My lady, and my coming interrupts you.
   I am not here to use unworthy art
   And make injustice pass for innocence;   1310
   That my own heart condemns me, is enough,
   And what I do not feel, I could not plead.
   I am to wed a Trojan woman: yes,
   And what is even worse, the heart I bring her
   I owe to you. Another man might urge
   That on the plains of Troy, when our two fathers
   Engaged our hands, our hearts were not consulted,
   And love was absent from the pact they made.
   But it suffices me that I consented;
   And when ambassadors promised you my heart   1320
   I did not disavow them, I endorsed them.
   I let them bring you home to my Epirus.
   Here, though another with her sovereign beauty
   Had conquered what your beauty should have
         claimed,
   I brushed aside that unexpected passion;
   I tried to will myself to faithfulness,
   Welcomed you as my Queen, and to this day
   I hoped my vows could take the place of love.
   But love has proved too strong. Andromache

Triumphs, and wins the heart she feared to gain,   1330
And each of us as helpless as the other
Is hurrying the other to that temple
To make reluctant vows of love unending.
So now, let all your rancour loose on one
Who sorrows at his treachery even as
He executes it. I shall not attempt
To quell an anger, which will bring relief,
And, as I think, no less to me than you.
Fling at me all the titles fit for perjurers.
I do not fear your taunts, I fear your silence;   1340
And anything that you forbear to say
I shall hear in the secret of my heart.
Hermione   These terms, so free of all unworthy art,
Do show, my lord, that you see what you are doing,
And, as you violate a most sacred pact,
You go about it as a criminal.
Why should a conquering hero, after all,
Stoop to the servitude of keeping faith?
No, treachery has much to recommend it;
And you are here, it seems, to tell me so.   1350
What, undeterred by promise or by duty,
You court a Greek and love a Trojan mistress?
You leave me, then return, and then go back
From Helen's daughter to the wife of Hector?
Dangle your crown at times before a slave,
Then a princess? Sacrifice Troy to Greece,
Then Greece to Hector's orphan? Noble signs
That show a hero captain of his soul,
Slave to no promises. Would you have liked
To flaunt as ornaments before your bride   1360
The names, perhaps, of traitor and deceiver?
Did you hope to find some pallor on my brow
That you could laugh at as you lay together?
Did you need me in tears to grace your triumph?
No. For one day, my lord, you ask too much,
And those distinctions that you have already
Are surely ample: who could wish for more?
— Such as the regal Priam in the dust,
Before his kinsfolk almost dead with horror
To see your sword probing his ancient breast   1370
For some drop of chill blood the years had spared;
Troy all ablaze and slaked in streams of blood;
Polýxena, whose life you took yourself
While your own army watched in outraged shame —

Who could remain unmoved at feats like these?
Pyrrhus   Let us not dwell too much on cruelties
That Helen's wrongs called forth. You have no need
To ask why blood was shed. But I am willing
That what is past be buried. And I am thankful
To find I have not harmed you by this love.   1380
I should have known you better, judged more calmly,
Instead of torturing myself for nothing.
It was presumption, and a grave injustice —
I was not loved, so how could I betray?
I've called myself a traitor, when perhaps
I've been your helper — for you did not want me;
There was no predetermined union
Between our hearts: I meant to do my duty,
You bowed to yours. What cause had you to love me?
Hermione   I did not love you? What do you think I
      did?   1390
I scorned the proffered hands of all our princes;
I came out here to you; and I remain,
Unmoved by all your infidelities,
Trying to check the outcry of my Greeks
Who gaze revolted at my weaknesses.
I made them hush up my humiliation;
I thought to see you, in a better mind,
Return one day remembering your duty
And beg me take the heart that was mine of right.
I loved you faithless — faithful, ah, what then?   1400
And even at this moment, as I hear
Those cruel lips so unconcernedly
Pronounce my mortal sentence, you deceiver,
How can I tell I do not love you still?
Even so, my lord, if it has come to this,
If Fate assigns the glory of your love
To someone else, marry her. But at least
Not in my presence. Hear a last request —
For it may be we shall not meet again —
Leave just one day, and all the rest is yours.   1410
You do not speak? You faithless cur, it's clear
Each moment spent with me is one too many;
You cannot bear to be away from her,
Your Trojan woman, you cannot spare a word
For anyone, every thought strays to her
And every glance. — What are you waiting for?
Go away, go. Repeat your vows to her
And take the high names of the Gods in vain.

Those Gods, those righteous Gods, will not forget
They heard such promises addressed to me.   1420
So, take your place with her before the altar,
Abandon me. Go, hurry; but beware
In case you meet Hermione there again!

Exit Hermione

Phoenix   You heard what she said. My lord, do not
          disdain
     A threat of vengeance from a woman scorned.
     She is not here alone: the cause of Greece
     Is joined with hers: Orestes loves her still,
     And if encouraged . . .
Pyrrhus   Phoenix, I am late.
     I go to Andromache. You guard her son.

ACT V

HERMIONE, alone

Hermione   Lost! What have I done? What shall I do?   1430
     Caught up distraught in who knows what despair,
     Aimlessly wandering in these empty halls,
     Why am I here? Ah, shall I ever know
     If it is hate or love, the pain I feel?
     What cruelty in his eyes as he dismissed me!
     And not a touch of kindness or of pity,
     Not even counterfeit! Was there one sign
     Of doubt or of relenting in his eyes?
     Or any sound of sorrow from his lips?
     Dumb to my sighs, unmoved at my distress,   1440
     Did he so much as notice I was weeping?
     And still I spare him? Even worse, my heart,
     My craven heart, forgets its injury
     And sides with him? And I, I cannot bear
     Even to imagine what awaits him,
     And on the point of my revenge, reprieve him?
     No, no, I will not pardon. Let him go:
     Is he not dead for ever in my eyes?
     He triumphs in his perfidy, and mocks,
     Thinking the storm will spend itself in tears   1450
     And I, still feeble and irresolute,
     Will always parry with the other hand
     Each stroke I deal. He thinks I am as I was.
     No, that's not true: he does not think of me.

What's it to him, exultant in that temple,
If someone else wants him alive or dead?
That grim dilemma he has left to me.
No, for the last time. Let Orestes strike
And let him die — he should have seen it coming,
And he has driven me to will his death.   1460
To will his death? What? I have ordered this?
This was the love-gift of Hermione
To one, whose exploits were my daily theme,
Over and over told for my delight;
To one whom I had chosen for myself
In secret, long before our fatal match?
And have I sought him over land and sea
Only for this, to plot against his life,
To watch him die? Oh, quickly, while there's time . . .

                              Enter Cleone

Hermione   What have I done, Cleone? What is your
                      news?   1470
What's Pyrrhus doing?
Cleone   He is beside himself,
The fondest and most glorious of lovers.
I watched as he advanced towards the temple,
Leading his conquest with a conqueror's air,
His eyes alight with joy and expectation,
Drunken with rapture simply at her sight.
Andromache meanwhile, amid the plaudits,
Bears in her heart the memory of Troy,
Incapable of love, forswearing hate,
She neither joys nor murmurs, but obeys.   1480
Hermione   But did you, Cleone, study his expression?
Was all his pleasure perfect and serene?
Did not his eyes turn once towards this palace?
Did you not let him see you? Did he blush,
Tell me, when he set eyes on you? Or show
In any feature that he felt remorse?
Or did he face it out until the end?
Cleone   He sees nothing, my lady, thinks of nothing,
Neither yourself, nor safety, nor good name;
He does not care who is about him, subjects   1490
Or enemies; all his thought is for his love.
His guard has gone to keep the son of Hector
As if he were the only one at hazard.
Phoenix has charge of them, and they are now
Far from us, far from Pyrrhus, in a stronghold.
After that, Pyrrhus has no other cares.

Hermione   Perfidy! He shall die. — What says Orestes?
Cleone   He has gone into the temple with his Greeks.
Hermione   Well, is he, or not, determined to revenge
        me?
Cleone   I cannot say.
Hermione   You cannot say! Orestes,   1500
    He too will fail me?
Cleone   No, he loves you dearly,
    But such remorse is raging in his mind
    That now his love, and now his scruple, leads him.
    In Pyrrhus he respects the royal name,
    Respects Achilles, yes, and Pyrrhus too.
    He fears the Greeks, and universal outrage.
    But he dreads himself, he says, the most of all.
    Proudly as he would take his life in battle,
    He shrinks in horror from the name 'assassin'.
    Still, he went in, doubting if he would leave   1510
    Guilty of murder, or a wedding-guest.
Hermione   Oh no, there's nothing they need fear from
        him:
    He will not mar their triumph or their joy.
    I know the secret of all his misgivings —
    He fears to die, there's nothing else he fears.
    To think my mother never stooped to plead,
    Yet every Greek took arms in her defence,
    And for her sake, in those ten years of war,
    Died twenty kings that she had never met!
    And I, who claim one traitor's punishment,   1520
    And put my cause into a lover's hands,
    Give him a safe and certain way to win me,
    Offer myself — I cannot be revenged?
    Well then, I'll take my cause in hand myself;
    I'll make their temple ring with shrieks and groans,
    Wipe out their wedding, end their union,
    As far as lies in me, before it starts.
    I'll strike out blindly in my hour of fury,
    See Pyrrhus everywhere — even in Orestes.
    Oh, I shall die, but not without revenge,   1530
    I shall not die alone, and there shall be
    Someone to go with me — .   *Enter* Orestes
Orestes   So, it is over,
    My task is done, and you have been obeyed.
    Pyrrhus is yielding up his guilty life
    Before the altar.
Hermione   Is he dead then?

Orestes   Dying.
   Our Greeks have wiped the score clean with his
         blood.
   You had my word for it: and though my heart
   Was sick with apprehension of the deed,
   I hurried to the place; I found our men
   Around the altar mingled with the crowd.   1540
   Pyrrhus observed me; but his face showed nothing
   Except resolve — perhaps to see me there
   And to flout all Greece in her ambassador
   Lent something splendid to his wedding rites.
   Himself with eager hands he laid his crown
   Upon the bent head of Andromache,
   Saying, 'Receive my kingdom and my heart,
   Andromache; be Queen over Epirus
   And over me. I promise to your son
   A father's loving care. By all the Gods   1550
   I swear it, in the presence of his mother;
   And I proclaim his title King of Troy.'
   His people all applauded, but the Greeks
   Howled in defiance, and clustered round about him
   So close, I could not find a place to strike
   So keenly did they vie to bring him down.
   I saw him face them, and struggle for some moments
   Streaming with blood, fighting to break away,
   And then at last fall headlong by the altar.
   At that I cleft the terror-stricken throng   1560
   To reach my love and carry her to safety
   Back to the haven, where our friends will gather
   Drenched in the blood I undertook to bring you.
Hermione   What have they done?
Orestes   Forgive their too much haste.
   I see it now — they ruined your revenge:
   Mine should have been the hand that touched him
         first,
   So that in death he knew he died your victim.
   But mine was the passion that inflamed them all,
   I led them there, led them for you alone,
   My lady, and the glory of the death   1570
   Is yours. They were the executioners,
   But you prepared the blow.
Hermione   Enough, you criminal;
   Keep all the credit of your parricide,
   Go and parade your deed before the Greeks,
   Go. I want none of it. I abhor your sight.

What have you done? What cruel, what savage
    madness
Made you cut off that noble, noble life?
You butchers, when you offered up that victim
Did not your own blood mutiny against you?
Speak up: who gave you the right to sentence him?   1580
Why did you do it? And for what? Why you?
Who told you to?
Orestes   Great Gods! but did you not
Command me, here, yourself, not an hour past?
Hermione   Did you believe the ravings of a lover?
Couldn't you try to read my true desires?
Couldn't you see that even in my raging
My heart unsaid the word before I spoke it?
And what if I said it? Was it for you to obey?
Why didn't you force me to repeat the word
A hundred times again? Why didn't you   1590
Make me reflect once more before the end,
Come back again — or better, keep away?
Couldn't you let me get my own revenge?
What brought you here at all? Who wants you here?
Look what has come of your accursed love —
The doom that clings to you, you brought to me.
You only, and your doubly fatal mission,
Made him decide for her, and choose his death.
He might be still irresolute between us —
He might love me; he might pretend to love me.   1600
You can go. Goodbye. I stay here in Epirus.
I've done with Sparta and I've done with Greece,
I've done with all my kindred. It's enough
For me that you are one of them, you monster!
                      Exit Hermione
Orestes, alone   What was that? Hermione? Were those
    her words?
Was it for this that so much blood was spilt?
She calls me treacherous, calls me murderer.
Is it Pyrrhus dying there? Am I Orestes?
So then, I silence conscience in my breast,
Breach in one day all sanctities at once,   1610
Those that encircle kings, ambassadors,
And every man and every human bond;
Even that altar, where I did not spare him.
I have committed murder, parricide,
I have committed sacrilege — and for whom?
For one without a heart, who makes me promise,

Who will not see me till she knows he's dead.
And so I serve her passion, and when I've done it
She turns upon me and demands from me
The blood I shed, the life I took for her!   1620
She loves him! I'm a madman, I'm a monster,
And she has passed for ever from my sight,
Tossing me as she passes for my wages
Each hideous title I assumed — for her!

      Enter Pylades, *with* Orestes' men

Pylades We must go quickly. Come away, my lord,
Unless you mean never to leave the palace.
Our Greeks still hold the gateway for a while,
But all the populace is after us.
The town is subject to Andromache,
And she, who held the king at bay so long,   1630
Pays him the duty of a faithful widow,
Calls for revenge for him — or else perhaps
Revenge for Hector by our punishment.
Come on, for very soon they will surround us.
Our men will join us later. While the people
Still cluster round to see Hermione,
This is the way, and we can still escape.

Orestes Not I. I must go to Hermione.
How can I live in her disdain and anger?
You go. The act was mine, I'll pay the price.   1640

Pylades Hermione, my lord? Better forget her.
Must you be nothing but her passion's tool
And now its victim? Do you mean to see,
Among the dead, how she can wrong you there?
And if she dies, what reason you should die?

Orestes She dies? O all you Gods!

Pylades   Did you not know?
As we came up, she passed us rushing out
In frenzy uncontrolled, towards the temple.
Finally she found the corpse of Pyrrhus
Carried by soldiers crying for revenge,   1650
And there her passion must have mastered her.
For looking from the gate we saw her next
Snatch up a dagger, bend above the King,
Look up, and stab, and fall.

Orestes   Why, Heaven be praised!
I've borne more than I ever thought I could.
You have done well, you patient justicers,
So unremitting in your torturer's task;
There is no peak of pain I have not touched —

Sport of your hatred, born to take upon me
All of your wrath and all the woes of men.   1660
I have fulfilled my fate, I die content.
Where are those lovers now? To crown my joy
I must end wallowing in their blood and mine;
I want to contemplate them while I die —
Three hearts at odds no more. — But, suddenly,
What is this darkness that comes over me?
What is this shuddering horror? Ah, thank Heaven,
A glint of light again. But Gods, what blood,
What gushing blood!

Pylades   Alas, my lord!
Orestes   Ha, Pyrrhus,
What are you doing here? Detested rival,   1670
Must you be everywhere? I saw you stabbed
A dozen times: how did you get away?
Take that, and that, the blows I saved for you.
— But what is this? Hermione enfolds him,
She drags him back and saves him from my sword,
And eyes me, Gods! with eyes I cannot face.
What rabble's that she rallies, snakes and demons?
Are you there too, gaunt Goddesses of Hell,
With whistling snakes set writhing in your locks?
Who do they seek? for whom have you prepared   1680
The hideous engines I can see behind you?
Was it to take me to the unending Night
You came? Come on, here is Orestes, take him!
But no, stand back, Hermione is there,
And she can rend me better than you all.
Here is my heart for her to gorge upon.

Pylades   Look, he has fainted. Hurry, take him up.
This is a happy chance, for time is pressing
And there is nothing we could do for him
If he regained his madness with his strength.   1690

IPHIGENIA
(1674)

INTRODUCTION

Like *Andromache*, this play is linked with the great legend of the Trojan war, but this time looks forward to it in the immediate future; and beyond the war, the bloodstained history of Iphigenia's parents and their son Orestes — set aside, as we have seen, in *Andromache* — is the subject of some grim tragic irony (lines 1672, 1680).

It is directly indebted to Euripides' *Iphigenia in Aulis*, but (as Racine does not say) very much also to a reworking of that tragedy by Jean Rotrou (1640), in which Achilles loves Iphigenia. In both plays they meet for the first time on the stage; the Greek hero expresses only admiration and pity for the girl, while the French one undergoes a *coup de foudre*. Public taste demanded a love-interest, and would not have understood it if such an obvious opportunity had been missed. But Racine treats it with such taste and discretion that the clash with ancient manners hardly irks a modern public: the couple are already betrothed, so the conventional coynesses of (seventeenth-century) courtship have been thrown back into the past, and the heroine can be sincere and direct; in any case, as always in Racine, danger presses and they have almost no time to talk of their love in peace.

Achilles has reflections of Homer's splendid figure. Agamemnon wavers and changes his resolve more often than in Euripides. The very moving relation between father and daughter, unique in Racine, owes much to the Greek tragedy, but the mixture of girlish spontaneity with high-born decorum and firmness of purpose in a tragic crisis in largely original and seems to me beautifully conveyed. She is, in her acts and reactions at least, the youngest of Racine's heroines. Her terrible mother, with her egotism and self-assertiveness, is already in Euripides. The motive for Iphigenia's final refusal to be rescued removes a blemish noted by Aristotle in Euripides — his heroine's sudden unexplained change from pleading to resignation (*Poetics* 15): it is not so much, or not only, because her father has forbidden her to see Achilles again, but because, as it has recently been pointed out, this is the only way to prevent a head-on collision between the two men she loves.

Of the difficulty of dramatising this story enough has been said (p. x). Without the Goddess who demands a human life, there would be no play; and the seventeenth century was coming to demand 'poetic justice' for innocent and guilty. Racine has defended his solution in his preface: it is both uneasy and over-ingenious. It involves nothing less than forging a passport for Eriphile (see note to *Dramatis personae*). Her part has to be built up, and though they have tragic value her scenes jar a little with the story on which they are grafted. The sub-plot culminates in a 'recognition', which is of the seventeenth-century and not the classical type, in that the audience as well as the characters had been in the dark, in spite of clues carefully planted. And we still do not know why Diana wanted her killed — must we think she foresaw the betrayal Eriphile had not yet committed?

The play was first given in the middle of one of Louis XIV's sumptuous *divertissements* at Versailles, in the fairly incongruous setting of an open-air stage in a long vista leading to the Orangerie, and cluttered with fountains, ponds, marble vases and gilded statues. Here, and later in Paris, it had the most triumphal reception of any play by its author.

There is nothing more celebrated among the poets than the
sacrifice of Iphigenia. But they are not all agreed on the most
important facts about this sacrifice. Some, like Aeschylus in
Agamemnon, Sophocles in *Electra*, and after them Lucretius,
Horace and many others, say that the blood of Iphigenia,
daughter of Agamemnon, was really shed and that she died in
Aulis. We have only to read Lucretius, at the beginning of his
first book:

By that Diana's cruel altar flow'd
With innocent and royal virgin's blood:
Unhappy maid . . .
Led by the Grecian chiefs in pomp and state, . . .

And Clytemnestra says in Aeschylus that her husband
Agamemnon, who has just died, will meet among the dead
Iphigenia, his daughter, whom he once sacrificed.

Others have related that Diana, taking pity on the young
princess, had carried her off into the Taurian country just as
she was being sacrificed, and substituted for her a hind, or
some such other victim. Euripides has followed that story, and
Ovid has put it among the *Metamorphoses*.

There is a third opinion, no less ancient than the two
others, about Iphigenia. A number of authors, among others
Stesichorus, one of the most famous and oldest of lyrical
poets, have written that it was quite true that a princess of the
name had been sacrificed, but that this Iphigenia was a
daughter whom Helen had borne to Theseus. Helen, say these
authors, had not dared to recognise her as her daughter
because she dared not confess to Menelaus that she had been
secretly married with Theseus. Pausanias reports both this
account and the names of the poets who were of this opinion.
And he adds that it was the common belief of the whole land
of Argos.

Homer, finally, the father of the poets, is so far from assert-
ing that Iphigenia the daughter of Agamemnon had been either
sacrificed at Aulis or carried into Scythia, that in the ninth
book of the *Iliad*, that is to say nearly ten years after the
arrival of the Greeks before Troy, Agamemnon offers in
marriage to Achilles his daughter Iphigenia, whom he says he
has left at home in Mycenae.

I have recorded all these opinions, so different from one another, and above all the passage from Pausanias, because it is to him that I owe the fortunate figure of Eriphile, without which I should never have ventured to attempt this tragedy. How could I contemplate polluting the stage with the horrible murder of a person as virtuous and lovable as I had to make Iphigenia? And on the other hand how could I make my denouement depend on a Goddess and a 'machine', and on a metamorphosis which might indeed find some credence in the time of Euripides, but would seem too absurd and incredible in our day?

I may say then that I have been very fortunate to find in ancient authors this other Iphigenia, whom I could show with whatever character I liked, and who, since she falls into the misfortune into which her jealousy made her wish to precipitate her rival, deserves her punishment in some degree, but without being altogether unworthy of compassion. Thus the denouement of the play is drawn from the matter of the play itself. And anyone who has seen it performed knows what pleasure I have given the audience, both by saving in the end a virtuous princess whose part they have taken so warmly all through the tragedy, and by doing so otherwise than by a miracle, which they could not have endured because they could never believe it.

Achilles' expedition to Lesbos, which he overpowers and from which he carries off Eriphile before coming to Aulis, is not without foundation either. Euphorion of Chalcis, a poet well known among the ancients, of whom Virgil and Quintilian make honourable mention, spoke of this Lesbos expedition. He said in one of his poems, according to Parthenius, that Achilles had conquered the island before joining the army of the Greeks, and even that he met there a princess who fell in love with him.

Those are the principal respects in which I have slightly diverged from the plan and the plot of Euripides. As regards the passions, I have taken care to follow him more closely. I confess that I owe him a number of the passages which have been most highly approved in my tragedy. And I confess it the more readily because these marks of approval have confirmed me in the esteem and veneration I have always had for the works which remain to us from antiquity. I have had the pleasure of realising, from the effect produced on our stage by whatever I have imitated from either Homer or Euripides, that good sense and reason are the same in every century. The taste of Paris has been found to agree with that of Athens. My audi-

ences have been moved by the same things that brought tears
to the eyes of the most civilised people in Greece, and caused
it to be said that among the poets Euripides was most tragic,
tragikotatos, in other words that he was wonderfully adept in
arousing compassion and terror, which are the true effects of
tragedy.

I am amazed, after that, that certain moderns have recently
shown so much distaste for this great poet, in the judgement
on his *Alcestis* that has been published . . .

[This was a comparison of the *Alcestis* with a new French
opera of the same name, published the same year by P.
Perrault. Racine seizes on parts of the criticism which he
can blame on a faulty understanding of Euripides, in particular a passage wrongly attributed (in some *Latin* text,
says Racine meaningly) to the grieving husband instead of
the dying wife. He concludes:]

I advise these gentlemen not to judge the works of the
ancients so light-heartedly in future. A man like Euripides
deserved at least to be studied if they wished to condemn him.
They should have remembered those wise words of Quintilian:
'We should be very prudent and restrained in pronouncing on
the works of these great men, lest we come, as many have, to
condemn what we do not understand. And if it is necessary to
go too far in one direction, it is better to err in admiring everything they wrote, rather than in blaming a great deal.'

DRAMATIS PERSONAE

Agamémnon
Achílles
Ulýsses
Clytemnéstra   wife of Agamemnon
Iphigenía   daughter of Agamemnon
Eriphílē   daughter of Helen and Theseus
Arcas   ⎫
Eurýbates   ⎬   officers of the household of Agamemnon
                   attendant on Clytemnestra
Aegína   attendant on Clytemnestra
Chloris   confidant of Eriphile

Detachment of Guards

The scene is at Aulis, in Agamemnon's tent.

ACT I

AGAMEMNON, ARCAS

Agamemnon   Yes, it is Agamemnon. Rouse yourself,
    Listen to me. Your King has need of you.
Arcas   What, is it you, my lord? What pressing cause
    Has brought you out so long before the daybreak
    In this pale dusk that hardly shows my way?
    No eyes but ours are open yet in Aulis;
    Was there some sound you noticed in the sky?
    Was it the wind that we so sorely need?
    — But all is hushed: Neptune, the troops, the air.
Agamemnon   Happy the man that loves his lowly state,   10
    Free of the gilded yoke that lies on me,
    And lives where Heaven hid him, unremarked!
Arcas   You never spoke like that before, my lord.
    Under your honours, is there a secret wound
    By which the Gods, with all their benefits,
    Have made you loathe their generosity?
    Happy as King, as husband, and as father,
    You rule the richest country of all Greece,
    Son of great Atreus, issued from the Gods
    On every side, and tied to them by marriage.   20
    And now the great Achilles woos your daughter —
    Achilles, whom the oracles acclaim
    With tales of marvels that he must perform —
    So that the flames of blazing Troy will serve
    To light the torches of their wedding day.
    But is there any triumph, any glory,
    Equal, my lord, to what this shore displays —
    Those thousand ships, those twenty kings, who wait
    Only a wind to sail at your command?
    This calm delays your victory, it's true.   30
    The winds, held now in leash above our heads
    For three months, keep you away from Ilium;
    Still, what does this mean, but that you are mortal,
    And cannot look, even amid your honours,
    To fickle fortune always for success?
    Soon now . . . But what is written in that letter,
    My lord, to make you shed the tears I see?

Is your Orestes threatened in his cradle?
Do you mourn Clytemnestra? Iphigenia?
What does it say? I beg you, let me hear.   40
Agamemnon   You shall not die! No, I can never let
        you!
Arcas   My lord . . .
Agamemnon   Yes, I am troubled. Hear the cause,
    Then tell me, friend, if this is time for sleep.
    You well remember when our mariners
    In Aulis thought the wind stood fair for us,
    And we put to sea, while countless shouts of joy
    Threatened the coasts of Troy with our advance.
    Then came that prodigy that struck us dumb —
    The wind had dropped before we left the port;
    We could not stir; even the oars in vain   50
    Struck at the unruffled surface of the sea.
    After this wonder past our understanding
    I sought the Goddess who is worshipped here;
    With Menelaus, Nestor and Ulysses
    I brought a secret offering to her shrine.
    What a response, Arcas! These were the words
    I had to hear, spoken by Calchas' lips:
    'Your force will never reach the Trojan walls
    Unless a maiden's blood of Helen's race
            In solemn tribute falls   60
    Upon Diana's altar in this place.
    To purchase that fair wind the Gods deny,
            Let Iphigenia die.'
Arcas   Your daughter!
                        Aghast, as you may well suppose,
    My blood ran chill, I had no voice, but only
    Unconquerable sobs that spoke my grief.
    I took the Gods to task, I shut my ears,
    And swore upon their altars to defy them.
    Would I had listened to my love and fear!
    I set about disbanding all the army.   70
    Ulysses listened, seeming to approve,
    Letting the early torrent pass, but soon,
    With all his cruel and cunning eloquence,
    He talked to me of honour and of country,
    The peoples and the Kings at my command,
    The rule of Asia in the grasp of Greece —
    Could I betray a nation for a daughter,
    Go back, grow old among my family,
    A King without his glory? I myself,

(Must I confess it?) my own power beguiled me,   80
My state obsessed me, and the lofty names
Of King of Kings and Captain of all Greece
Flattered the pride and folly of my breast.
And this was not the worst; for every night
No sooner had I lost my cares in sleep,
The Gods appeared, to vindicate their altar,
Assert its ghastly claim, denounce my pity
As sacrilege, brandish the thunderbolt
And dare me to revolt. Arcas, I yielded.
Ulysses wore me down; and though I wept   90
I gave the order that my child should die.
But then I had to tear her from her mother.
I hit upon a shameful subterfuge —
To fetch her here more easily from Argos
I hid behind Achilles' name; I wrote
That he desired to see the girl again
And marry her, before he sailed for Troy.

Arcas   But did you count without Achilles' rage?
Did you think such a man could hold his peace,
With love and justice on his side, to let you   100
Misuse his name to perpetrate a murder,
And see his love butchered before his eyes?

Agamemnon   Achilles was away. His father Peleus,
If you remember, had recalled him home
Because he feared the invasion of a neighbour.
The war that followed, Arcas, should have kept him
Away from Aulis longer than it did.
But what can stop that torrent in its spate?
Achilles went to war, triumphed at once,
And close behind the fame of his success   110
Came back last night into our camp again.
But there is more than this to give me pause —
My child, who comes so eagerly to her death,
Never suspecting who pronounced her doom
But joyful that she has so kind a father;
My child — but it is not the name of daughter,
It's not her youth, my blood that flows in her,
These are not what grieve me; no, I think
Of so much goodness, so much love between us,
Her willing duty, and my tenderness,   120
Respect for me that nothing can disturb —
How much I hoped to have repaid it better!
No, no, ye Gods, it cannot be your justice
Approves the senseless horror of this deed.

You gave your oracle to try my heart,
And you would strike me down if I obeyed.
   So, Arcas, I am trusting in your care
And your devotion, for I know their worth;
I know the Queen in Sparta found you faithful
Before she chose you for the place you hold.   130
Take this letter, haste towards Mycenae,
And never stop until you meet the Queen.
Bar her way the moment that you see her,
And make her read the message I have sent.
Take a good guide: you must not lose your way:
If once my daughter sets a foot in Aulis
Her life is forfeit. Calchas will seize upon her,
Condemn our mercy in the name of Heaven
And rally all the Greeks behind religion
To combat and chastise our sacrilege.   140
Intriguers, too, offended by my glory,
Will take the chance to call it into question;
They may well take it from me. Go, I say,
Save her from what my weakness brings upon her —
But do not, this I beg you, say too much;
Hold back my dreadful secret. She must never
Suspect the peril I have put her in.
Protect me from a mother's wild reproaches,
And let your words confirm the words I wrote.
What I have told them, in the hope that they   150
Will take offence and turn at once for home,
Is that Achilles now has changed his mind;
The marriage that he seemed to want so much,
He will not celebrate till he returns.
You can add this, that underhand reports
Suggest that the reluctance of Achilles
May show the influence of a certain captive,
Eriphile, a girl he took on Lesbos
And left at Argos in my daughter's care.
Leave it at that; the rest, keep to yourself.   160
And now, the day is dawning, it is lighter.
Men are about. Someone is coming here;
It is Achilles. Go, be off. Ah Gods,
Ulysses with him!

Exit Arcas
Enter Achilles *and* Ulysses
        Can it be, my lord,
That victory has brought you back so swiftly?
Are these the first steps of an untried courage?

What noble triumphs, then, await you now!
The whole of Thessaly crushed or overawed,
Like Lesbos, seized before our army came,
Are feats enough to make a man immortal,   170
But, to Achilles, sport for holidays!
Achilles   Oh, feeble exploits that you prize too highly,
My lord. I pray that Heaven will set us free
To seek that nobler field by you laid open
To hearts like mine that only breathe for glory. —
But let me ask, my lord, if I may credit
Reports that fill me with surprise and joy;
Have you been so propitious to my wishes
That I shall have the good I most desire?
They say Iphigenia's here already   180
So that a wedding-bond may make us one.
Agamemnon   My child? Who told you she was coming
          here?
Achilles   What is there that amazes you in this?
Agamemnon (*to* Ulysses)   Ah Heaven, can he know of
          my deception?
Ulysses   My lord, the King is right to be amazed.
Have you forgotten the perils that we face?
Is this a time, ye Gods, for marrying?
When still the sea's forbidden to the fleet,
Greece is dismayed, the army rots away;
When to buy off the unkindness of the Gods   190
May cost us blood, and blood who knows how dear?
And still Achilles feeds on lover's thoughts
And in the face of all our people's fears
Calls on our leader to outrage the Gods
By ordering a wedding, and a feast!
Can you feel nothing more than this, my lord,
For our mishaps? Is this your love for Greece?
Achilles   On Phrygian fields I shall be glad to try
Who loves her more, Ulysses or myself.
Till then, go on, parade your pure devotion,   200
Go and make all the vows you please for Greece,
Heap altars high with offerings and blood,
Inspect the entrails of the beasts yourself
To learn the secret causes of the calm.
These cares belong to Calchas, not to me;
While, by your leave, by your kind leave, my lord,
I'll make my best endeavours to advance
A wedding that will not offend the Gods.
Then, for I cannot bear to linger idle,

I shall be back at once upon the port;   210
    For it would grieve me if another warrior
    Leapt down before me on the Trojan strand.
Agamemnon   Heaven, why is it that your dark designs
    Deny such men access to Asian shores?
    Must I admire this fine impetuous rage
    Only to turn more bitterly away?
Ulysses   Gods, what is this?
Achilles   What can you mean, my lord?
Agamemnon   That we must part, Princes; we all must
        part.
    We have hoped too long, too fondly, for the winds
    We are denied. Heaven is shielding Troy   220
    And warns us clearly not to brave its anger.
Achilles   What fearful omens tell us of this anger?
Agamemnon   Only consider what's foretold for you.
    Why not speak plainly? For we know the Gods
    Will not give Ilium to us but for you;
    We also know that as the price we pay
    You are to find your grave in foreign fields.
    Long life, great fortune, anywhere beside
    Await you: there, you fall before your prime.
Achilles   So, all the Kings that gathered in your cause   230
    Must run away crowned with eternal shame,
    While Paris in his insolent adventure
    Keeps your wife's sister with impunity?
Agamemnon   Not so; that brilliant foretaste of your
        valour
    Avenged us all before we struck a blow.
    The woes of Lesbos that your hands have ravaged
    Are still the terror of the Aegean sea.
    Troy saw the flames; and into Trojan ports
    The sea throws up its wreckage and its dead.
    Not only that: Troy lost a second Helen   240
    In that young captive you sent home to Argos.
    For who can doubt her beauty and her bearing
    Betray a secret that she seeks to hide?
    Her very silence speaks her a Princess.
Achilles   No no, your explanations are too clever,
    Too certain of the secrets of the Gods.
    Am I a man to let himself be stopped
    While you pursue the path where honour calls?
    Yes, it is true, the Fates once told my mother
    When she received a mortal in her bed,   250
    I must choose either long inglorious life

Or few short years with ages of renown.
But the same tomb awaits us young or old;
Shall I then live a burden to the earth,
Afraid to shed the blood a Goddess gave me,
Go back to my father, and await, unknown,
A slow decay? and die, inglorious,
A total death, and nothing left behind?
Away with all these base impediments!
If honour calls, that is my oracle.   260
The Gods may well mete out our length of days,
But not our glory: that is in our hands.
Their high designs concern themselves alone.
They are not for us to know; we only study
To make ourselves immortal by our deeds
And carve ourselves a place as high as theirs.
Troy gives me that; and I forget the Fates
And only pray the favour of a wind.
What would I care if I should have to fight
The war alone? We'll bring you back your vengeance,   270
Patróclus and myself. — But no, for Destiny
Saves that for you, my lord; I only ask
The honour of appearing in your ranks.
I cease to claim indulgence for a love
Which would have kept me absent from your fleet.
That love, which prompts me to protect your fame,
Tells me to set an example to the army,
And more than everything, to save you from
The cowardice of some of your advisers.

                                    Exit Achilles

Ulysses   You see, my lord. He is all set on Troy   280
Whatever it may cost. We feared his love;
But he himself, so luckily deceived,
Gives us the arms to fight against his wishes.
Agamemnon   Alas!
Ulysses   Tell me how I must read that sigh.
Can you not rule the impulse of your blood?
Has one night shaken what I thought resolved?
Was it your heart that spoke just now? Consider:
You owe your child to Greece; you promised her,
And on your promise, Calchas day by day
Swears to the Greeks who cluster to consult him   290
That the winds will blow again infallibly.
And if the future goes against his words
Can you expect that he will hold his peace
To do you pleasure? Will he keep your secret

And let them mock the oracles of Heaven?
If once they know that you withheld their victim
What may they not attempt, and think it just?
Take care not to compel them in their fury,
My lord, to choose between the Gods and you.
And whose but yours the pleadings that recruited   300
All of our band to seek the plains of Troy?
City by city, didn't you call out
All Helen's suitors to make good the oaths
They all had sworn to Tyndarus her father
When they all wooed the bride your brother wed?
Whoever was the man that won her hand,
We swore that moment to uphold his right,
And promised him, if any dared defraud him,
To bring him back the head of the offender.
Without your pains, this oath inspired by love,   310
Who would have honoured it when love was cold?
You were the man who called us from new passions,
Young wives, young children; you have brought us
          here
With one thought only burning in our hearts —
The honour of assuring your revenge.
Now Greece has recognised your guiding hand
By naming you the Captain of her host;
And all the other Kings resign their claims
Ready to shed their hearts' last drops of blood
To serve King Agamemnon. He alone   320
Refuses so much glory; shrinks from offering
A little blood for such a victory;
At the first step he falters; his first order
Will be to tell the armies to disperse.
Agamemnon   Easy for you, my lord, to be heroic —
You are untouched by all that crushes me;
But could we see your son Telemachus
Blindfolded, and led forward to the altar,
Should we not see you change your lofty tone,
Weep as I weep and suffer as I suffer,   330
And throw yourself between the priest and him?
As you know well, my lord, I gave my word;
So, if my daughter comes, I yield her up.
But if some chance, in spite of all I did,
Keeps her at home, or holds her back from Aulis,
Release me then from this barbarity.
Let me interpret the impediment
In favour of my blood, and let me bless

Some milder God that watches over her.
I have been too subservient to your counsels,   340
And now . . .   *Enter* Eurybates
Eurybates   My lord, . . .
Agamemnon   Ah! what have you to tell me?
Eurybates   The Queen is here. I came before to
        announce her.
    She comes to bring her daughter to your side.
    They are near already; but we lost our way
    Under the shadow of those woods that seemed
    To form a barrier before the camp.
Agamemnon   Heaven!
Eurybates   She also brings Eriphile,
    That prisoner Achilles sent from Lesbos,
    Who never learnt her parents or her country
    And says she wants to question Calchas here.   350
    News of their coming spreads across the camp.
    Already soldiers gather to admire
    Iphigenia's beauty and her grace,
    Calling on Heaven to bring her happiness.
    Some went to lend their escort to the Queen;
    Some stopped to ask me what has brought her here;
    But all confessed that if the Gods had never
    Given a throne to a more glorious King,
    They never, in the secret of his house,
    Made a man happier in his child than you.   360
Agamemnon   It is well, Eurybates. Now you may go.
    The rest is my concern. I shall perform it.
                                Exit Eurybates
Agamemnon   Just Heaven, you have punished me, and
        broken
    Every expedient of human wit!
    If I had but, in this extremity,
    Freedom to soothe my sorrows with my tears!
    Dire fate of kings! Slaves as we all must be
    To what Heaven orders and what men may say,
    We act our part always before their eyes,
    And the most sorrowful must weep the least.   370
Ulysses   I have a child, my lord. I too am weak,
    And put myself most readily in your place.
    I tremble at the blow that makes you groan,
    Nor can I blame the tears I almost share.
    But you are left without your last excuse —
    Calchas receives his victim from the Gods;
    He knows, he is waiting. If he waits too long

He'll wait no more, but call for her aloud.
While we are still alone, make haste, and shed
Those tears a father's eye cannot restrain.   380
Weep for your own blood, weep. But no, be firm,
Think of the honour that will follow it.
See our oars churn the Hellespont to whiteness,
See faithless Troy given over to the flames,
Its folk your captives, Priam at your knees,
Helen by you surrendered to her husband.
See all your ships with garlands at the prow
Return with you at last again to Aulis;
And dwell upon that triumph which will be
The eternal theme of ages yet to come.   390
Agamemnon   My lord, I see that I can do no more.
I must let the Gods destroy the innocent.
The victim shall be with you very soon.
Go on. But see that Calchas does not speak;
Help me to cover up the hideous truth
And keep a mother from her daughter's death.

ACT II

ERIPHILE, CHLORIS

Eriphile   Leave them alone, Chloris, let them enjoy
The embraces of a father and a husband;
And in this moment of enraptured greetings
Let them indulge their joy, and me my grief.   400
Chloris   Are you still dwelling on your sufferings,
My lady? Do you look for no relief?
I know all things are hateful to a captive,
And pleasure dies where freedom is denied;
But in those earlier most bitter times
When we left Lesbos in the conqueror's ship,
When, shrinking and in bonds, you found yourself
Close to the murderous captor of the isle,
Your eyes were — dare I say it? — dryer then,
You brooded less over your sufferings.   410
And now the worst is done. Iphigenia
Has welcomed you with open-hearted kindness,
She treats you as a sister, feels for you;
You could not live more happily in Troy.
Now, when her father calls her out to Aulis,
You ask to come as well; she brings you here.

And yet, and this is hard to understand,
Each step towards Aulis brings you deeper pain.
Eriphile   What, do you think Eriphile can bear
To stand and watch another's happiness?   420
You think my sorrow ought to fade away
Before a joy in which I have no part?
Iphigenia's in a father's arms,
The only pride of an exultant mother,
And I, from peril into peril tossed,
Reared up from infancy in strangers' hands,
No father, since I breathed the light of day,
No mother's face, have ever smiled on me.
I wonder who I am, and dare not search
For fear of that sinister oracle   430
That warns me not to wish to know my blood,
For knowing it I shall most surely die.
Chloris   You must not take it so, you must search on,
For words of oracles are always dark
And the first meaning often will deceive.
You find your name, you lose the one you bear
(Which, as we know, is false and not your own) —
That is the only danger you can fear;
Surely that is the death that threatens you.
Eriphile   Such is the only knowledge that I have.   440
Your poor unhappy father knew the rest
And never let me penetrate the secret.
Alas, in Troy where he was taking me
He promised me a glorious revelation:
My name, my rank restored, and in my veins
The blood of greater monarchs than I dream!
Already I had almost reached the city:
On Lesbos falls the pitiless Achilles.
Nothing can stand the fury of his arms.
Your father's buried with the countless dead.   450
I live in bonds, his secret still untold;
And out of all the splendours I awaited,
Bond-servant to the Greeks, remains but this,
Pride in a blood that I can never prove.
Chloris   With such a witness lost, and such a guardian,
How must you hate the hand that struck him down!
But you have Calchas here, the famous Calchas,
Who reads the secrets of the Gods above:
They speak to him, and learned in their lore
He knows all that has been and all that shall be.   460
He cannot fail to tell who gave you birth.

Why, all this camp is filled with friends and helpers;
Iphigenia, as Achilles' bride,
Will give you his protection for your safety —
She promised to, and I have heard her swear it:
He has engaged it as a wedding-gift.
Eriphile   What if that wedding, Chloris, was to me
Worse than the sum of all my other ills?
Chloris   But how, my lady?
Eriphile   It is strange to you
That nothing can console me. Listen then,   470
And you will marvel that I even live.
Alien, unknown, a captive — that is nothing.
But this destroyer of unhappy Lesbos,
Achilles, guilty of all your ills and mine,
Whose bloody hand dragged me into my bondage,
Who robbed me of my parentage and your father,
Whose very name should be abhorrent to me —
I love him as I never thought to love.
Chloris   Can this be?
Eriphile   I never meant to speak. I hoped
Unending silence would conceal my folly.   480
But it lays too much weight upon my heart:
I tell it now, and never shall again.
You need not ask me whether any hope
Fostered the fatal love that grows in me.
I will not blame Achilles that he showed
Some semblance of compassion for my fate.
I think the Gods took an inhuman pleasure
In venting all their hate on me alone.
That day of horror when we lost our freedom —
Must I recall the dreadful dream again? —   490
After the savage violence of our capture
I lay for hours, seeing and feeling nothing.
At last I looked into the light again.
A bloodstained arm constrained me; and I shuddered,
Chloris, and turned away to avoid the sight
Of a barbaric victor's countenance.
I went aboard his ship; I cursed his rage
And never yet had looked him in the face.
Then, I did; I found there nothing savage.
My protestations died upon my lips.   500
My heart rebelled and took his side against me.
My anger fell, and I could only weep.
I was obedient to one so kind;
I loved him there, I love him still in Aulis.

Iphigenia may be charitable,
Protect me, pity and encourage me —
How can she understand that I am mad,
Tormented? When I take her proffered favours,
It is as weapons to attack her with
And thwart a happiness I cannot bear.   510
Chloris   How could your hate do anything against her?
Why could you not have stayed alone in Argos,
Fighting a passion you can never show,
Rather than seek inevitable torment?
Eriphile   That was my wish. Why should I come with
           her
To watch her glorying in her happiness?
But something drew me; I could not resist;
A voice within me ordered me to come,
Telling me my unwanted presence here
Might be a way of spreading my misfortune;   520
That if I could approach those happy lovers
Some of my grief might chance to fall on them.
That is why I am here; not out of haste
To know the riddle of my unhappy birth;
Or rather, my plans depend upon this wedding —
If they wed, well and good: my life is over.
I shall die, Chloris, die immediately,
The darkness of the grave will hide my shame.
For why seek parents that I never knew,
Now my mad passion has dishonoured them?   530
Chloris   How I feel for you, my lady! How the
           force . . .
Eriphile   This is King Agamemnon with his daughter.
                Enter Agamemnon, *followed by* Iphigenia
Iphigenia   Dear lord, why run away? What can it be
That forces you to fly from our embraces?
Is something wrong, to make you leave so soon?
I waited for the Queen to express her joy,
But is there not a moment left for me?
May I not talk to you about my pleasure?
Can't you . . .
Agamemnon   Well then, my child, embrace your father;
He loves you still.
Iphigenia   And how I prize that love!   540
How I rejoice to see you, and enjoy
The splendid signs that tell of your new greatness!
What honours! and what power! Yes, I had heard
Astonishing reports before we came;

But now I see you close and drink it in,
That pleasure, that astonishment redouble.
Gods! how the whole of Greece loves and reveres you!
How good to be the child of such a father!

Agamemnon   You well deserved a happier one, my
          child.

Iphigenia   What happiness is not within your reach?   550
     Can any king want greater weight of honours?
     I thought my only prayers should be thanksgiving.

Agamemnon   Great Gods! Should I prepare her for her
          fate?

Iphigenia   You hide your face, my lord; you seem to
          sigh;
     You act as if you could not bear to see me.
     Did we do wrong? didn't you want us here?

Agamemnon   My child, you mean as much to me as
          ever;
     But times have changed, just as the place is different.
     Here I find cruel pains that kill my pleasure.

Iphigenia   Oh father, come, forget your kingly state.   560
     A long and bitter absence lies before us.
     Are you ashamed to act the part of father
     One moment? There is no one here to watch us
     Except this young Princess, who has heard me tell
     A hundred times how kind you are to me;
     I boasted of the favours I enjoyed,
     And promised you would help her for my sake.
     What will she think to see you now so cold?
     Have I made promises I cannot keep?
     Will you not smooth that brow so charged with care?   570

Agamemnon   Ah, child!

Iphigenia   What, my lord? Tell me, speak.

Agamemnon   I cannot.

Iphigenia   Destruction to the Trojan that dismays you!

Agamemnon   Many a tear must fall to buy his doom.

Iphigenia   Your life at least the Gods defend and bless!

Agamemnon   These days, the Gods are deaf and harsh
          to me.

Iphigenia   Calchas, they say, plans some great sacrifice?

Agamemnon   Unless I first appease their tyranny!

Iphigenia   Will it be offered soon?

Agamemnon   Only too soon.

Iphigenia   And will they let me add my prayers to
          yours?
     Will your proud family stand at the altar?   580

Agamemnon   Alas!
Iphigenia   You do not answer?
Agamemnon   You will be there,
My child. — Goodbye.

                                Exit Agamemnon
Iphigenia   What can I think of this?
I am left shuddering with inward horror.
I cannot help but fear some unknown evil.
Just Gods, you know what name is in my prayers!
Eriphile   What, in the cares that must oppress him now
You let a little coldness make you tremble!
Ah me, what of the sorrows I must bear? —
I, all my life rejected by my parents,
Who never knew a home, who never even   590
At birth, perhaps, received a look of love!
You, if a father brushes you aside,
At least find solace in a mother's arms;
And should the woes you weep be numberless,
What are the tears a lover cannot dry?
Iphigenia   Yes, I confess it, fair Eriphile,
Achilles could have quickly dried these tears.
My heart is his by every kind of reason —
His glory and his love, my father's bidding,
My duty. But Achilles, what of him?   600
This eager lover, burning for my sight,
Refusing to be parted from these shores,
Making my father call me from so far,
Is he so anxious to enjoy the meeting
I thought he longed for? I, these last two days,
As we drew near to Aulis and began
At last to see the journey's end we longed for,
I sought him everywhere. Along the roads
My tremulous gaze went searching for his form,
My heart was ranging far beyond my eyes.   610
Nothing I saw but seemed to hide Achilles.
I have come all the way: he has not met me,
Though strangers came, clustering round our path.
Only he was not there. And my poor father
Seems fearful to pronounce his name before me.
What holds him back? What can explain this riddle?
And will the lover, when I find him, prove
As chilling as my father was? Can war
And all its cares so drain the hearts of men,
In one short day, of tenderness and love?   620
No. I've no right to think it. But for me

He never would have come to join the war.
When Helen's father made her suitors swear
That oath in Sparta, he was not among them.
He is not bound, alone of all the Greeks,
And if he goes to Troy, it is for me.
That is enough for him; and he even asks
To carry there the title of my husband.

Enter Clytemnestra

Clytemnestra   We must go, child, without a moment's
      pause,
   Or our fair name is lost, both yours and mine.   630
   I do not wonder that your father seemed
   Distracted and constrained when we appeared:
   Here is a letter he had sent by Arcas
   To head us off from meeting this rebuff;
   But Arcas missed us when we lost our way,
   And only now has he delivered it.
   I tell you again, our fair name is at stake:
   Achilles says that he has changed his mind,
   Declines the honour we accorded him,
   And does not wish to wed till he returns.   640

Eriphile   What is this?

Clytemnestra   I see you flush at the affront.
   Summon your pride to help your resolution.
   I had myself approved this fickle suitor,
   Presented him to you myself in Argos,
   Charmed and delighted that so great a man,
   Son of a Goddess, sought you for his bride.
   But since, unworthy of his boasted birth,
   He breaks his word and shamefully withdraws,
   It is for us to show him what we are,
   And treat him as the meanest of mankind.   650
   Is he to see us linger here, and think
   That in your heart you want him back again?
   The wedding he delays, we break off, gladly.
   I've sent to tell your father what I plan,
   And only wait to take my leave of him.
   Meanwhile I'll give my orders, then we'll go.
   (*To* Eriphile) I shall not press you to return with us,
   My lady. You'll be happier here alone.
   Do not suppose your true intent is hidden:
   Calchas was not the cause that made you come.   660

Exit Clytemnestra

Iphigenia   What dreadful news, what dreadful blow to
      me!

So he has changed his mind about the wedding;
I must go back under this slight to Argos;
And you are here for someone else than Calchas!
Eriphile   I have not understood a word of this.
Iphigenia   Oh, you can understand me if you want to.
   If unjust fate deprives me of a husband
   Will you leave me, my lady, to my grief?
   You would not stay at home and let me go,
   But now the Queen and I must leave you here?   670
Eriphile   I had intended to see Calchas first.
Iphigenia   Then why delay, my lady, to send word?
Eriphile   It seems you are leaving at this very moment.
Iphigenia   Sometimes a moment settles many a doubt.
   But it is wrong, I see, to press you further.
   I see, what I refused to think — Achilles . . .
   You cannot wait to be without me here.
Eriphile   I? You suspect me of such treachery?
   You think I could love a brutal conqueror,
   One I shall always see with blood upon him,   680
   Flame in his hand and murder in his heart,
   The ravager of Lesbos . . .
Iphigenia   Yes, you love him!
   And all the savage picture that you draw
   Of bloody arms and corpses, fire and ashes —
   Love used these tools to engrave him in your heart.
   They are not memories you cannot bear,
   They are a tale you love to dwell upon.
   You never cease to talk to me about it.
   Already, more than once, I should have seen
   What these laments concealed — and I did see;   690
   But I reproached myself for unkind thoughts
   And slipped the bandage back over my eyes.
   You love him. I was blind! What was I doing?
   How could I clutch a rival to my breast?
   I even loved her; and I promised her,
   Even today, my fickle lover's help.
   Such was the triumph into which you tricked me;
   — Not you: I bound myself behind your wheels.
   I can forgive this love you stand to gain from,
   I can forgive the heart you've filched from me;   700
   But when you let me cross the whole of Greece
   To meet, without one warning of my fate,
   The man who waits only to cast me off —
   Is that an outrage that I can forgive,
   Impostor?

Eriphile   Such words I never heard before,
 My lady, nor expected I should hear.
 The Gods, whose anger darkens all my days,
 Had never yet subjected me to this.
 But I forgive injustice from a lover.
 — What did you think I should have warned you of? 710
 Would you have thought that it was possible
 The great Achilles would reject the blood
 Of Agamemnon, for a nameless girl
 Who guesses only this of all her fate,
 That hers is a blood Achilles lusts to shed?
Iphigenia You mock me, and exult over my pain.
 Only now can I feel what I have lost.
 You paint my fortune and your homelessness
 Only to give more lustre to your victory.
 But do not be too quick to savour it.   720
 This Agamemnon that you name in scorn,
 He is Captain of the Greeks, he is my father,
 He loves me; this will grieve him more than me.
 He felt my tears even before I shed them;
 I heard the sighs he sought to hide from me.
 — To think that I accused him to his face
 Of a cold greeting and a lack of love!

            Enter Achilles
Achilles So it is true, my lady, you are here!
 I thought that all the army must be wrong.
 In Aulis, you! What are you doing here?   730
 And how is it that Agamemnon swore
 That you were not?
Iphigenia   My lord, you need not fear.
 Iphigenia will not spoil your pleasure
 For long.

            Exit Iphigenia
Achilles She flies me! Do I wake or dream?
 Into what strange confusion am I thrown!
 — I do not know, my lady, if Achilles
 Can face your sight and not arouse your anger;
 But if an enemy may plead for help,
 An enemy who often showed you pity,
 You surely know what purpose brought them here; 740
 You know . . .
Eriphile   But you know too, my lord, you must,
 You who, a month ago, would wait no longer
 And sent for them to come at once to Aulis.
Achilles A month ago I left the coasts of Aulis;

Only last night did I return again.
Eriphile   What, then when Agamemnon wrote to Argos,
It was not you whose love guided his hand?
What, you, the ardent suitor of his daughter . . .
Achilles   More ardent, as you see me now, than ever,
My lady; and if thinking could have done it   750
I should have been in Argos first. And yet
She will not speak to me. What have I done?
Why all around me are there enemies?
A moment past, Ulysses, Nestor, Calchas,
Were wasting all their force of eloquence
To fight against my love, and prove to me
That honour forces me to give it up.
What is this plot that seems to be afoot?
Has all the army made a fool of me?
I will go back and force the truth from them.   760

Exit Achilles

Eriphile   Where shall I hide, ye Gods, in my confusion?
Proud rival, you are loved, and you complain.
Can I bear both your fortune and your insults?
I'd rather . . . But, Chloris, I deceive myself
Or else some frightful tempest threatens them.
I am not blind. They are not out of trouble.
Iphigenia does not know the truth,
Achilles neither. Agamemnon grieves.
There is much to hope; and if her destiny
Is half as bitter as the hate I bear,   770
From their collusion may I not contrive
Some subterfuge, whereby at least I may
Not weep alone, nor die without revenge?

ACT III

AGAMEMNON, CLYTEMNESTRA

Clytemnestra   Yes, we were going home. I was so angry
I meant to leave Achilles and the camp
And take my child to nurse her wounded pride
At home in Argos. But the Prince himself,
Astounded at my resolution, stopped us
With protestations that I could not doubt:
The wedding that they said he had delayed   780
He seeks with passion. He is looking for you
To put an end to this outrageous lie,

To learn who spread it, and to punish him.
You will dispel these slanders and suspicions?
Agamemnon   My lady, say no more. Let us believe him.
I recognise that we had been deceived,
And I share your joy as much as I am able.
You wish for Calchas to unite the pair;
So you may let your child go to the altar:
I will await her. But, while we are here,   790
Let me say certain things to you in private.
You see what place it is you have brought her to,
Where all things speak of war and not of marriage —
All this tumultuous camp, soldiers and seamen,
An altar bristling with massed spears and lances,
This pomp of war, well fitting for Achilles,
Is too disordered to befit your eyes;
And Greece must not behold her Captain's Queen
In scenes unworthy of yourself or me.
Be ruled by me: stay away, let your women   800
Attend our daughter to her wedding-rites.
Clytemnestra   Who, I? Relinquish her to the care of
          others?
Let others crown the work I have begun?
I bring my child to Aulis out of Argos,
Then leave her for the journey to the altar?
Have you more right than I to stand near Calchas?
Then who will give my daughter to her groom?
Who else will order all the holy rites?
Agamemnon   This is not the palace of my father
          Atreus.
This is a camp . . .
Clytemnestra   Where you are in command,   810
Where in your hands you hold the doom of Asia,
Where every Greek is marching at your orders,
Where Thetis' son desires to call me mother.
What is the palace where I could appear
In half the dignity that Aulis lends me?
Agamemnon   My lady, by the Gods that sired our race,
I beg you to concede this to my love;
I have my reasons.
Clytemnestra   By those Gods, my lord,
I beg you not to rob me of this joy —
As if my presence were a cause of shame.   820
Agamemnon   I hoped that I should find you more
          compliant.
But now, since reason has no power to move you,

Since even my requests are made in vain —
You have heard, my lady, what it is I ask:
It is my wish, and it is my command.
Do it.

Exit Agamemnon

Clytemnestra   Why is the King so cruel, so anxious
Not to permit me to approach the altar?
Has his new dignity so turned his head
That I appear unworthy to attend him?
Or is he so uncertain of his power   830
That he dare not be seen with Helen's sister?
But what is she to me? And is it just
That I should suffer for the shame she bears?
No matter. If he wills it I submit
And let your happiness, my child, console me.
Achilles will be yours — Oh joyful thought
That you will bear the name . . . But here he is!

Enter Achilles

Achilles   My lady, every obstacle is down.
The King desired no other form of proof,
My eager words sufficed. He barely listened,   840
And barely answered, and with one embrace
Accepted me for bridegroom to your daughter.
But has he told you of the happy change
Your coming has produced? The Gods relent!
Calchas, at least, within an hour from now,
Has promised to appease them; and the winds
And Neptune will content our ardent prayers
As soon as he has shed that blood they claim.
The mariners are shaking out their sails,
The ships, upon his word, are faced towards Troy.   850
And as for me, although my love could wish
That Heaven would hold back that wind awhile,
Though I shall grieve to quit these happy shores
That see the torches of my wedding-day,
Must I not bless this opportunity
To seal that sacred bond with blood of Troy
And bury in the ruins of her walls
The slight upon a name allied to mine?

Enter Iphigenia, Eriphile, Chloris, Aegina

If you are willing, nothing else can part us,
Princess, your father calls you to the altar;   860
Come, and accept this heart that beats for you.

Iphigenia   There is still time, my lord, before we go.
The Queen will not forbid me to require

One proof of love, and you will surely grant it.
Here I present to you a young Princess;
Her dignity is written on her face,
She spends her days in weeping her misfortunes;
I need not tell you what they are — you caused them.
But I too — I was angered, I was blind —
I have inflamed wounds that I should respect.   870
Would I had power to give such timely help
As might repair the injustice of my words!
All I can do is plead for her. But you,
My lord, have power to undo what you have done.
She is your prisoner, and when you will
You can remove the bonds I grieve to see.
So, may our happiness begin with this?
May she be free to look on us no more?
Show that the King I follow to the altar
Is one not only dreadful to his foes,   880
Not glorious only for a ravaged city,
But one who lets the pity of his bride
Sometimes disarm him, and by showing mercy
Comes even nearer to the Gods his forebears?

Eriphile   Yes, you can heal the bitterest of my sorrows,
My lord. You took me prisoner on Lesbos,
But it exceeds all rights of war and conquest
To make me suffer what I suffer here.

Achilles   You suffer . . . ?

Eriphile   Yes, and, to forget the rest,
Can you inflict on me a harsher doom   890
Than that of watching, in adversity,
All the felicity of my oppressors?
From every side I hear my country threatened;
I see the furious armies that assail her;
I see this wedding, which to me is torment,
Put in your hands a flame that will destroy us.
Grant me the right, far from the camp, and you,
Nameless as ever, desolate as ever,
To seek some refuge for a fate, more dreadful
Than anything these tears have told you of.   900

Achilles   No more. Come, fair Princess, follow us now.
Achilles will release you in the sight
Of all the Greeks; and this my happiest moment
Shall be the moment of your liberty.

                                              Enter Arcas

Arcas   The preparations are complete, my lady.
The King is at the altar, and awaits

Iphigenia. I am sent to bring her.
— Or rather, I come to beg your help, my lord,
Against him.
Achilles   What's that, Arcas?
Clytemnestra   What is happening,
  Ye Gods?
Arcas   There is none but you can save her now.   910
Achilles   Save her! From . . . ?
Arcas   Would that I need not accuse him.
  As much as lay in me, I kept his secret.
  But now the knife, the blindfold and the fire
  Are there; and should it all recoil on me
  I must speak out.
Clytemnestra   I tremble. Arcas, speak.
Achilles   Whoever it may be, speak, do not fear him.
Arcas   You are her lover, and you are her mother:
  You must not send the Princess to the King.
Clytemnestra   Why should we fear him?
Achilles   Why should I distrust him?
Arcas   The King is waiting there to sacrifice her.   920
Achilles   What, he!
Clytemnestra   My child!   ·
Iphigenia   My father!
Eriphile   Gods, what news!
Achilles   What senseless rage could have set him against
          her?
  How can one hear of it without abhorrence?
Arcas   Would to the Gods, my lord, that it was false!
  Calchas says the oracle demands her,
  And will accept no other offering.
  The Gods are shielding Paris. No other price
  Will purchase us our vengeance, or a wind.
Clytemnestra   The Gods! demand murder unspeakable?
Iphigenia   Heaven, what have I done to suffer this?   930
Clytemnestra   No wonder if the King's express
          command
  Kept me so cruelly from the altar's side!
Iphigenia (*to* Achilles)   This was the wedding that
          awaited me!
Arcas   It was the King's pretext to bring you here;
  And even now the whole camp thinks it true.
Clytemnestra   So then, my lord, I fall before your
          knees . . .
Achilles (*raising her*)   My lady, I beg . . .
Clytemnestra   Forget my dignity,

This is the posture fitting to my fortune;
Too happy if my tears can move your pity!
A mother feels no shame to kneel to you.   940
She is your bride: they tear her from your arms.
For you, for this sweet hope, I brought her up;
We made this fatal journey here for you;
Your name is what has lured her to her fate.
Is she to go and pray the Gods for justice
At altars decked for her approaching death?
You are all she has, she looks to you alone
As father, husband, sanctuary, Gods.
I see that you are moved. — Stay here, my child,
Wait with your bridegroom. And, my lord, I pray you, 950
Stay at her side until I come again.
I'm going to confront my treacherous husband.
He will not hold against the rage that drives me.
Calchas must find another sacrifice;
Or else, my child, if everything should fail,
They must take me and sacrifice me first.

              Exeunt all but Achilles *and* Iphigenia

Achilles   My lady, what am I to say to this?
Such words to me? And can she know Achilles?
A mother thinks she must beg my help for you?
A Queen prostrates her greatness at my feet?   960
Dishonours me with doubts of my intent,
And lets me see her tears to move my pity?
Who should your life mean more to than to me?
Indeed you may depend on my devotion!
This crime touches my honour; come what may
I answer for a life I link with mine.
But that's not all, the injury goes further —
Defend you, yes of course; and I'll avenge you,
And in the act punish that insolence
That dared to take my name to do you wrong.   970
Iphigenia   My lord, one moment! Stop, I beg, and
        listen.
Achilles   What, let myself be outraged by a savage?
He sees I long to take revenge for Helen;
He knows I was the first to raise my voice
To put him over twenty Kings his rivals;
And as reward for all I've thought and done,
As all my thanks for a resounding triumph
Which leaves him rich, avenged and glorious,
I gloried only in the name of husband
Asking the honour only to be yours.   980

And now the bloody treacherous dissembler
Not only breaks the bonds of love and nature,
Not only means to make me watch your heart
Transfixed, and reeking on an altar slab;
He dresses up the ritual as a wedding,
He uses me to lead you to your doom
And guide the knife with my unwitting hand,
No longer groom but executioner.
What sort of bloody wedding would be yours
Had I come one day later? Think of it —   990
This moment, helpless in these madmen's hands,
You would be looking round for me, in vain,
And, as you felt the unsuspected knife,
Blaming my name in which you put your trust!
For this design, this treacherous design,
I must call him to account, and publicly.
Your husband's honour is, my lady, yours;
And surely you will see it must be so.
The butcher who has slighted me shall learn
Who bears the name he dares to take in vain.   1000
Iphigenia   Ah, if you love me, if you deign to hear
As a last show of love, a last request,
This is the time, my lord, when you must prove it.
For think, this butcher that you would defy,
This enemy, cruel, savage and unjust,
Think, be he what he may, he is my father.
Achilles   He your father? After what has passed
I call him nothing but your murderer.
Iphigenia   I say again, my lord, he is my father.
He is a father that I love, a father   1010
I worship, and himself he holds me dear.
Never until today have I received
Anything from his hand but marks of love.
Always I have looked up to him since childhood,
And all that hurts him cannot fail to move me.
And shall I now change suddenly, and approve
The wildness and the fury you have shown?
Still more, add fuel to them by words of mine?
Trust me, had I not loved you as I love you
I never could have endured those hateful names   1020
Your love has made you fling at him before me.
And why can you suppose him so inhuman
As not to grieve at what they do to me?
Does any father shed his own blood gladly?
Why should he have me killed if he could save me?

I tell you I have seen his eyes drop tears.
Can you condemn him and not even hear him?
Alas, while all these horrors fall on him,
Must he be harried by your hate as well?

Achilles   My lady, with a world of things to dread,   1030
Are these the only ones to fill your mind?
A butcher (yes, I know no other word)
Prepares to have you felled by Calchas' hand;
And when I set my love against his rage
You care for nothing but his peace of mind!
I must not speak! He is forgiven, pitied;
You fear for him, and I am what you fear?
Have I gained no more ground? And is Achilles,
My lady, still no more to you than this?

Iphigenia   Oh, you are cruel! This love you put in
                doubt,   1040
Have you seen none of it before today?
You saw how calmly and how tranquilly
I took the dreadful tidings of my death.
I did not pale. If only you had seen,
But now, when we had hardly reached the camp,
When I was told that you had cast me off,
My wild extremes of heartbreak and despair!
The agony, the floods of fierce reproach
Addressed to men and all the Gods at once!
For if you had, I need not tell you now   1050
How much more precious to my heart than life
I count your love. Who knows even, who knows
If Heaven was not offended by such bliss?
Alas, possession of a love like ours
Seemed to uplift me over mortal fate.

Achilles   Princess, if I am dear to you, then live!
                              Enter Clytemnestra *and* Aegina
Clytemnestra   My lord, unless you save us, all is lost.
The King's afraid to meet me and avoids me.
He cuts me off from access to the altar;
And guards, that he himself has posted there   1060
On every side, forbid us to advance.
My grief is more than his hard heart can face.

Achilles   Well then, it is my turn to go instead.
He will see me, my lady, and will hear me.

Iphigenia   My lady, no! My lord, what will you do?

Achilles   What right have you to stop me with these
                pleadings?
Shall I for ever have to fight you first?

Clytemnestra   What is your thought, child?
Iphigenia   Oh, for all the Gods
  My lady, stop a lover in his rage.
  We cannot let him go to this fatal meeting.   1070
  My lord, your protests would be too impassioned —
  I know a lover's anger has no limits —
  And my father stands on his authority:
  Who does not know the pride of the Atrídae?
  Leave it to gentler voices to complain.
  He will be here to see why I delay;
  He'll meet the pleas of a grief-stricken mother;
  And who can tell the words that I may find
  To save so many tears you all would shed,
  To end your quarrel, and to live for you?   1080
Achilles   If nothing else will please you, then I yield.
  Advise him, both of you, with words of prudence.
  Appeal to reason till he is convinced —
  For your good, and for mine, but most for his.
  I let the moment pass in useless talk,
  When it is time to act and hold our tongues.
  (*To* Clytemnestra) My lady, I shall put in readiness
  Everything that your service may require.
  Meanwhile go to your quarters, take some rest.
  Your child shall live, that much I can predict.   1090
  Be sure at least, be sure, that while I breathe
  The Gods' decree will never touch her head;
  And this is truer than Calchas' oracle.

ACT IV

ERIPHILE, CHLORIS

Chloris   What are you saying? Are you in your senses?
  You, to feel jealous of Iphigenia!
  She dies within the hour. And yet you say
  You never envied her good fortune more.
  I don't believe it. How, my lady, could you . . . ?
Eriphile   Chloris, I never spoke a truer word;
  And never did the suffering I endure   1100
  So move my mind to envy of her fortune.
  Danger as fruitful as my hope was vain!
  Did you not see her triumph, his emotion?
  I did; so clear, I could not bear to see it.
  A hero, that inspires the world with terror,

Knowing no tears, save those his victims shed,
Inured against them from his earliest days,
When, if report be true, he sucked for milk
The blood of lions and of mountain bears,
Has known, for her, the experience of fear!   1110
She saw him weep, she saw his face go pale —
You pity her, Chloris? What would I give
To have inspired those tears instead of her,
Were I like her to expire within the hour.
Expire, did I say? She will not die, not she.
Defended by Achilles, she is safe.
Do you suppose Achilles will stand by,
And none will pay for having made him blench?
You'll see, that oracle came from the Gods
For nothing else but this, to multiply   1120
At once her glory and my bitterness,
And make her fairer in her lover's eyes.
Haven't you seen all that they do for her?
No one's divulged the doom pronounced by Heaven;
And though the fire is ready to be lit
No one knows yet what offering it must burn.
The whole camp waits for news. What is that, Chloris,
But proof that still her father's mind's uncertain?
What could he do, though? What kind of fortitude
Could face the onslaughts he must face today —   1130
A mother beside herself, a daughter weeping,
The clamour, the despair of all his kin,
The voice of his own blood, which must betray him,
Backed with the menace of Achilles' wrath?
Ah no, be sure, in vain the Gods condemned her:
I take the brunt alone, I always shall.
Ah, if I did what . . .

Chloris   What is in your mind?

Eriphile   I'd like to know what stops me going out
To put an end to all this secrecy
By making public what the Gods have said,   1140
And what rebellious plots are being brewed
Against their altars and their majesty.

Chloris   What a design!

Eriphile   But, Chloris, what delight!
What incense would be burnt on Trojan altars
If I could throw the Greeks into confusion
And, in revenge for my captivity,
Set Agamemnon up against Achilles,
Turn all their hate and all their marshalled force

Away from Troy into intestine war,
And make this camp, by what I can disclose,   1150
A sacrifice to save my fatherland!
Chloris   There are voices, coming this way. —
      Clytemnestra.
Restrain yourself, my lady, or avoid her.
Eriphile   Come then. — If I disrupt this hateful
      marriage
My anger has the sanction of the Gods.

          Exeunt Eriphile *and* Chloris
          Enter Clytemnestra *and* Aegina

Clytemnestra   You see that there is nothing I can do:
She will not weep or tremble in her peril,
Simply defends her father; and even now
Thinks I am wrong to blame the hand that strikes her.
Such fortitude, such respect! — Which he repays   1160
By chiding her, because she keeps him waiting!
I shall receive him. He will soon be here
To ask me why she's late; he still expects
That we have not discovered his deception.
Here he is. I shall keep my wrath in check
And see if he can face it out before me.

          Enter Agamemnon

Agamemnon   What is this, my lady? Why is your
      daughter
Not here with you to meet me at this place?
Arcas brought word she was to come to me:
Why has she not? Was it you held her back?   1170
Would you resist what I see fit to order?
Cannot she come unless you walk before her?
Explain.
Clytemnestra   If it is time, my child is ready.
But you, my lord, does nothing hold you back?
Agamemnon   Me?
Clytemnestra   Have you seen to everything you need?
Agamemnon   Calchas is there, the altar is adorned;
I have provided what is right and fit.
Clytemnestra   You have not spoken of the offering.
Agamemnon   What do you mean? And why do you
      presume . . . ?

          Enter Iphigenia

Clytemnestra   Come, child, for only you are lacking
      now.   1180
Come here, come; speak your thanks to a loving father
Who will himself conduct you to the altar

Agamemnon   What's this? What words! And you, my
           child, in tears,
    Whose downcast eyes seem to avoid my own;
    Distraught; and both in tears, mother and child!
    Accursed Arcas, you've betrayed me.
Iphigenia   Father,
    Be reassured. You have not been betrayed.
    Whenever you command, I shall obey.
    My life belongs to you. You wish to take it.
    You could have called for it without disguise.   1190
    As cheerfully and as respectfully
    As I received a bridegroom from your hand,
    Now, if need be, as a submissive victim,
    I shall bare a blameless throat to Calchas' blade,
    And, honouring the stroke decreed by you,
    Return you all the blood you gave me first.
    Yet, if respect and if obedience
    Seem in your eyes to merit something better,
    If you have mercy on a mother's grief,
    I venture to say this: in such a moment   1200
    Perhaps the honours that have lit my life
    Have made me loath to think that it should cease,
    And that the Destiny that marks its end
    Will cut it off so near to its beginning.
    I first, the eldest child of Agamemnon,
    Called you, my lord, by that sweet name of father.
    I, who was all the pleasure of your eyes,
    I made you thank the Heavens for that name;
    I that you fondled often, unashamed
    To yield to nature and the voice of blood —   1210
    Ah, and how eagerly I made you tell
    The names of all the lands you would subdue,
    And could not wait the fall of Ilium
    To plan the feast for that triumphant day!
    Little I knew that, if it was to come,
    My blood would be the first you had to shed!
    Do not suppose that fear of what awaits me
    Makes me recall your kindness in the past.
    Fear not: I am too jealous of your honour
    Ever to shame a father such as you;   1220
    And if my life alone had been at stake
    I could have stilled those tender memories.
    But my unhappy fate, you know, my lord,
    Meant joy or pain to mother and to lover.
    A King who is not unworthy of your name

Had hoped today would see our wedding-rites.
He knew my heart responded to his own,
And he was happy; you had given me leave.
He knows what you intend: judge of his fears.
Here is my mother, and you see her grief.   1230
Forgive such efforts as I have essayed
To save them from the tears that I shall cause them.

Agamemnon   My child, it is the truth. For what
        offence
The Gods are angered and require a victim
I do not know. But they have named your name.
A pitiless oracle demands your blood
Here, on an altar. To defend your life
A loving father had no need of pleadings.
I shall not tell how long I fought for you —
Judge by that love which you yourself appeal to.   1240
Even last night once more — perhaps you know —
I had revoked the doom they made me sign,
Preferring you to Greece and all her claims.
For you I sacrificed my rank, my safety.
Arcas went out to warn you from the camp.
Heaven willed that he should miss you on the road
And all the efforts of my love were foiled
To save, in spite of all, what Heaven had sentenced.
Do not rely on any power I hold.
What could restrain a people, when the Gods   1250
Deliver us to its unthinking zeal
And free it from a yoke it never loved?
My child, we have lost the fight. Your hour has come.
Think of the lofty station that you fill
— Though these are words almost too hard for me,
And you will die today no more than I.
Show them whose daughter gives her life for them,
And shame the Gods who bring you to this end.
Go: force your executioners to confess
The blood that gushes from your wound is mine.   1260

Clytemnestra   You are true son of that accursed blood!
You are the race of Atreus and Thyestes!
Butcher of your own child, what stops you now
From making her a banquet for her mother?
Savage, was this the auspicious sacrifice
You were preparing with such careful art?
What, you could bring yourself to sign that order
And not for very horror stay your hand?
Why act a show of sorrow for us now?

Is it with tears that you would prove you love her?   1270
Where are the battles you have fought for her?
Where are the streams of blood that you have shed,
And shattered relics of some desperate stand?
What piles of corpses shame me into silence?
That would be evidence that could convince me,
Brute, that you cared and tried at least to save her.
— But Fate has spoken in an oracle!
Do oracles say all they seem to say?
Do Gods, those just Gods, take delight in murder
Or thirst to drink the blood of innocents?   1280
If Helen's kin must bleed for Helen's fault
Then send to Sparta for Hermione
Her daughter; let the daughter pay the price
For Menelaus to reclaim the wife
He loves so much and so unworthily.
Why should you pay the ransom for her lust?
Why be so mad as seek to right her wrong?
And why should I rend my own flesh apart
To shed the purest of my blood, for her?
For after all, this cause of strife, this Helen   1290
That sets all Europe and Asia by the ears,
What has she done to make her the reward
Of all your exploits? We have blushed for her
Again and again. Before your brother took her
(Would he had not!) Theseus made off with her.
You know, for Calchas told you countless times,
That from the secret love between those two
Was born a daughter that her mother hid,
And Greece has never seen that princely babe.
But what is that to you? A brother's honour   1300
Counts less than nothing in your purposes:
A thirst of power unappeasable,
Pride to have twenty Kings to serve and fear you,
Possession of the Captaincy of Greece —
These are your Gods to whom you sacrifice,
Savage. You do not want to avoid this blow.
You turn its horror to your own account;
You fear so much the rivals of your office
That you rejoice to buy it with your blood,
Hoping to find no other man that dares   1310
Set his ambition at so high a price.
Call yourself father? Ah, my mind gives way
At the atrocity of this betrayal!
So then, a priest before a gloating crowd

Will lay his murderous hand upon my child,
Hack her breast open, and with curious gaze
Read the Gods' pleasure in her throbbing heart?
While I go back, alone and desperate,
The way she came, exultant, adulated,
Along the roads still odorous with the breath   1320
Of all the blossoms strewn beneath her feet!
Never. Rather than leave her here to die
I'll make a second victim for these Greeks.
No fear, no piety will tear me from her;
You'll have to pluck her from my dying grasp.
Come if you dare, and show me no more mercy
Than you have her, and see if you can take her.
Meanwhile, my child, go in. At least today
Obey my words, this once and never more.

Exeunt both

Agamemnon   I had no cause to hope for less than this.   1330
Yes, yes; such clamours I had feared to meet.
Too happy, if in my perplexity
There had been nothing worse to fear than words!
But when you laid your dread commands upon me,
Great Gods, why leave me with a father's heart?

Enter Achilles

Achilles   Certain most strange reports have come to me,
My lord; I cannot think them worth belief.
They say — with horror I repeat the words —
That here, today, and by your own command,
Iphigenia dies; that you yourself   1340
Have stifled love and all humanity,
And Calchas will receive her from your hand.
They say my name was used to bring her there
Before an altar where she will be killed,
On pretext of a wedding — death to her,
And foulest shame to me that served as lure.
Tell me, my lord, what do you say to this?
What must I think? Will you not disavow
Tales that bring such dishonour on your name?

Agamemnon   I owe no man account of my designs,   1350
My lord. My child has not received her orders;
And when the time has come for her to hear
You too shall hear, the army shall be told.

Achilles   Too well I know what you will do with her.

Agamemnon   Why do you ask then, if you know so
well?

Achilles   Why do I ask? Great Heavens, are you saying

That you confess this mad and wicked plan?
Do you suppose I shall stand idly by
And let you kill your daughter in my sight,
Forgetful of my vows, my love, my honour?   1360
Agamemnon   But you, who speak in these insulting
          tones,
Have you forgotten who it is you question?
Achilles   Have you forgotten who I love and who
You wrong so foully?
Agamemnon   And who gave you charge
Over my house? May I not deal with her
Without consulting you? Is she not mine
And I her father still? Are you her husband?
Can she not . . . ?
Achilles   No, she is no longer yours.
No man makes empty promises to me.
As long as any blood is in my veins,   1370
Since every moment of her life is mine —
You swore it — I shall stand upon my rights.
Did you not bring her here because of me?
Agamemnon   Then blame the Gods, who ordered me
          to bring her.
Blame Calchas, blame Ulysses, Menelaus,
The army, and yourself the most of all.
Achilles   Me?
Agamemnon   You who will hear of nothing but the war,
And daily fret against the Gods' delays;
You who found fault with my well-judged alarm
And spread your mutinous rage throughout our force. 1380
My love for her found you a way to save her,
But nothing will content you, only Troy.
I barred the field in which you wish to shine:
Go to it, sail; her death removes the bar.
Achilles   Justice of Heaven! Can I hear such talk?
Not only do you give me lies, but insults. —
I longed to sail although it cost her life?
What have they ever done to me, these Trojans?
Why do I rush to fight beneath their walls?
Why was I deaf to a Goddess mother's words,   1390
Why did I spurn the pleadings of a father,
To go and court the death so long foretold me?
Did any Trojan ship from the Scamander
Ever approach the plains of Thessaly?
Did any base adventurer ever come
To rob me of wife or sister in Larissa?

What have I lost? What wrongs have I endured?
I go for you, you savage, only you;
For you, to whom alone of all the Greeks
I am not bound, you, that I made them all   1400
Elect their chief and mine; you I avenged
When I put Lesbos to the sword and flame
Before you had an army fit to march.
And what design has brought us all together?
What, but to get back Helen for her husband?
And shall I, helpless in my own behalf,
Be parted, think you, from a wife I cherish?
Is there no man entitled, save your brother,
To take revenge when outraged in his love?
I loved your daughter, wooed and made her love me,   1410
I made her vows, to her and her alone.
Well pleased to win her hand, I offered all —
Soldiers, ships, arms — to her, not Menelaus.
Let him go on if that is what he wants,
Let him pursue this wife that he has lost,
And triumphs, that no blood can buy but mine.
I do not care for Priam, Helen, Paris.
I sought your child, I will not sail for less.
Agamemnon   Go then, go home. Sail back to Thessaly.
I set you free from any oath that binds you.   1420
I shall not lack for others, less unruly,
To pluck the laurels offered first to you,
Reverse the Fates' decree by force of arms
And bring to Troy her day of destiny.
I see your pride; your speech has made it plain
How dearly I should pay your lordly help.
You see yourself the arbiter of Greece
And me, a helpless puppet of her Kings.
You are our champion, and you intend
Us all to serve, obey and cringe to you.   1430
A good deed boasted of is an offence.
I want less valour and more discipline.
Go home. I do not fear your harmless rage.
I break all bonds that ever tied me to you.
Achilles   Be thankful for the only bond that holds me:
I still regard Iphigenia's father.
But for that name, the Chief of all those Kings
Might have defied Achilles once too often.
Just one more word: listen if you are wise.
Two things I prize, your daughter and my honour.   1440
Before you reach that heart you mean to pierce

This is the gate that you must batter down.

Exit Achilles

Agamemnon, alone   After that there is nothing which
    can save her.
I feared my daughter by herself much more.
You, with your overweening love, your threats,
Hasten the very thing you would prevent.
There is no more to say. He has defied me;
My honour is at stake and turns the scale.
I cannot let Achilles threaten me,
I cannot show pity which would pass for fear.   1450
Hallo, guards, here!

Enter Eurybates and guards

Eurybates   My lord.
Agamemnon   What shall I tell them?
Do I pronounce the order for her death?
Cruel — but are you cruel enough for this?
What is this fight, what is this enemy?
A mother who has passed beyond all fear, awaits me
To save her own blood from a father's knife.
Less barbarous than I, these men will shrink
To drag their own King's daughter from her arms.
What if Achilles threatens me and slights me?
Is she the less submissive to my will?   1460
Will she attempt to shirk the sacrifice?
Has she complained of what I mean to do?
— Do I? What could I gain from sacrilege?
What could I pray for, after offering her?
What pleasure can I take in victories,
In glorious laurels sprinkled with her blood?
— I must placate the cruelty of the Gods?
Ah! which of them could plague me like my
    thoughts?
I cannot do it. A father's love's too strong;
Why be ashamed to yield to just compassion?   1470
She shall live. But then, must I neglect my honour
And let Achilles triumph over me?
I shall only feed his mutinous arrogance —
He'll think I yield because he has made me tremble.
A paltry thought, unworthy of my mind!
As if I could not tame Achilles' pride!
My child shall be to him a cause of pain.
He loves her: she shall live, but not for him.
Eurybates, call the Princess and the Queen.
They need not fear.   Exit Eurybates

Agamemnon (*continues*)   Now, great Gods, if your
    hatred   1480
  Will not relent, if you must snatch her from me,
  What can a mortal do? A father's struggles
  Harm her the more; I know. And yet, great Gods,
  For such a sacrifice, is it not right
  You should review the cruelty of your sentence
  And claim her from my arms a second time?
                        Enter Clytemnestra, Iphigenia,
                        Eriphile, Eurybates, Chloris
Agamemnon   Take her, my lady, take her. Guard her
    well.
  I give you back your child into your care.
  Convey her quickly from this place of terror.
  My guards go with you, Arcas at their head.   1490
  I pardon him his fortunate indiscretion.
  Now all depends on secrecy and speed.
  Ulysses has not spoken yet, nor Calchas —
  See to it they hear nothing of your going,
  And hide your daughter, so that all may think
  I keep her here and send you back alone.
  Go now, and may the Gods accept my tears
  And keep her long away from these sad eyes.
  Guards, go with the Queen.
Clytemnestra   Oh, my lord!
Iphigenia   Oh, my father!
Agamemnon   Keep clear of Calchas and his cruel zeal;   1500
  Be gone, and quickly, while I keep him busy
  With specious arguments to give you time.
  I shall demand at least today for respite
  And make him adjourn the fatal festival.
                 Exeunt all except Eriphile *and* Chloris
Eriphile   Come with me, Chloris. That is not our way.
Chloris   Not go with them?
Eriphile   I can resist no more.
  Now I have seen Achilles and his love
  The fury in my heart demands a victim.
  Do not resist. Either she dies, or I.
  Come on, I say. Calchas shall learn of this.   1510

ACT V

IPHIGENIA, AEGINA

Iphigenia   Let me alone. Go to the Queen, Aegina.
  I must placate the anger of the Gods.
  Look what a storm has gathered over us
  Because men would have robbed them of my blood.
  Consider what has happened to my mother;
  See how the army will not let us pass
  But insolently rush from every side
  To flash their sharpened lances in our faces —
  Our guards flung back, the Queen fainted away . . .
  She must endure no more; so let me leave her,   1520
  Renounce the help she cannot give me now
  And do what she would hinder if she could.
  Even my father, if I have to say it,
  My father saves me only to condemn me.
Aegina   Your father? How is that? What has he done?
Iphigenia   I think Achilles' ardour must have galled
      him.
  The King hates him, and means that I should hate him.
  He sent his orders by the mouth of Arcas,
  Aegina: I am not to speak to him
  Ever again.
Aegina   My lady!
Iphigenia   Cruellest sentence!   1530
  Gods, you have been more merciful, you asked
  Only my life. So, I obey, I die.
  — But who is here? O Gods, what do I see?
  Achilles!

                                        Enter Achilles
Achilles   My lady, follow me at once.
  Fear not the shouts, fear not the powerless throng
  Of soldiery that jostle round the tent.
  Come out. They will not wait to meet my sword,
  The stormy waves will part to let you through.
  Patróclus, with some other of my captains,
  Brings you the cream of my Thessalian force,   1540
  And all the rest are ranged about my standard,
  A wall impregnable for your defence.
  My tents will shelter you from your assailants —
  Let them attempt to take you if they dare.
  Is this, my lady, all the help you give me?

You weep; only your tears reply to me.
Are you still trusting to so weak a weapon?
Hasten. Your father saw you weep before.
Iphigenia   I know, my lord; and so my only hope,
Now, is the fated stroke by which I die.   1550
Achilles   You die! No more of that. Do you forget
The sacred oath that binds us one to other?
To cut the matter short, do you forget
Achilles' happiness hangs on your life?
Iphigenia   No, my poor life has no such privilege:
Your happiness does not depend on this.
Our love has blinded us; for Fate has made
That happiness dependent on my death.
Think, my lord, think what harvests of renown
Victory holds to put into your hands —   1560
That field of glory that attracts you all
Can yield no fruit till watered by my blood.
Such is the law the Gods spoke to my father;
In vain he fought with Calchas and defied it.
The voice of all these Greeks is clear enough
In confirmation of their ruthless will.
Leave me and sail: I hinder your renown.
Go and make good those oracles of yours;
Show Greece the hero that they promised her,
And turn your bitterness on her enemies.   1570
Already Priam pales; Troy quakes to see
My funeral fire, she trembles at your tears.
Go; in her battered and unpeopled walls
Let widows' wailings be my burial chant.
Calm in this hope, I die well satisfied.
If I have never lived Achilles' wife,
At least I trust some happy future time
Will join my name with your immortal deeds;
Some day my death, that sets your glory free,
Will stand as prologue to that tale of wonder.   1580
Goodbye, my Prince. Live, offspring of the Gods.
Achilles   No, I'll have none of these last parting sighs.
Vainly your cruel skill would seek to take
Your father's side, and disappoint my love.
Vainly you cling to death and try to prove
My honour forces me to give you up.
These laurels, conquests, harvests of renown,
Are here to gather if I serve your cause.
And who would ever look to me for help
If I am helpless to defend my bride?   1590

Honour and love both call on you to live.
So come, my lady; hear their voice and come.
Iphigenia   Who? I? Rebel against a father's will?
If I refused this death I should deserve it.
What of my duty, what of that respect . . .?
Achilles   You will come with the husband that he gave
        you to.
He cannot take that name away from me.
Are all his oaths made only to be broken?
And you, so loyal to so harsh a duty,
When he bestows you, is he not your father?   1600
Do you observe his absolute commands
Only when he forgets his part, and wrongs you?
We stay too long, my Princess; I am fearful . . .
Iphigenia   What, would you stoop, my lord, to show
        me violence?
Would you add further to my misery
By listening to the voice of lawless passion?
Would you prefer my life above my honour?
Be generous, my lord, and spare me this.
Under that duty that I must acknowledge
I am at fault even to hear you speak.   1610
But take no more advantage of my weakness;
Or, since I must, with these two hands I shall
Sacrifice myself to my fair fame
Rather than take a help so full of danger.
Achilles   So be it then. Glory in your obedience.
Choose death since it attracts you. Take your father
The heart he claims. I know that in it lives
Less deference to him than hate for me.
Now I have nothing left in me but fury. —
Go to the altar: I'll be there before you.   1620
And if the Gods want blood and human corpses
Then they shall have more blood than ever yet.
I shall be blind, my love will stay at nothing;
The first I immolate shall be the priest,
I'll wreck and overturn the funeral pyre
And float its timbers on the assistants' blood;
And if in all the terror of the conflict
Your father should be felled and meet his death,
Then you will see at least what you have done
With these fine virtues of respect and duty.   1630
                       Exit Achilles
Iphigenia   No, no, my lord! You would not . . . He has
        gone.

— Heaven, just heaven, who hast willed my death,
Strike now, I am alone. End life and terror.
Strike me, and spare the others with your shafts.

        Enter Clytemnestra, Eurybates *and* guards

Clytemnestra   Let the whole army come, I will defend
    her.
Cowards, will you betray your Queen in need?

Eurybates   Never, my lady. You have but to speak
And we will lay our lives down at your feet.
But what can our poor efforts do to help you?
And what can shield you from these enemies?   1640
This is no riot of a shifting crowd,
But all the camp, made murderous by zeal.
Pity is dead. Calchas is king and leader,
And harsh religion calls aloud for blood.
The King is not the king, his power is gone,
He makes us yield, himself, before the torrent.
Achilles the invincible, Achilles
Would fail if he should try to stem its rage.
What can he do, my lady? Who can scatter
These floods of enemies that will engulf us?   1650

Clytemnestra   Then let them glut their impious zeal on
    me,
And rob me of what little life remains.
I'll bind her to me with my arms' embrace
And death alone shall break these bonds apart.
Yes, they can part my body from my soul
Before they ever . . . Ah, my child!   (*Sees* Iphigenia)

Iphigenia   My lady!
What unkind star looked down upon the birth
Of this unfortunate you have loved for nothing?
But in this pass, what is there left to do?
You have to face both Gods and mortal men.   1660
Would you oppose a rabble in its fury?
Do not, amid a camp of mutineers,
Dragged back, perhaps, by the base hands of soldiers
In vain attempts to keep me from my death —
Do not force me, now after all you have done,
To see what I would rather die than see.
Go, leave the Greeks to do what they must do
And turn from this unhappy strand for ever.
The funeral fire that waits me is too near:
Its blaze would strike too fiercely on your eyes.   1670
This above all: as you have loved me, mother,
Never hold my death against my father.

Clytemnestra   Your father, who will clutch and hand
          to Calchas . . . !
Iphigenia   What did he leave undone to save me for
          you?
Clytemnestra   After the treachery of his betrayal!
Iphigenia   The Gods that gave me made him give me back.
     But I am not the only token living
     Of all your love and all your years together.
     You will still see me when you see my brother
     Orestes — ah! may he bring you less pain!   1680
     — You hear the cries of an impatient crowd.
     Take me now and enfold me, I entreat you,
     For the last time, my lady, in your arms;
     And call upon that lofty heart . . . Lead on,
     Eurybates, take the offering to the altar.
                              Exeunt Iphigenia *and* Eurybates
Clytemnestra   You shall not go alone. I will not let . . .
     But all this multitude has barred my path.
     Traitors! assuage your thirst for blood with mine!
Aegina   Where would you go, my lady? What are you
          doing?
Clytemnestra   Alas, I waste my strength to no avail.   1690
     I feel myself fall back into the horror
     That swallowed me before and nearly drowned me.
     So many deaths, and can I never die?
Aegina   But do you know the crime, and who betrayed
          you,
     My lady? Do you know what thankless snake
     Iphigenia sheltered in her breast?
     That same Eriphile you brought to Aulis,
     She alone, told the Greeks of your escape.
Clytemnestra   Monster, from the womb of fell Megaera!
     Monster that Hell has spewed across our path!   1700
     Is there no death for you? What, will such crime . . . ?
     But why do I concern myself with her?
     Will you not yawn and open new abysses,
     You seas, to overwhelm those Greeks at once
     With all those thousand ships? Will not the winds
     As soon as Aulis vomits from its port
     Their crime-polluted fleet, these very winds
     They raged against so long, bespatter you
     With shattered wreckage of each stricken ship?
     Sun, thou bright Sun, who seest in this place   1710
     The one successor and true son of Atreus,
     Thou who didst shrink to light the father's banquet,

Turn back, turn back as they have taught you to!
But at this moment — can a mother say it? —
My child is crowned with hateful flowers, she bares
Her throat to knives her father has prepared.
Calchas will plunge his hand — . Stay, savages,
This is the purest blood of thundering Jove! . . .
That is his bolt that roars. All earth is quaking.
A God, a God of vengeance deals these blows.   1720

Enter Arcas

Arcas   Assuredly, my lady, a God is with you.
Your prayers are being answered by Achilles;
The Grecian ranks have broken down before him.
He stands at the altar. Calchas is aghast,
And still the dreadful sacrifice delays.
Threats fly, men charge, sounds fill the air, steel
          flashes,
Achilles posts his friends around your child
And they will do his bidding to the end.
The King despairs, and fearful to support him,
Whether to shut away the sights he fears,   1730
Or else to hide his tears, has veiled his face.
Come, since he will do nothing, come at least
To add your voice to our defender's deeds.
Come and receive out of his bloodstained hands
The maid he loves and saves. He sent me for you.
Fear nothing.
Clytemnestra   Fear? Who, I? No, quickly, Arcas;
There is no peril that can make me pale.
I will go anywhere. But, O ye Gods,
What do I see? Ulysses? Yes, it is.
My child is dead, Arcas; it is too late.   1740

Enter Ulysses

Ulysses   No, your child lives. The Gods have been
          appeased.
Be of good cheer. They give her back to you.
Clytemnestra   She is alive, and you have come to tell
          me!
Ulysses   Yes, I, who saw it as my task to steel
Your husband's mind against your child and you;
Whose stern and urgent promptings caused your tears
Rather than stain the honour of our arms.
I now, since now the Heavens are content,
Have come to heal the anguish I have brought.
Clytemnestra   Oh Prince, my child! Heaven! How can
          it be?   1750

What God, what miracle, has brought her back?
Ulysses   Myself no less than you, this happy moment,
    I am lost in wonderment and holy awe.
    Never was day more threatening to Greece.
    Discord already reigned over the camp,
    Her deadly blindfold laid on every eye,
    And raised the signal for the clash of arms.
    Your helpless daughter in this fearful scene
    Counted none but Achilles on her side,
    Against her, all the army: but Achilles   1760
    Had cowed the host, divided the Immortals.
    The air was darkened by the shafts that flew,
    Blood had been drawn, the carnage had begun.
    Then, where the two sides faced each other, Calchas
    Stood forth, fierce, glowering, every hair upraised,
    Terrible to behold, filled with his God.
    'Achilles, and you Greeks', he said, 'be still.
    The God who now instructs you by my voice
    Makes plain his oracle and names his choice.
    It is another of the blood of Helen,   1770
    Another Iphigenia, who must die
    And shed her blood as victim on this strand.
    For Helen once was carried off by Theseus;
    A secret union followed their adventure,
    A child was born, and hidden by her mother;
    She too received the name Iphigenia;
    And I myself, I saw this child of theirs
    And prophesied terrible things for her.
    This evil fate, joined with her own black heart,
    Has brought her here under another name.   1780
    She hears me now. She stands there in your sight;
    And it is she the voice of Heaven demands.'
        Thus Calchas spoke. The whole camp seized with
            fear
    Stood motionless and watched Eriphile.
    She was by the altar, chafing (so I think)
    To see the fatal stroke so long delayed.
    (For it was she that lately, in great haste,
    Had come to tell the Greeks of your departure.)
    We wonder at her story and her fate;
    But since her death delivers Troy to us   1790
    The army with one voice takes part against her
    And calls the priest to execute her doom.
    Calchas had moved to lay his hands upon her:
    'Stay where you are,' she cried, 'and come no nearer.

If I am born of that heroic blood
What need have I of your unworthy arm
To shed it now?' And then with one wild bound
She snatched the knife from off the altar slab
And plunged it in her breast. As the first blood
Flowed from the wound to redden all the ground,   1800
Thunder fell from Heaven on the altar;
The air was filled with the stirring of the winds,
The water roared in answer, while afar
The spume flew white along the sounding shore.
The flames leapt up unbidden from the pyre.
The sky, lurid with lightning, parted, pouring
Into our midst a holy healing awe.
The wondering soldiers swear they saw Diana
Herself descend in clouds over the blaze;
They think that rising with the smoke again   1810
She bore on high our incense and our prayers.
All run to the ships. Only Iphigenia
While we rejoice, weeps for her enemy.
Come now, and take her from a father's hand;
Come. For Achilles and the King together
Await you eagerly, their discord ended,
And ready now to ratify with oaths
The solemn bond that makes your houses one.
Clytemnestra   What can I give, O Gods, what incense
        burn,
To pay Achilles and requite your mercy?   1820

PHAEDRA
(1677)

INTRODUCTION

The Phaedra of Euripides was not the central figure of *Hippolytus*. There, Aphrodite (Venus) hates Hippolytus, who refuses her the worship that is her due and follows Artemis (Diana), living like her as a chaste huntsman. Phaedra's guilty love for him, his rejection of her, and her accusation of rape, left in writing when she takes her own life, are means used by the Goddess to destroy her enemy. Phaedra, an unimportant tool, has one long pathetic scene, and dies before her husband returns. In the *Phaedra* of the Roman Seneca on the other hand, the heroine is the victim; it is her family, not Hippolytus, that Venus hates; and Phaedra has a long dramatic confrontation with the youth, and dies, on stage, only after he has been banished and cursed and the news of his death has been brought in. Several French adaptations, before Racine, had drawn on Seneca almost exclusively. Racine marries the two versions, taking, as my notes will show, the most affecting scenes of each; his heroine contrives to unite the essential purity of Euripides' Phaedra with the lustful acts of Seneca's. Racine has dared to return to two themes which his contemporaries had feared to touch in the prevailing atmosphere of squeamish decorum – the guilty love of a married woman, and an explicit accusation of (attempted) rape.

But even Racine does not keep a Hippolytus hostile to love – his character has been like that, but he has fallen like the rest, to a highly suitable young princess with whom his brief idyll forms a prelude and parallel to Phaedra's two confessions of her love – to her nurse in Act I, and to himself in Act II. This Aricia is cleverly fitted up by the poet with a family and background (which he found in legend, but which has no connection with the Virgilian Aricia whom he mentions in his preface); and these provide the play with a 'political' dimension of dynastic struggle, cutting across the love-interest, such as is found almost universally in tragedies at this time.

All this revision and modern colouring is compensated by a dwelling on the legendary background for its own sake (because it is 'full of the stuff of poetry' as the preface says) – not to mention all the references to Venus, there are Theramenes' journeyings, Theseus' exploits (all in I 1); references to Minerva, patroness of Athens where Theseus reigns, and to Neptune his own patron; and above all the overwhelming presence, in Phaedra's conscience, of the Gods her forebears (IV 6, a scene which could not have existed without the invention of Aricia).

No earlier play by Racine shows this preoccupation half so much. One is left wondering how he would have continued, if he had continued, his playwright's career, or whether he had said all it was in him to say; whether the cruelty of Phaedra's fate had not shocked the poet himself, who can never, I think, have believed in a universe like this. The God of his Jansenist ex-teachers was inscrutable, severe, but utterly just, and could never tempt a mortal into sin.

The answer will never be known. He left working for the stage at this point, drawn by a prestigious appointment as historiographer of the King's reign, aided (perhaps) by his growing moral scruples. *Phaedra* was greeted almost at once as the great play it is. Racine remained willing to revise his works for new editions, since the reading of plays was not condemned by those who condemned the stage; but he added to them only the two religious plays, written after a twelve-year interval, for private performance under high patronage.

PREFACE
(1677)

Here is another tragedy on a subject taken from Euripides. The action follows a somewhat different course, but I have enriched my play with everything in his that I considered most strikingly beautiful. Had I borrowed no more than the conception of Phaedra's character, I might say I owe him the most reasonable thing, perhaps, that I have given to the theatre. I am not surprised that this character was so successful in Euripides' time, and now again in our own, considering that it has every quality required by Aristotle in the tragic hero, and proper to arouse compassion and terror. For Phaedra is not altogether guilty, and not altogether innocent. She is drawn by her destiny, and the anger of the Gods, into an unlawful passion which she is the first to hold in horror. She makes every endeavour to overcome it. She chooses death rather than disclose it to anyone. And when forced to reveal it, she speaks of it with such shame and confusion as leave no doubt that her crime is rather a punishment from the Gods, than an impulse of her own will.

I have even taken pains to make her a little less odious than she is in the tragedies of antiquity, where she brings herself, unprompted, to accuse Hippolytus. I felt that a false testimony was something too base, too black, to put into the mouth of a Princess possessed otherwise of sentiments so noble and virtuous. Such baseness seemed to me more fitting to a Nurse, who might have more slave-like propensities; though even she only enters upon the lying accusation to save the life and honour of her mistress. If Phaedra acquiesces, it is because she is beside herself in the agitation of her thoughts, and the next moment she comes on with the intention of vindicating the guiltless and publishing the truth.

Hippolytus is accused, in Euripides and in Seneca, of actually raping his step-mother — *vim corpus tulit*; here, of no more than the intention. I desired to spare Theseus a sense of shame which might have made him less acceptable to my audience.

As for the figure of Hippolytus, I had read in ancient authors that Euripides was blamed for depicting him as a philosopher free of all imperfection — so that the death of the youthful Prince gave rise to far more indignation than pity. I felt I should give him a failing that might render him somewhat guilty towards his father, without detracting at all from that magnanimity which makes him spare Phaedra's honour and go to his doom without accusing her. By failing I mean his involuntary passion for Aricia, the daughter and the sister of his father's mortal enemies.

This Aricia is not a child of my invention. Virgil relates that Hippolytus married her, and she bore him a son, after Aesculapius had brought him back to life. And I have read too, in certain authors, that Hippolytus had married and brought into Italy an Athenian maiden of high birth, named Aricia, who had given her name to an Italian township.

I adduce these authorities, because I have most scrupulously endeavoured to keep close to the legend. I have even taken the history of Theseus just as it is in Plutarch.

It is this historian who mentions that the belief in Theseus' descent to the underworld to abduct Proserpine, was occasioned by a journey he made into Epirus towards the source of the Acheron, where a King, whose wife Pirithous sought to carry off, held Theseus prisoner after putting Pirithous to death. Thus I have tried to retain the verisimilitude of history, and yet to lose none of the embellishments of fable, so rich in the stuff of poetry. And the rumour of Theseus' death, based on the legendary journey, gives rise to that declaration of Phaedra's love which proves one of the principal causes of her unhappy plight, and which she would never have dared utter while she believed her husband to be alive.

For the rest, I dare not yet assert this play to be in truth the best of my tragedies. I leave my readers, and time, to set its rightful price upon it. What I can assert is that I have composed none where virtue is shown to more advantage than here. The slightest faults are severely punished. The bare thought of crime is regarded with no less horror than crime itself. The failings of love are treated as real failings. The passions are offered to view only to show all the ravage they create. And vice is everywhere painted in such hues, that its hideous face may be recognised and loathed. Here is the proper aim for every man to keep in sight who works for the public. And this, above all, was the purpose of the earliest tragic poets. Their stage was a school where virtue was taught no less well than in the schools of the philosophers. Thus Aristotle consented to draw up the rules of the dramatic poem; Socrates, the sagest of the philosophers, thought it no shame to set his hand to the tragedies of Euripides. It were much to be desired that our works should be found as serious and as full of useful instruction as the pages of those poets. It might bring about a reconciliation between the tragic art and a number of persons, noted for their religion and learning, who have denounced it of late, but might well look upon it with less disfavour if authors cared as much to instruct as to entertain their audience, and carried out thereby the true purpose of tragedy.

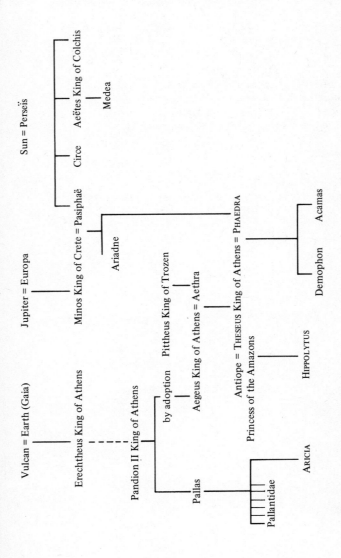

Genealogical table for *Phaedra*

DRAMATIS PERSONAE

Theseus	son of Aegeus, King of Athens
Phaedra	wife of Theseus, daughter of Minos and Pasiphaë
Hippŏlytus	son of Theseus by Antiope Queen of the Amazons
Arícia	daughter of Pallas, descended from the ancient kings of Athens
Oenone	nurse and confidant of Phaedra
Theramenes	governor of Hippolytus
Isméne	confidant of Aricia
Pánope	one of Phaedra's women

Guards

The scene is in Trozen, a town in the Peloponnese.

ACT I

HIPPOLYTUS, THERAMENES

Hippolytus   My mind's made up: I sail, Theramenes.
No more for me the tranquil days of Trozen,
For in the mortal tempest of my doubts
I am dishonoured if I linger here.
Six months ago my father sailed and left me
Ignorant what befalls a head so cherished,
Ignorant even where he may be hidden —
Theramenes   So where will you go to look for him, my
        lord?
Already, to relieve a fear I shared,
I have scoured the two seas that Corinth holds
        asunder,   10
Demanded Theseus of the tribes that live
Where Ácheron drives down headlong into Hell,
Searched Elis, skirted Taēnarum, and even
Traversed the waves where Icarus fell and perished.
What hope new-risen or what happier skies
Will light you to his footsteps? Why, perhaps,
Who knows, perhaps the King your father wishes
Not to unveil the mystery of his venture,
And while his peril fills your thought and ours,
Serene, weaving the latest of his loves,   20
The hero waits to seize the unguarded moment —
Hippolytus   Stop, good Theramenes. You slander
        Theseus;
There is a nobler cause for these delays;
After the follies of forgotten youth
The wanderings of his inconstant heart
Are fixed at length, and Phaedra fears no rival.
So once more — I shall go where duty points
And fly a land I cannot bear to see.
Theramenes   But my lord, how long have you despised
        the presence
Of these calm fields, the pleasure of your childhood   30
Whose solitude was dearer to you than
The splendid stir of Athens and the court?
What fear has banished you, or else what heartache?

Hippolytus   Those days are past. Pleasure and peace
       have vanished
     Since first the Gods directed to our shore
     The child of Minos and Pasíphaë.
Theramenes   I see: there is the cause, the hated
       presence —
     Phaedra, who came, your father's dangerous bride,
     Looked on you once, and by your prompt exile
     Gave the first measure of her new-won power.   40
     But all that dogged hate and old aversion
     Has passed with time, passed or at least abated;
     And after all what danger lies in her,
     A woman dying, crying out for death?
     Stricken by ills that none can make her utter,
     Tired of her life, tired of the day that lights her,
     What can she do to you?
Hippolytus   I do not fear
     Anything her aversion could devise.
     I sail to fly another enemy,
     I do admit: I fly Aricia,   50
     The youngest and the last of all that house
     In fatal league against ours.
Theramenes   You, my lord,
     Are turned against her too? But Pallas' daughter
     Surely had no part in her brothers' treason,
     And must you hate that unoffending grace?
Hippolytus   I would not fly her if I hated her.
Theramenes   My lord, have I permission to interpret
     Your flight? Must I suppose that you are not
     The old implacable Hippolytus,
     The outlaw of Love's empire, he that vowed   60
     Never to wear the yoke his father wore?
     Can it be that a slighted and a smarting Goddess
     Will press you to the service of her shrine,
     Reduce you to the rank of common men
     And vindicate that father by your fate?
     Can it be love, my lord?
Hippolytus   How can you say it,
     My friend, that knew the childhood of my heart
     And all its growth in pride and fierce resolve?
     Shall I dishonour it, disown myself?
     First, as a babe, at an Amazonian breast   70
     I drank the resolution that astounds you,
     But once of age to look upon myself
     I wished to be no other than I was.

Then, in the faithful service of your kindness
As you rehearsed for me my father's story,
Do you remember how my soul blazed up
At each particular in the noble toils
Of the intrepid hero, as you showed him
Turning the world from thoughts of lost Alcídes
By monsters strangled and by brigands slain —   80
Procrustes, Sinnis, Sciro, Cércyon
And Epidaurus scattered with the limbs
Of her gigantic tyrant, and the gore
Reeking from all Crete, of the Minotaur?
But when you told other ignobler feats —
A faith so cheaply pledged, and ever new,
Helen torn from a mother's arms in Sparta,
In Salamis the sighs of Periboẽa,
So many more than he can even name,
Victims too credulous of a lover's tongue;   90
What barren rocks heard Ariadne's sorrows;
How Phaedra, last and under happier auspice,
Followed him — then I wished the tale untold;
Often I urged you hasten and be done;
And would my wishes had redeemed from fame
That darker half of such a fair renown!
And now, by the spite of Heaven, shall I be
Degraded to the same indignity?
— Baseness beyond excuse, for those were frailties
Unseen amid a multitude of honours,   100
While not one trophy of a monster slain
Entitles me to fail as he has failed.
Even if I lost my freedom and my pride
How could I yield them to Aricia?
How could my disobedient sense forget
That which divides us irremovably?
The King denies her, denies her fallen brothers,
By violent laws, continuance of their line;
Their name must die for ever in her death,
Their guilty branch must bear no other fruit,   110
And till the tomb, submissive and sequestered,
The torch of wedlock must not burn for her.
Am I to oppose my father and his wrath?
Embrace her claims? and give a precedent
To treason? and embark my youth —
Theramenes   My lord,
If the marked hour draws on, our arguments
Escape the notice of the incurious Heavens.

No. Theseus wished you blind, and gave you eyes;
His hate inflames the passion he forbids you,
And adds enchantment to his prisoner's charms.   120
But come, why look askance at honest love?
Why not make trial where its sweetness lies?
Why be enchained by vain and foolish scruples?
Who fears to stray that follows Hercules?
Many a stubborn heart has Venus bent —
Where would you be yourself and your defiance
Had chaste Antíope been as chaste as you
And never warmed to Theseus' flame? But why
Face out a falsehood with the pride of words?
Confess how things have changed: not now as once,   130
Aloof, intractable, we see you guide
A skimming chariot along the beaches
Or, adept in the mystery Neptune taught,
Break an unmastered courser to the curb;
Less often our halloos awake the forests;
Your eyes droop, weighted with a secret fire . . .
The case is clear — you are in love, in flame,
In torment, and you will not show your wound.
Is it Aricia?
Hippolytus   Theramenes,
I sail today, and go to find my father.   140
Theramenes   Without an audience of Phaedra?
Hippolytus   No.
I will see her; I cannot well do less.
You may send word. — But what is the fresh mis-
        fortune
Disturbs her favourite Oenone so?

                                        Enter Oenone
Oenone   Alas, my lord, what grief can equal mine?
The Queen is near her utmost bourne of fate;
She that I watch by night and day unsleeping
Dies in my arms, and will not tell her sickness.
Her thought is all at variance with itself;
Her sick disquiet drives her from her bed   150
To see the light of day. But by her orders
No eye of man may see her suffering.
— Here she is.
Hippolytus   Very well; then I retire
Not to offend with this unwelcome face.
                        Exeunt Hippolytus *and* Theramenes
                                        Enter Phaedra
Phaedra   No more, for I can move no more, Oenone.

Let me rest; I am faint, my strength has left me.
My darkened eyes are dazzled by the light,
My wavering knees are weak beneath my weight.
Ah me!   *Sits*
Oenone   High Gods, relent and see our tears!
Phaedra   These fripperies, these veils, they hang so
              heavy!   160
Whose was the unkind hand that piled and bound
These clustering locks that weigh upon my brow?
So feeble and so weary, all these things
Grieve me and weary me.
Oenone   How can we please you?
Yourself, repentant of your wicked thoughts,
You called in haste for clothes and ornaments;
Yourself you rallied your forgotten vigour,
You wanted to be out and see the sunlight.
Now you are here, my lady, and it seems
You loathe the very light that you desired.   170
Phaedra   Splendid begetter of a seed afflicted,
Father from whom my mother claimed her birth,
O blushing Sun ashamed of my despair,
Now, for the last time, I salute thy face.
Oenone   What, still possessed of such a fearful
              purpose?
Shall I for ever see you, turned from life,
Enact the mournful ritual of your death?
Phaedra   Oh give me the shadow of the forest glades!
Or let my eye piercing the glorious dust
Follow the wheeling chariot in the course!   180
Oenone   My lady?
Phaedra   Oh, I am mad. What have I said?
Where am I, where are my thoughts, my wandering
              mind?
Lost, for the Gods have taken it away.
My face is hot, Oenone, with my shame;
I cannot hide my guilty sufferings
And tears descend that I cannot restrain.
Oenone   Blush if you must, but blush to keep a silence
That doubles all the misery you suffer.
Rebellious to all tending, deaf to all pleas,
Will you unpitying allow your life   190
To flow away? What madness cuts it short?
What spell, what poison stanches up its course?
Thrice has the sky been muffled up in shade
And still is sleep a stranger to your eyes;

Thrice has the day displaced the gloom of night
And still you fast, and still your body wastes.
What dark temptation leads you on? What right
Invests you with the power to take your life —
Wronging the Gods from whom you draw your being,
Failing the husband who received your promise,   200
Failing still more your helpless children, doomed
To bitter lives of bondage; for reflect,
The very day that takes their mother from them
Rebuilds the hope of that Barbarian's child,
That arrogant enemy of you and yours,
The boy the Amazonian stranger bore,
Hippolytus —

Phaedra O Gods!
Oenone   That charge strikes home!
Phaedra Woman, how dare you name that name to me?
Oenone Why, now your anger is most justly roused.
It heartens me that you should shrink to hear   210
That fatal name. Then live. For love, for duty,
Live; if you would not have the Scythian's son,
Bending your children to his hated yoke,
Lord it over the fairest blood of Greece
And of the Gods. But do not wait, each moment
You die. Rally, betimes, your prostrate vigour
While yet your almost spent and guttering life
Still glows, and may be kindled once again.
Phaedra I have outlived the right to live already.
Oenone Why, is there some remorse that feeds upon
  you?   220
What have you done that drives you so distraught?
Your hands have never dipped in guiltless blood?
Phaedra I thank the Gods my hands are free of evil.
Would that my heart were innocent as they!
Oenone What resolution, then, have you conceived
To terrify your heart before the time?
Phaedra I have said enough. Ask me no more, have
  pity;
For if I die it is to keep within me
This dreadful secret.
Oenone   Keep it then, and die;
But other hands, not mine, will close your eyes.   230
Yours is a weak and flickering fire, but I
Will lose my spirit first among the dead;
There are many avenues and all unbarred;
An injured heart will soon perceive the best. —

Ungrateful mistress, when did I betray you?
Have you forgotten that these hands received you
When you were born? My children and my home,
I have left all for you: and all for this.

Phaedra   What do you think to gain by this beseeching?
You will shrink with horror if I break my silence.   240

Oenone   What can you tell me then more horrible
Than thus to see you die before my face?

Phaedra   And when you know my destiny and my
        weakness
Still I shall die, and only die more guilty.

Oenone   My lady, by the tears I shed for you,
By these your trembling knees I hold entwined,
Deliver me from deadly fear and doubt.

Phaedra   You wish it. Rise.

Oenone   Speak on, and I will listen.

Phaedra   How shall I tell, ye Gods, or where begin?

Oenone   Your fears are insults to my loyalty.   250

Phaedra   O deathless hate of Venus, fatal vengeance!
O heavy doom of love upon my mother!

Oenone   Forget, my lady. Hide that memory
And keep it from the ears of later times.

Phaedra   Love left thee dying, sweet sister Ariadne,
Lying forsaken by the alien waters.

Oenone   Let be, my lady. Must your mortal grief
Be vented on the dearest of your blood?

Phaedra   Of this doomed blood, I, by the will of Venus,
I perish now the last and most accursed.   260

Oenone   You love!

Phaedra   To madness and to ecstasy.

Oenone   Who?

Phaedra   There's the horror that surpasses horror:
I love . . . at the fatal name I blench and tremble —
I love . . .

Oenone   But who?

Phaedra   You know the Amazon's son,
The young Prince who endured so much, through
        me . . .

Oenone   O Gods! Hippolytus!

Phaedra   You spoke the name!

Oenone   Sweet Heavens! You have chilled my very
        blood.
O race polluted, hopeless, lamentable!
Woe worth the day that brought us to these shores!
Why did we venture?

Phaedra   It was long ago   270
    And far from here. When first the rite of Hymen
    Bound my obedience to the son of Aegeus —
    My happiness, my peace then seemed so plain —
    Careless in Athens stood my conqueror.
    I saw and gazed, I blushed and paled again,
    A blind amazement rose and blurred my mind;
    My eyes were dim, my lips forgot to speak,
    This, I knew, was the awful flame of Venus,
    The fated torment of her chosen victims.
    I tried to ward it off with prayers, with vows   280
    And offerings, a temple built and decked,
    And in the midst of endless sacrifices
    I searched the entrails for my erring wisdom.
    Weak drugs for irremediable love!
    Even as my hand spilt incense at the shrine,
    Even as my lips invoked the name of Venus
    I prayed Hippolytus, my eyes beheld
    Hippolytus, and while the altars steamed
    I offered all to him I dared not name.
    I fled him everywhere. O bitterness,   290
    He looked upon me in his father's features.
    At last, I turned upon myself. I forced
    Myself to play the torturer against
    The dreaded enemy I loved too well,
    Put on the bride's abhorrence of the stepson,
    Pleaded and pressed until I banished him
    Out of his father's arms, his father's heart.
    Once more I breathed; and after this, Oenone,
    My life, serener, flowed in blameless ways,
    Pleasing my husband, covering my pain,   300
    Tending the fruits of his unhappy bed:
    Foolish expedients! and inexorable
    Hardness of destiny! — My lord himself
    Brought me to Trozen and my banished foe.
    The ancient wound gaped deep, and bled again.
    No longer is it a secret flame that flickers
    About my veins: headlong in onset Venus
    Hangs on her quarry! I abhorred my guilt,
    Life was a curse, my love a misery;
    I looked for death to save my name, and bury   310
    Far from the day the darkness of these fires.
    I could not face your strivings and your tears.
    Now you know all; and it is well, if you
    Stand but aside from my advancing death,

Abstain at last from undeserved reproaches,
And leave your useless effort to revive
The embers of a fast-expiring fire.

Enter Panope

Panope   I wish that I could hide the news, my lady,
That I am forced to bring you. Death has taken
Your lord, our most indomitable King;   320
And you alone are ignorant of your loss.
Oenone   What is this, Panope?

My lady's prayers
Will never now bring Theseus back to Athens,
And mariners that landed here today
Have told Hippolytus that he is dead.
Phaedra   Gods!
Panope   Athens wavers in the choice of masters.
One boasts allegiance to the Prince your son;
One, reckless of the statutes of the land,
Presumes to favour the Barbarian's child,
My lady; and they say a rank sedition   330
Proclaims Aricia and the blood of Pallas.
I knew it was my duty to report
Such perils. Hippolytus is ready now
To sail, and many fear if he arrives
In this tempestuous season, he will sway
A fickle multitude.
Oenone   Panope, thank you:
Your news was precious, and the Queen has heard.

Exit Panope

Oenone   My lady, I had thrown away all pleadings,
All hope to move you, and my only thought
Was to attend you past the gates of the tomb,   340
But new disaster points new purposes,
An altered fortune, and an altered duty.
     Theseus is dead, and you are his successor,
My lady, with a son that looks to you —
A slave alone, and if you live a king.
No other will uphold his friendless quarrel,
No other wipe away his orphan tears;
Only in Heaven will his hearers be
The Gods, your judges and his ancestors.
Live then, in liberty from all misgiving;   350
Your love is now as unremarkable
As any love, for death disjoins the bond
That made its foulness and its infamy.
Henceforth the image of Hippolytus

Is not so terrible, and you may see him
With perfect guiltlessness. But what if now,
Despairing of a better understanding,
He takes command of these rebellious throngs?
Open his eyes, soften that stubborn heart.
Prince of these smiling coasts, his patrimony   360
Is here in Trozen, but he knows the laws;
He knows that they deliver to your son
The queenly ramparts that Minerva reared.
Your rightful enemy is also his:
Unite your forces to defeat Aricia.
Phaedra   So be it. I commit my way to you.
I will live, if I still have strength to live
And if a mother's love can even now
Revive in my wasted flesh the seeds of life.

ACT II

ARICIA, ISMENE

Aricia   He asked to see me here? Hippolytus   370
Wanted to see me and to say farewell?
Are you quite certain? Is this true, Ismene?
Ismene   Much more than this, now that the King is
       dead.
Prepare yourself, my lady; all the hearts
He kept at bay will cluster at your feet.
All Greece will bring its tributes to Aricia,
Enfranchised now and sovereign of her fortunes.
Aricia   So then, Ismene, it is no idle talk
And I have no oppressor and no foe?
Ismene   My lady, none. The Heavens have relented   380
And Theseus walks among your fathers' shades.
Aricia   What enterprise has brought him to his death?
Do they say?
Ismene   Rumours wild and past belief:
Some say that in a lover's last adventure
The seas have claimed this ever-wandering husband;
Some say, and everywhere the news is sown,
That with Pirithous he went down to Hell,
Saw the Cocýtus and the coasts of darkness
And stood alive amid a world of shadows,
But could not scale the gloomy track again   390
Nor pass the bourne men never pass but once.

Aricia   Shall mortal men, before the last leave-taking,
        Fathom those sullen deeps of the Departed?
        What sorcery lured him to their awful shore?
Ismene   My lady, he is dead, and you alone
        Doubt it. All Athens grieves for him, all Trozen
        Knows, and salutes Hippolytus for Prince.
        And in these walls, despairing for her son,
        Phaedra takes counsel of her trembling friends.
Aricia   And you suppose that, kinder than his
            father,   400
        Hippolytus will make my bondage sweeter
        And pity me?
Ismene   My lady, yes, I do.
Aricia   But do you know the hard Hippolytus?
        What makes you fancy he could feel compassion
        For me alone, who never felt for woman?
        He never joins our customary paths
        And hides himself wherever we are not.
Ismene   Oh, I know all the legend of his coldness;
        But when you met the proud Hippolytus
        I own the strangeness of his reputation   410
        Sharpened the edge of my curiosity.
        I saw a face at variance with the fable;
        At once your eyes disturbed that hard assurance
        And his, avoiding you but all in vain,
        Melted at once, and could not turn away.
        His pride may yet refuse the name of lover
        But I'll believe his looks, and not his tongue.
Aricia   Ah, sweet Ismene, how my heart devours
        The unhoped-for comfort of a mere perhaps!
        You that have known me, did you once imagine   420
        This heart, the plaything of unpitying Fortune,
        Starved of all sustenance except despair,
        Would learn of love and the wild woes of love?
        Child of Earth's child, last of a royal lineage,
        Sole remnant spared by battlefield and hatred,
        I lost the last proud blossoms of our tree,
        Six brothers, in the springtime of their year.
        The steel reaped all, and Earth's unwilling furrows
        Drank her own blood, the blood of her Erechtheus.
        Since then you know what rigorous decree   430
        Defies all Greeks to lift their eyes to mine —
        For a mutinous ardour in the sister's breast
        Might wake the embers in her brothers' urns —
        And you remember how I laughed to scorn

Those calculations of the victor's fear;
I held that love itself was slavery
And even thanked the King for a constraint
So fit and favourable to my distaste —
Then, yes; but then I had not seen his son.
Not that subservient to the eye's seduction   440
I love him for that beauty, that demeanour,
Graces of partial Nature, gifts that he
Ignores, if ever he has noticed them;
I see richer and dearer treasures in him —
His father's parts, and not his father's failings;
For I confess I love the manly pride
That never bent under the yoke of Love.
Phaedra was flattered by the doubtful glory
Of Theseus' courtly sighs: but I am prouder
And will not stoop to share an easy prize   450
Or occupy an undefended heart.
No, but to shape a will as yet unbending,
To waken pain in a proof-armoured bosom,
To lead a slave that never thought to serve,
Vainly at war against the pleasing chain —
There's a reward worthy of my ambition;
Hercules was an easier adversary
Who readily disarmed and quick to yield
Lent no such lustre to his overthrow.
But dear Ismene, these are reckless dreams: 460
Resistance there will be, and all too stubborn,
And you shall hear me soon in humbler strain
Lament the coldness that I praise today.
He love, Hippolytus? What heights of fortune
Could ever bring him —

Ismene   Only let him speak;
He is coming now.

                                              Enter Hippolytus

Hippolytus   My lady, before I sail
I owe you some account of my intentions.
My father's dead: and well enough my fears
Foretold the causes of his late homecoming —
Death only, and the closure of his toils   470
Could hold him from the world so long. The Gods
At last abandon to the fatal Spinners
Alcides' friend, his fellow, his successor.
— I know your enmity will not forbid
His son to assert these titles he has earned. —
One hope alleviates my deepest sorrow,

For I can end a harsh and long subjection:
I here revoke laws that have caused me grief —
The full bestowal of your life and hand
Is yours alone, and in my patrimony,   480
This Trozen, seat of Pittheus my grandfather,
Which willingly defers his crown to me
I leave you free and freer than its Prince.
Aricia   Show me less kindness, I could bear it better.
So much regard for me in my abjection
Binds me, my lord, more even than you know,
To that constraint you would have put away.
Hippolytus   Doubtful who stands the next in title,
Athens
Canvasses you, and me, and Phaedra's son.
Aricia   Me, my lord?
Hippolytus   I have never shut my eyes   490
To arrogant laws that seem to bar my claim:
The Greeks reject me for my mother's race.
But if my brother were my only rival
I could appeal to certain natural laws
And make them good against the law's caprice.
I have a better reason to refrain:
To you I yield, say rather I restore
The seat, the sceptre, that your fathers held
Of the illustrious mortal, son of Earth.
It only passed to Aegeus by adoption;   500
And next my father, Athens' second founder,
Was hailed and crowned for all his benefits
While your unhappy brothers lay forgotten.
Now, Athens calls you home within her ramparts,
Too long the ancient quarrel lives in pain,
Too long your blood, that flowed along her fields,
Reeks from the furrows where it found its birth. —
Trozen I hold. As for the son of Phaedra
The Cretan acres yield him rich retirement.
Attica falls to you. I sail, to join   510
My partisans with yours, in your support.
Aricia   At every word more troubled and bewildered,
Can I, or dare I, think I heard you rightly?
Have I my senses, is this your intent?
What God, my lord, what God inspired your mind?
Rightly your glory sounds in every climate
But reputation falls behind the truth.
What, will you cheat yourself on my behalf?
It was enough indeed to think that you

Hated me not, and held a mind untainted   520
  By this long enmity —
Hippolytus   How could I hate you?
  Men may deride this proud unconquered heart
  But do they think a monster gave me birth?
  What brutishness or what inveterate malice
  Could see your face and not forget its fury?
  And how should I withstand the subtle spell —
Aricia   My lord! . . .
Hippolytus   My tongue has carried me too far;
  But wisdom fails and yields to the compulsion . . .
  Now that my silence has been partly broken,
  My lady, I must needs go on, and speak   530
  The secret that my soul cannot contain. —
  Here stands a Prince of all men most unhappy,
  A monument of overthrown presumption;
  I, long a truant from the law of love
  And long a mocker of its votaries,
  That stayed ashore watching the luckless sailor
  And never thought myself to fight the tempest,
  Levelled at last beneath the common fate
  By strange tides I am borne far from myself.
  My wanton liberty has learnt to yield   540
  And in an instant this bold heart was tamed.
  Six months or nearly, in despair and shame,
  I've borne the arrow burning in my side;
  Vainly I pit my strength against myself
  And you. I fly you where you are, and find you
  Where you are not; deep in the forest glade
  Your picture chases me; sunlight and shade
  Alike retrace your features and alike
  Betray the fugitive that would be free,
  And I, for all my fruitless pains, look round   550
  To find Hippolytus, and know him not.
  My bow, my bounds, my spear, my chariot,
  Weary me. Neptune's lessons are forgotten;
  Only my lamentations fill the groves,
  My stabled coursers know my voice no more.
     Perhaps this tale I tell of uncouth passion
  Will make you blush to own your handiwork:
  Wild terms, indeed, to offer up a heart!
  And chains too fair for such a slave to claim!
  And yet my tribute therefore ranks the higher;   560
  Consider that I speak an unknown language
  And do not spurn these faltered words of love

That you alone could teach Hippolytus.
                                    Enter Theramenes
Theramenes   Close on my heels, my lord, the Queen
        approaches
    Asking for you.
Hippolytus   For me?
Theramenes   In what intention
    I do not know, but messengers have come
    Bidding you wait on her before you sail.
Hippolytus   The Queen? What should I say to her? Or
        she . . .
Aricia   You cannot disappoint her wish, my lord.
    Even to such an enemy is due   570
    Some sign of formal pity for her grief.
Hippolytus   So you go. And I sail. And still I know not
    Whether my worship has incensed my goddess,
    Whether this heart I leave in your two hands . . .
Aricia   Sail, Prince. Pursue your noble purposes;
    Bring me the realm of Athens for dominion;
    Whatever gift you make shall be accepted,
    But that imperial, that unhoped-for state
    Is not the dearest of your offerings.
                            Exeunt Aricia *and* Ismene
Hippolytus   Good friend, are all things ready? — But I
        hear   580
    The Queen. — Have all things ordered for our sailing.
    Send out the signal. Haste, command, return
    And free me from the burden of this meeting.
                                    Exit Theramenes
                            Enter Phaedra *and* Oenone
Phaedra   He is here. My blood retreats toward my heart.
    I see him, and forget what I should speak.
Oenone   Be mindful of the son that trusts in you!
Phaedra   They say that you are taking ship at once,
    My lord. I came to join my grief with yours,
    And with the story of a mother's terrors —
    My child is fatherless, and soon the day   590
    Will dawn that brings him to another deathbed;
    So fiercely even now assailed and threatened,
    Your strength alone can champion his weakness. —
    But deep within me throbs the preying thought
    That his complaint will never reach your ear,
    That through my child your angry justice soon
    Will strike a hated memory.
Hippolytus   My lady,

So infamous a wish was never mine.
Phaedra   But you have seen me unremittingly
    Pursue your hate, my lord; and how could you   600
    Explore the bottom of my soul and read
    My secret there? I threw myself upon
    Your just resentment; I would not suffer you
    Within the self-same frontiers; privily
    And openly I waged my war, and set
    The width of seas between your path and mine.
    I even gave explicit orders not
    To breathe your name before my presence. Yet,
    If by the wrong the penalty were measured,
    If only hatred could achieve your hatred,   610
    Never did woman more deserve your tears,
    My lord, and less your enmity.
Hippolytus   No mother
    That watches for her children's interest
    Forgives the other children of her house;
    I know, my lady. Untoward mistrust
    Is always near when men have married twice.
    Another in your place would have conceived
    No less suspicion, and I might have suffered
    Deeper indignities.
Phaedra   Ah but, my lord,
    The Gods — as now they stand my witnesses —   620
    Deigned to release me from this general law.
    How different are the thoughts that ravage me!
Hippolytus   It is too soon, my lady, for such thoughts;
    The sunshine may still light your husband's eye,
    And Heaven still may yield him to our prayers;
    Neptune's his friend, and that high patronage
    Will not in vain be canvassed by my father.
Phaedra   No man has twice explored the coasts of
    Death,
    My lord. If Theseus touched the sullen shores
    Vainly we look for Gods to send him home: 630
    Harsh Acheron is grasping and holds fast
    His prey. But did I say that he is dead?
    He breathes again in you; I see the King,
    See him, speak to him, thrill . . . My mind is
        wandering,
    My lord, my madness speaks the thing it should not.
Hippolytus   This is a prodigy of loyal love:
    Theseus is gone, yet lives within your mind
    And fires the ardour of your loving heart.

Phaedra   Yes, Prince, for him indeed I yearn, I
             languish;
    I love him — not the man that Hell has claimed,   640
    The butterfly that every beauty lured,
    The adulterous ravisher that would have stained
    The God of Hell's own bed; but faithful, fine,
    Sometimes aloof, and pure, gallant and gay,
    Young, stealing every heart upon his road —
    So do they character our Gods, and so
    I see you now; those eyes, that voice, were his,
    That generous red of virtue in your cheek,
    When first he drove across the Cretan foam,
    Meet meditation for the virgin dreams   650
    Of Minos' daughters. You, where were you then
    Among the flower and chivalry of Greece?
    Where was Hippolytus — alas, too young —
    The day his vessel grounded on our shore?
    You would have slain the terror of the island,
    The monster lapped in labyrinthine wiles;
    Into your hand my sister would have thrust,
    To unweave those riddling and deceitful ways,
    The thread of life and death. But no, she would not —
    Love would have found a readier wit in me,   660
    And I, Prince, I, devoted and assured,
    Could have resolved the devious Labyrinth;
    What would I not have done for that sweet head?
    How should a thread content your fearful lover?
    Half-claimant in the peril that you claimed
    I would have walked before you in the way,
    And Phaedra, steadfast in the Labyrinth,
    Would have returned again with you, or else
    With you remained.
Hippolytus   Great Gods, what have you said?
    My lady, can it be that you forget   670
    That Theseus is my father, and your husband?
Phaedra   And why do you suppose I had forgotten,
    Prince? Do I appear so careless of my honour?
Hippolytus   Forgive, my lady. I own, I blush to own
    How blameless are the words that I reproved.
    My shame can face it out no more before you,
    So let me go . . .
Phaedra   Ah, leave your heartless lying.
    You understand and you have heard enough.
    Very well then, you shall learn what Phaedra is
    And all her frenzy. Yes; I am in love.   680

But never think that even while I love you
I can absolve myself, or hide my face
From my own guiltiness. And never think
The wanton love that blurs my better mind
Grew with the treachery of my consent.
I, singled out for a celestial vengeance,
Unpitied victim, I abhor myself
More than you hate me. Let the Gods bear witness,
Those Gods that set the fire within my breast,
The fatal fire of my accursed line;   690
Those Gods whose majesty and might exulted
In the beguiling of a mortal's weakness.
Turn back the past yourself; how I have laboured
To seem malignant, savage, how I fostered
Your hatred as my ally in the fight.
Did I escape you? No, I banished you.
What fruit repaid these unavailing cares?
You loathed me more, I could not love you less;
Your suffering doubled the spell that binds me,
The withering ravage of my flames, my tears.   700
Your eyes can testify that this is true —
If for one moment they could bear my sight.
Why, this confession of my bitter secret,
My shameful secret, do you think that I
Have made it willingly? I came in fear
For one defenceless that I dare not fail:
I came to pray you not to hate my child.
Precarious resolution of a mind
Too full of what it loves! I came, and spoke
Of nothing else but you. So now, do justice.   710
Punish me for this execrable passion.
Approve yourself a hero's son indeed
And sweep this monster from the universe.
Dare Theseus' widow love Hippolytus?
Truly so vile a monster must not live.
My heart is here, and here is where you strike.
Eager to make atonement for its fault
I feel it swell and bound to meet your hand:
Strike. Or am I unworthy of your steel,
Or will your hate refuse to sweet a doom,   720
Or would ignoble blood sully your fingers?
Then hold your hand and let me have your sword.
Give it me.
Oenone   Stop, my lady. Heavenly powers!
What would you do? But somebody is coming:

Escape their sight, be quick, come back, or face
Inevitable shame.

Exeunt Phaedra *and* Oenone
Enter Theramenes

Theramenes   Was that the Queen
Half dragged, half rushing out? What, my lord, what
Are all these marks of grief? You stand disarmed,
Dumb, pale . . .
Hippolytus   Come, let us go, Theramenes.
I cannot think of what I have heard and witnessed;   730
I cannot see myself without disgust.
Phaedra . . . No more, great Gods! Oblivion
Must shroud away the secret and the shame.
Theramenes   If you would leave, my lord, the sail
                hangs ready;
But Athens is beforehand with her answer:
Her chiefs have counted votes among the tribes;
Your brother has their suffrage, Phaedra wins.
Hippolytus   Phaedra!
Theramenes   A herald of the will of Athens
Will bring the reins of state into her hands.
Her son is King.
Hippolytus   Ye Gods that know her heart,   740
Is it her righteousness you would repay?
Theramenes   And now dark rumours speak again of
                Theseus:
Some tell that men have seen him in Epirus
Alive; though I, who went to seek him there,
I know full well, my lord . . .
Hippolytus   It may be so.
But I would hear whatever rumour tells,
Consult this public cry, divine its sources.
If it be worthless to delay our journey
We sail; and cost the venture what it will
I'll save the sceptre for a worthy hand.   750

ACT III

PHAEDRA, OENONE

Phaedra   Send them away, these heralds and these
                honours.
Have they a balm to ease a tortured mind?
Unkind, is Phaedra fit for public show?

Rather conceal me, for my secret's out:
Intemperate desire has seen the light,
And what these lips had never thought to utter
He heard. Immortal Gods! and how he listened,
How long he parried, how deviously he turned
To baffle the approaches of my speech!
How visibly he yearned to leave my presence!   760
How painfully his blush revived my shame!
Why did you disappoint me of my death?
Ah, when his weapon pointed at my breast
Did he blench? Did he stir to snatch it back?
Enough for him my fingers at the hilt
And in his heartless reckoning it was vile,
Profaned, a blade that would defile his hand.

Oenone   And so complaining, dwelling on your sorrow,
You feed a fire that wisdom would have quenched.
Should not a worthy child of Minos' blood   770
Look for serenity in nobler tasks,
Fly from a struggle that you cannot win,
Learn to assume the guidance of a kingdom
And be a Queen?

Phaedra   Queen, I? And hold command,
While my own senses rage in mutiny,
While in my soul wisdom has lost dominion,
While shame and slavery has bowed my head,
And death is waiting?

Oenone   Fly.

Phaedra   I cannot leave him.

Oenone   You drove him away, and cannot go from
          him?

Phaedra   I cannot now. He has seen my raging soul,   780
Seen me transgress the rigid pale of virtue;
Before those stony eyes I have poured out
My shame, and now, unbidden, secret hope
Has slipped into my breast. Ay, you yourself,
Rallying the wasted forces of my life,
The parting spirit ready on my lips,
Wooed me from death with false and soothing words;
You half persuaded me that I might love.

Oenone   Ah, call me guilty, or call me innocent,
I would do worse if anything could save you.   790
But, if resentment ever stung your mind,
Can you forget the blow of his rebuff,
The insolence, the icy cruelty
That eyed you all but prostrate at his feet,

The arrogant disdain? — how odious
Had Phaedra only seen him as I saw!
Phaedra   What if he lost this arrogance, Oenone?
He has the harshness of his forest ways,
And in his arduous life Hippolytus
Has never heard of love until today.   800
What if surprise had robbed him of his speech?
What if we blamed him more than he deserved?
Oenone   He was conceived in a Barbarian's womb.
Phaedra   Barbarian, Scythian, still she learned to love.
Oenone   He hates our sex with firm and deadly hate.
Phaedra   So I shall never fear another woman.
Enough: such counsels had their season once;
My passion now commands you, and not my reason.
Though hard and inaccessible to love,
Another side lies weaker to attack —   810
The sweets of empire tempted him, I think;
Athens allured him more than he could hide.
His ships already turned their prows to sea
With canvas rigged and offered to the breeze.
Find him, Oenone, find the ambitious boy,
Show him the glitter of the Athenian crown,
Bid him assume the diadem and the glory;
I only ask to lay it on his brow,
Into his hand descends authority
I cannot grasp, and he shall teach my son   820
The science of command — even he might
Look as a father on him. In his power
I now resign the orphan and the mother.
Incline his heart by any means you know,
Use — do not blush — the voice of supplication,
I sanction all. I have no other hope;
Go, till you come again I cannot tell
What else I have to do.
                                              Exit Oenone
Phaedra, alone   O Thou, that knowest
How deep in shame my soul is overwhelmed,
Venus, O Venus unappeasable,   830
This is the consummation of thy hatred.
These must be the limits of thy cruelty.
Thy triumph is entire, each shot has told.
Art thou not sated yet with victory?
Find tougher quarry then: Hippolytus
Rejects thy deity, derides thy wrath,
He never bent the knee before thy altar;

Thy name seems hideous in his stubborn ears,
Goddess, avenge; our grievances are one!
Teach him to love . . . Oenone, here so soon?   840
I am rejected then, you were not heard.

Enter Oenone

Oenone   Stifle the memory of a hopeless passion,
My lady; summon up your earlier virtue.
The King's not dead, and you will see him soon.
Theseus has landed. He is coming here.
The populace are rushing to salute him,
And as I passed obedient to your mission
Unending cheers rose up on every hand —
Phaedra   He is not dead. Nothing else signifies,
Oenone. I revealed a lawless love   850
That wounds him in his honour. And he lives.
What needs there more?
Oenone   But yet —
Phaedra   I told you so;
And you would not. Foreboding and remorse
Have yielded to your tears. Only this morning
My death was not unworthy to be pitied:
I took your counsel, and I die disgraced.
Oenone   Die?
Phaedra   Righteous Gods! The things this day has seen!
And now, as I meet my husband and his son
I know this witness of adulterous passion
Studies my countenance before his father —   860
My heart heavy with sighs he would not hear,
My eyelids drenched with tears that he despised.
Do you think his tenderness for Theseus' honour
Would hide away the memory of my falsehood,
My treason to a father and a King?
Will he repress the loathing I inspire?
What if he did? I know my treachery,
Oenone. And if there are intrepid women
Who taste a flawless quietude in crime
And force their countenance to show no shame,   870
I am not such. My misdeeds rise before me;
And even now these over-arching walls
Seem full of tongues, impatient to accuse me
Before my husband, and proclaim his wrong.
Oh for a death, and surcease from this anguish!
Is life so precious and so hard to leave?
Need the tormented hesitate to die?
Only I fear the name I leave behind —

The legacy of horror for my children,
Whose blood, the very blood of Jupiter,   880
Should swell their hearts with pride: now they must
    lift
The burden of a mother's infamy.
My soul foretells that malice, soon or late,
Will throw my black reproach into their faces,
And crushed so cruelly they may never dare
To look with level eyes upon their kind.
Oenone   It is most true. They both are to be pitied,
And never sorrow was foretold more surely.
But why abandon them to the ordeal?
Why be the witness that betrays your cause?   890
For all is lost; and all the world will judge
That Phaedra knows her guilt, and dare not wait
The awful presence of an outraged husband.
Hippolytus should thank you for a deed
Stronger than all his words on his behalf;
And what can I respond to your accuser?
Confounded, tongue-tied, I must live to see
Him taste a hideous triumph undisturbed
And chronicle your shame to all mankind.
May fire from Heaven fall upon me sooner!   900
But tell me this, and tell without dissembling:
Do you still love him, this presumptuous Prince?
How does he now appear . . . ?
Phaedra   I see him now
Grim as a monster and as terrible.
Oenone   Then why concede him victory unresisted?
Do you fear him? Attack before he strikes
And use the imputation he prepares
For you. What can refute you? Every sign
Informs against him — first his sword that Fortune
Leaves in your hands, and then this day's distress,   910
And those disconsolate months of misery,
And long ago his father's mind prepared
When long ago you claimed his banishment.
Phaedra   Shall I defame and murder innocence?
Oenone   Lend me but silence and my zeal suffices.
Like you I shudder at my remedy
And dread it deeper than a thousand deaths.
But either this, or else I lose my mistress,
And in your loss all other values fade.
So I will speak. Theseus will rage, but still   920
He'll take no more revenge than banishment.

A father punishing is still a father
Whose love is louder than the voice of justice;
But guiltless blood is nothing in the scales
Against the imperilled honour of your name.
That is a jewel far too dear to hazard;
It is a law we dare not disobey;
And when our honour stands at such a cost
Virtue itself must go for sacrifice.
— Here they are. I see Theseus.

Phaedra   And I see   930
Hippolytus, and his unflinching eyes
Spell my dishonour. Do what you will, Oenone.
I am in your hands. In this tormented hour
To save myself is more than I can do.

        Enter Theseus, Hippolytus, *and* Theramenes

Theseus   Fortune has smiled again, my dearest lady,
And now your sweet embrace —

Phaedra   No, Theseus; stop,
Do not pollute this love and this delight.
No longer I deserve this tenderness.
You have been wronged. The jealousy of Fortune
Has not respected her you left behind you;   940
And now, unworthy to approach your love,
My sole desire must be for solitude.

                                        Exit Phaedra

Theseus   What is this cheerless welcome that I find
        here,
My son?

Hippolytus   A riddle Phaedra must interpret,
No one else can. But now if prayers can move
I ask but this, my lord, never to see
Her face again, but to live out my life
Safe, far away, forgotten by the Queen.

Theseus   Now you, my son, forsake me!

Hippolytus   For you know
I never sought her, but you brought her here   950
At your departure; and the coasts of Trozen
Became the dwelling of Aricia
And of the Queen. I was to be their guardian.
But now what duty keeps me from my life?
Inglorious victories among the forests
Weary my idle youth, my wasted skill.
I long to waken from obscurity
And tip my hunter's spear in a nobler red.
Before you had spent the years that I have counted

What robbers, what oppressors, and what monsters   960
Had known the weight of that revengeful arm,
Victor and scourge of wanton insolence!
While on the quiet shore of either sea
The traveller learnt to take his road in peace;
Hercules heard your prowess and drew breath,
Leaving his triumphs and his toils to you —
And I, the unknown son of such a father,
Have much to do to reach my mother's footsteps.
Now let my unfledged valour learn to dare;
Let me, if anywhere some monster yet   970
Escapes you, drag its trophy to your feet,
Or by the record of a glorious failure
Find life for ever in a fitting death
And show posterity I was your son.

Theseus   What is it, what invading blast of fear
Empties my very home at my approach?
Why, O ye Gods, to face these shrinking looks,
This lack of love, did ye deliver me?
I had one friend. His unregarding passion
Conspired to carry back from far Epirus   980
The tyrant's Queen. I helped, against my will,
But Fate was pitiless, and we were blind.
The villain caught me all unarmed, unwatching,
And these two eyes — that weep him yet — beheld
Pirithous under the fangs of beasts
Fatted on human slaughter; and I spent
Deep in the sightless silence of his dungeons
Down near the horrible empire of the Dead,
Six months. Then Heaven thought on me again.
I tricked the watchful eyes. I purged creation   990
Of one perfidious enemy, and his blood
Glutted his own fell monsters. Now at length
Free, and restored to all that's left to love,
Now that my soul aspires to nothing more
Than the enjoyment of their blessed sight,
Grief and lament is all my salutation,
None will abide to suffer my embraces;
And, chilled by the contagion of the fears
That breathe about my path, I'd rather be
A prisoner again and in Epirus.   1000
      Speak out. Phaedra declares I've been betrayed.
Who wronged me? Why is not the wrong avenged?
Has Greece, so long beholden to this arm,
Offered a refuge to the criminal?

— You will not answer? Is my son, my son,
A shield and ally of my enemies?
I will go in, for this suspense unmans me.
I will find out the culprit and the offence.
Phaedra must tell me what her sorrow is.

Exit Theseus

Hippolytus   What did her words portend? They froze
  my blood: 1010
 Would Phaedra in her ecstasy of frenzy
 Denounce her guilt and give her case away?
 Gods, when the King is told! Death-dealing Love,
 What blighting mists thou hast wrapped around his
  house!
 And I with my secret of disloyal passion,
 What was I once, what will he think me now!
 My mind is dark with unaccomplished shapes
 Of evil: but need innocence be afraid?
 I must look for better times and better ways
 To move my father's heart, and then reveal   1020
 Love he may doom to parting and to tears
 But fixed beyond his force to overthrow.

ACT IV

THESEUS, OENONE

Theseus   Ah! What have you said? The rebel, the
  betrayer
 Conceived this outrage on his father's honour?
 How unrelenting is thy hand upon me,
 O Destiny! I know not where I go,
 I know not what I do. All my long kindness
 Wasted, paid with this hideous wanton plot!
 And with the argument and threat of steel
 To enforce his dark design! I know that sword, 1030
 I gave it him, I strapped it to his side —
 For nobler work than this. Not all the bonds
 Of blood itself could hold him back; and she
 Could hesitate to punish, and her silence
 Showed mercy to the wrongdoer!
Oenone   Say rather
 Showed mercy to a father's suffering.
 Shamed by a lover's frenzy, and ashamed
 That her chaste eyes could kindle such a fire,

She would have died, my lord, and dimmed for ever
Herself the innocent lustre of those eyes.   1040
The arm was raised. I hastened, I preserved
Her life for the embraces of her lord,
And pitying your fears and her confusion
Became the unwilling spokesman of her tears.
Theseus   The perfidy! Yes, for all his craft, he paled;
He quaked with fear, I saw it as he came;
I marvelled then to feel his joylessness
And froze against the chill of his embrace.
— Did you not say, the love that burns in him
Had shown itself in Athens long before?   1050
Oenone   My lord, remember how the Queen abhorred
     him;
It was unhallowed love that caused her hatred.
Theseus   And now, in Trozen, it has flared again?
Oenone   I have told you all, my lord; but I have left
My lady too long now with her deadly sorrow,
And, by your leave, my place is at her side.

                                        Exit Oenone
                                        Enter Hippolytus
Theseus   So, here he comes. Great Gods, that noble
     carriage
Would it not blind another's eye, as mine?
Then sacrilegious and adulterous heads
May flaunt the sacred emblem of the pure?   1060
Why is there no infallible badge to blazon
The minds of our dissembling race of men?
Hippolytus   May I not know, my lord, why such a
     weight
Of cloud darkens the majesty of your brow?
Must this be secret from my loyalty?
Theseus   Dissembler! Dare you come so near to me?
Monster the thunderbolts reprieve too long,
Corrupted straggler of the brigand race
I cleansed the earth of once, how dare you still
Parade that odious face, here where your frenzy   1070
Clutched at a father's bed? How dare you pace
These halls where all things tell of your dishonour?
Why are you not far hence, where skies unknown
Illumine coasts that never knew my name?
Away, you traitor. Do not stand and tempt
A hate, an anger hardly to be stayed.
Enough for me the indelible reproach
Of fathering you, without the soil of murder

To smother my bright deeds from memory.
— Away. And if you would not share the sentence   1080
Of all the villains that this hand has felled
Take care that never again the sun that lights us
Finds your rebellious feet upon this shore.
Away, I tell you, out of my dominions
And cleanse them for ever of your loathsome
          presence.
        And now hear, Neptune, hear. If once my courage
Scoured off a scum of bandits from thy coasts
Remember thou hast sworn in recompense
To grant one prayer. In long and stern confinement
I called not thy undying power; I saved thee   1090
Thrifty of all the aid I hoped for, till
A greater need. Today I pray: avenge
A mourning father. To thy wrath I leave
This profligate. Still his lust in his blood.
Let Theseus read thy kindness in thy rage.

Hippolytus   With such a love Hippolytus is charged
     By Phaedra! Weight of horror crushes me;
     So many assaults unlooked-for, stroke on stroke,
     Leave me no words.

Theseus   And so you judged that Phaedra's
     Compliant silence would have muffled up   1100
     Your savage insolence. You might have waited
     To gather up the sword that now, in her hands,
     Helps to convict you. Or why not, better still,
     Heap up the measure of your infamy
     With one good blow to finish breath and life?

Hippolytus   After a calumny so infamous
     I should let truth be heard — but for a secret
     That touches you, my lord. I beg you sanction
     Respect that silences what I might say;
     Labour no more to probe into your pain,   1110
     Look on my life, consider what I am:
     The greatest crimes have lesser crimes before them;
     The rest is easy when the way is known;
     Like virtue, vice is gradual. No one day
     Made any good man vile, murderous, incestuous,
     And innocence is slow to dare, and slow
     To push beyond the boundaries of law.
     I had a mother, as chaste as she was valiant,
     Nor have I derogated from my blood;
     Pittheus, wise among men, took up my nurture   1120
     After her hands. I would not praise myself,

But, if one virtue was allotted mine,
May I not claim, my lord, to loathe that act
My enemies presume to speak of? This
Has made Hippolytus his name in Greece —
Unstudied honour rude in its excess,
Rugged, intractable austerity.
The daylight is no cleaner than the deeps
Of this my heart. What, sacrilegious lust
Could stain Hippolytus?
Theseus   And this condemns you: 1130
That was the foul source fed your vaunted coldness —
No one but Phaedra could bewitch your eyes;
No other woman's love was worth your interest
Unless it offered pleasures more than lawful.
Hippolytus   No, father, you shall hear the truth. This
             heart
Has not refused an honourable yoke.
Here at your feet I will confess — I love,
And love in disobedience to your will.
Aricia's beauty holds my heart enslaved
And Pallas' daughter has subdued your son.   1140
I worship her, forgetful of my duty
And have no room to feel another passion.
Theseus   You love her! No — a pitiful pretence;
You feign that crime to clear yourself of this.
Hippolytus   These six months I have hid from love,
             and loved,
My lord; I came here to confess to you
In trembling. But is it so? Will nothing move you?
What fearful oath will win you to believe?
Witness the Earth, the Heavens, and all Nature . . .
Theseus   What felon ever feared a perjury?   1150
Peace, peace. Waste no more time on idle stories
If that fine virtue rests on aids like these.
Hippolytus   You see it as a mockery, a lie:
But Phaedra in her heart of hearts knows better.
Theseus   Shall I endure so much effrontery?
Hippolytus   What place of exile, and how long a time
Do you appoint?
Theseus   Past the Pillars of Hercules
A traitor's presence is too close for me.
Hippolytus   What friendship shall I find to comfort me
When you have cast me out, dishonoured thus?   1160
Theseus   Find yourself friends whose dangerous regard
Goes to adultery and honours incest,

Deceivers, ingrates, free of law and shame,
Fit to protect a criminal like you.
Hippolytus   And still you taunt me with adultery
And incest. How can I reply? But Phaedra
Came of a mother, Phaedra's is a blood,
My lord, you do not need me to recall it,
More laden with their awful taint than mine.
Theseus   How dare you go so far before my face?   1170
For the last time, villain, avoid my sight,
Leave me; or force a father in his rage
To have you flung with infamy from the place.

                                        Exit Hippolytus

And now you go towards your waiting doom
Irrevocably. For by that River's name
Terrible even to the immortal Gods,
Neptune has sworn his oath, and will perform it.
Yes, and I loved you, and in spite of all,
Before the hour is come, my bowels yearn
For pity of you. But I have too much cause —   1180
Did ever a deeper injury wound a father?
Ye righteous Gods, that see me thus prostrated,
Did I give being to a son like this?

                                        Enter Phaedra

Phaedra   My lord, you see me here impelled by terror:
Just now, when that terrible voice assailed my ears,
I thought the threat might come to a fulfilment.
Let me beg you, if there still is time, have pity
On your own race, your own blood; do not force me,
My lord, to hear it crying from the earth.
Spare me the endless misery of laying   1190
That fearful stain on a paternal hand.
Theseus   My lady, I have kept my hand unstained
And still the unnatural boy has not escaped;
Immortal hands will undertake his doom,
Neptune's my debtor; you shall be avenged.
Phaedra   Your debtor, Neptune! Then your prayer of
            hate . . .
Theseus   Are you afraid it might be heard too soon?
No, join your own entreaty with my curses,
Paint me his crimes once more in all their blackness
Inflame my faint and still-too-sluggish rage —   1200
He has added guilt more than the guilt you knew;
His frenzy spends itself in railing on you,
He swears that all your words are perjuries,
He says Aricia claims his heart, his love,

    His loyalty.
Phaedra   No, my lord!
Theseus   That is what he told me;
    Not that a flimsy lie could impose on me.
    I hope to hear that Neptune's justice falls
    Swiftly, and till that hour I'll ply his altars
    And keep him mindful of his undying word.

                                        Exit Theseus
Phaedra   He leaves me, with this dreadful news, alone.   1210
    Ah Gods, the fire that I dreamed was safely stifled
    To wake no more! Dreadful, unlooked-for news!
    All trepidation and remorse, all speed
    Out of Oenone's clinging arms of fear
    I came to save his son. And who can tell
    What might have been had conscience had its way?
    Whether I might have spoken of my guilt,
    Might have let slip, had he but left me time,
    The entire and awful truth? — He has felt love,
    Hippolytus, who never felt for me;   1220
    Aricia claims his loyalty, his heart . . .
    Gods! while I pleaded, while my prayer beat
    On those rigid eyes, that unrelenting brow,
    I thought he bore impenetrable armour
    Always the same and closed to all alike.
    And now another has overthrown his pride,
    Another finds favour in the tyrant's eyes;
    Perhaps his heart is easy to entreat
    And condescends to any plea but mine.
    And I am fool enough to be his friend!   1230
                             Enter Oenone
    — Oenone, do you know what I have heard?
Oenone   No; I have tried to find you in alarm,
    Wondering what sudden impulse drove you here
    And how it may imperil you . . .
Phaedra   Oenone,
    Who would have thought there was another woman?
Oenone   You say —
Phaedra   Hippolytus, I tell you, loves —
    The adversary I could never shake,
    Vexed by submission, impatient of complaining,
    The ogre that I never could encounter
    Undaunted; he is tamed and brought to heel,   1240
    Aricia has forced the access to his heart.
Oenone   Aricia!
Phaedra   Oh, I never thought of these,

These newest tortures that I live to taste:
All the old despairs, the ecstasies, the broodings,
Raging of flame, and horror of remorse,
And that slight of unendurable denial
Were barely foretastes of my torment here.
They, lovers! Did they bewitch these watchful eyes?
What time did they find to meet? Since when? What
        place?
What furtive means? You knew. Why was I left   1250
To treasure foolish dreams? You might have told me
Of their stolen pleasure. Were they often seen
Speaking, or lingering? Was it the forest shades
That sheltered them? Ah, but they had liberty
To see the face they sought. The Heavens smiled
On the innocence of their embrace, no fear
Restrained their eager steps, and each fair day
Rose clear and candid on their love. And I
Disowned, dishonoured in the whole creation
I fled the sun, I could not face the daylight,   1260
Death was the only godhead I could pray;
Gall on my tongue, and tears my only drink;
Happy, if any privacy of grief
Had left me this one pitiable solace,
To taste a last precarious luxury;
But the forced travesty of a smiling face
Deprived me even of the right to weep.
Oenone   They reap no harvest of their vain desires:
They'll meet no more.
Phaedra   They'll love for evermore.
Now as I speak — the poison of the thought! —   1270
Mocking the fury of a rival wronged,
Forgetful of the exile that divides them,
They swear a thousand times never to part.
No, I will not yield to the insult of their joy,
Oenone. Help me, pity my jealousy.
Aricia must be crushed. I must stir up
My husband's wrath against that hated house —
No feeble sentence serves, the sister's crime
Is more than all her brothers'. I'll entreat him
In rage and jealousy.
                    What am I doing?   1280
Where is reason in my wandering mind? I, jealous?
I, entreat Theseus? He, my husband, lives
And still I burn — for whom? Still yearn — for whom?
At every word each separate hair lifts up

Upon my head. My guilt has filled the measure —
I crave for incest, dream of calumny,
My murderous hands, avid of vengeance, burn
To bathe in the blood of innocence. Misery!
And dare I live, and dare I face the sight
Of that sacred Sun, the giver of my life,   1290
I, grandchild of the high Father of the Gods,
My forebears crowding Heaven and all creation?
Where may I hide? Flee to the night of Hell?
No, no, not there; for there my father's hands
Inexorable lift the doomsday urn,
They say, and Minos stands in deathly justice
Over the pallid multitudes of men.
Will that great shade not start in ghastly anger
When I in shame before his awful gaze,
His daughter, plead my guilt, and deeds perhaps   1300
Unheard in all the calendar of Hell?
Father, what will you say to these? I see
The tremendous urn roll thundering at your feet;
I see you ponder unknown penalties
To execute yourself upon your own . . .
Forgive. A cruel God detests your seed,
A heavenly vengeance breathed in me the frenzy
You see. Alas, and still of all the guilt
And all the shame that never will release me
My fearful heart has never reaped the sweets.   1310
Pursued while yet I breathe by ceaseless evils
I wait to yield a bruised and broken life.
Oenone   My lady, come, dismiss a causeless terror,
Be more indulgent to a venial failing —
You love; but driven by a fatal charm.
It is not ours to challenge Destiny.
Was this a wonder never seen till now?
Were you the first that Love has overthrown?
Weakness was ever part of man's condition;
So, mortal, bow to a mortal's destiny.   1320
You struggle against an immemorial yoke:
Even the Gods that live in high Olympus
Whose judgements hold a guilty world in dread
Have loved, and sometimes loved against the law.
Phaedra   Still you dare speak? And this is your advice,
And till the end you mean to drug my mind?
I hate you. All your help has been my downfall.
You dragged me back to the unbearable sunshine;
Your prayers were louder than the voice of right;

The man that I had shunned, you made me see.   1330
Was it your business? And now have all the lies
Of those false lips dared blacken such a life?
You may have killed him. His father's impious vows
And blind revenge perhaps are gratified
Already. I'll hear no more. Leave me alone,
Loathly inhuman monster; leave my sight,
Leave me alone to shape my bitter future.
On you I pray the justice of the Gods;
And may they make you the eternal warning
Of all cringing cunning sycophants that nourish   1340
Their masters' dearest weakness, urge the way
Their cravings tend, and smooth the slope of crime;
Accursed flatterers, deadliest gift of all
That angry Heaven inflicts upon a King!   *Exit*

Oenone, alone   O ye Gods! To have borne so much for
      her, forgone
So much! — This is my pay. And it is just.

ACT V

HIPPOLYTUS, ARICIA, ISMENE

Aricia   And in this extremity you will not speak
And will not undeceive a loving father?
Cruel, if you can disregard my tears
And lightly say goodbye to me for ever,   1350
Then sail, and leave Aricia with her grief;
But do not go in certainty of death.
Fight the foul imputation on your honour,
Constrain your father to unsay his curses.
There is time yet. What reason, or what folly
Makes you leave all the advantage to the accuser?
Tell Theseus what you know.
Hippolytus   Have I not told
What may be told? Would you have me reveal
To light the shameful mystery of his bed
Or by too scrupulous report bring down   1360
Confusion on a father's honoured head?
Alone you know this horror. You, and the Gods,
Alone receive the outpouring of my heart.
See if I love you: I have shown to you
What I would fain have veiled from my own thoughts.
But under what a seal, you know. Forget,

My lady, if you can, that I have spoken;
Let me believe this hideous affair
Will never be breathed between those blameless lips.
We set our trust upon the righteous Heavens.   1370
My cause is theirs; and Phaedra, whether soon
Or in the slow procedure of their justice,
Will not escape disgrace. This deference
I ask of you; and all the rest I sweep
Before the liberty of my wrath. I bid you
No longer be a slave. I bid you dare
To come with me, dare to be banned with me.
Break from a poisoned house where Virtue breathes
A deathly and a desecrated air;
Turn into profit for a headlong flight   1380
All the disorder following on my fall.
The means I offer: you have still no guard
But my own men. Most powerful patrons wait us —
Argos extends her arms, and Sparta welcomes;
Let common friends receive our just laments,
Otherwise Phaedra rakes our wreckage up,
Evicts us both from a throne our fathers left us,
And strips us both for spoils to deck her son.
The moment beckons, grasp it. But what fear
Restrains you? What suspends your doubtful mind?   1390
Only for your sake have I dared so far.
When I am all on fire, why are you ice?
Are you unwilling to adventure on
An outlaw's path?

Aricia   Oh, but how happily,
My lord, I'd taste of exile so; how eagerly
Embrace a life forgotten of all beside
And linked with yours! But lacking that sweet bond
Can I in honour join your wanderings?
I know the sternest laws do not forbid me
To fly your father's power: he is not mine,   1400
I owe him no obedience; and to fly
From an oppressor is the right of all.
But you, my lord, love me. And anxious honour . . .

Hippolytus   And can you think I rate that honour
                    cheaply?
No, no. I came with worthier designs —
Escape your foes, and follow as my bride.
Free in adversity, since Heaven has freed us,
Our pledges need no words but ours, and Hymen
Robbed of his torchlit rites is Hymen still.

By Trozen's gates, among those sepulchres,   1410
Antique memorials of my father's pride,
A wayside temple holy and renowned
Stands grim protector of the plighted word;
There falsehood dare not raise her voice, or falls
Blasted at once, and certitude of death
Lays chains invincible on perjury.
May we not there with solemn mutual oath
Give and receive our hearts' enduring faith
Before the shrine, and pray the Deity
For his protection and paternal love?   1420
I will invoke each mighty God to hear me —
Maiden Diana, Juno's majesty,
And every name whose present patronage
Shall seal and sanctify my true intent.

Aricia　　The King is here. Fly, Prince, depart at once.
I shall remain awhile to hide my purpose.
Away — but send me back a trusty servant
To guide my footsteps safely to your side.

　　　　　　　　　　　　　　Exit Hippolytus
　　　　　　　　　　　　　　Enter Theseus

Theseus　　Lighten the mists, ye Gods, and show my eyes
The truth they seek for here!

　　　　　　　　　　　　Now, sweet Ismene,   1430
See everything is done. Be ready quickly.

　　　　　　　　　　　　　　Exit Ismene

Theseus　　You seem disturbed, your colour fails, my
　　　　　lady.
What was Hippolytus doing in this place?

Aricia　　Taking an everlasting leave, my lord.

Theseus　　And so your eyes have tamed that rebel heart
And brought him to his earliest thoughts of love.

Aricia　　I must not hide the truth from you, my lord.
He has not learnt your unjust hate from you;
He did not treat me like a criminal.

Theseus　　You mean he vowed you everlasting passion.   1440
I should not build on that unsettled heart.
He swore as deep to others.

Aricia　　　　　　　　　　He, my lord?

Theseus　　I wish you could have taught him constancy.
How could you bear that loathsome competition?

Aricia　　And how can you bear loathsome calumnies
To blacken all the lustre of his fame?
Have you so little knowledge of his nature?
Can you not tell the guiltless from the guilty?

Only your eyes are darkened by a cloud
That lets his goodness gleam on all the world.   1450
Oh stop, relent. He must not be the victim
Of false accusers. Repent your murderous curses.
Tremble, my lord, tremble, lest frowning Heaven
Hate you enough to take you at your word —
Gods may accept our offerings in anger
And punish with the presents we entreated.

Theseus   No, blind as you are with ill-requited love
You will not blind me to his villainy;
For I have witnesses, beyond reproach,
Beyond suspicion — I have seen tears flow,   1460
Tears that were true.

Aricia   Look to yourself, my lord:
Your matchless weight of arm redeemed mankind
From monsters past all counting — but not all,
The breed is not destroyed, and you have saved
One . . . I must say no more; your son forbids me.
Knowing what deference his heart still holds
I should increase his suffering too much
Dared I continue. Let me imitate
His generous scruple, and excuse myself
While nothing forces me to break my silence.   1470

                              Exit Aricia

Theseus, alone   But what is in her mind? What lurks
              below
A tale so often broached, and never told?
Is it a stratagem without a meaning?
Is it conspiracy to bind me on
A rack of doubt? And secret in my heart
Steeled to be cruel, what is the small voice
That pleads for mercy, and unmans my wrath,
Perplexes me and tears me? — I must see
Her woman once again; I know too little.
— Guard! Fetch Oenone, and send her in alone.   1480

                              Enter Panope

Panope   I cannot say what thoughts are in her heart,
But the distracted motions of the Queen
Fill me with fear, my lord. Death and despair
Are painted on her face, and the deathly tint
Sits even now upon her cheeks. Already
Pursued with scorn and chiding from her side,
Oenone has plunged to death among the waves.
None knows what wild will drove her, and her voice
Is covered in the murmur of the tide.

Theseus   What have you said?
Panope   Her going gave no peace;   1490
   Confusion gains in the Queen's divided soul:
   One moment, soothing her mysterious grief,
   She takes her children, bathes them in her tears;
   And suddenly, her motherhood dismissed,
   She drives them from her with a look of loathing.
   Her restless steps come and go purposeless
   And we are strangers in her fevered eyes.
   Thrice she has written, only to repent,
   And thrice destroyed the message uncompleted.
   My lord, be gracious: see her, comfort her.   1500
Theseus   Is it so? Oenone's dead, and Phaedra waits
   For death? Call for my son, let him plead his cause,
   Let him speak to me, and I will listen.   *Exit* Panope
                                  Neptune,
   Delay thy deadly gift, be not too sudden,
   Rather refuse it utterly. What if
   I was seduced too soon by worthless words?
   What if my cruel hands were raised too rashly?
   What wretchedness would follow from that vow!
                                Enter Theramenes
Theseus   Is it you, Theramenes? Where is my son?
   What have you done with him? His careful tending   1510
   Has been your charge from earliest infancy.
   But why the tears I see upon your cheeks?
   What of my son?
Theramenes   O late, O vain regret,
   O useless love! Hippolytus is no more.
Theseus   Oh Gods!
Theramenes   I saw him die, the best and sweetest
   Of human kind — and, let me say, my lord,
   The purest also.
Theseus   Is my son dead? Now,
   Now that these arms reached out for him, the Gods
   Impatient urged his execution on?
   How did I lose him? What immortal stroke . . . ?   1520
Theramenes   Still close behind us lay the gates of
      Trozen.
   He drove his chariot, his grieving guard
   Matching his silence, marched on either hand.
   Sunk in his thought, the loose reins lying free,
   He brought us on the causeway to Mycénae;
   And the noble beasts, so eager once to leap
   At the least inflexion of a master's voice,

Now bent dull eyes to earth and drooping crests
As if communing with his bitter mood.
— Suddenly from the sea an awful cry   1530
Shattered the silence of the air. And then
A second voice wailed answer from the landward.
Our blood was frozen in our inmost hearts.
Stiffly rose up the listening horses' manes.
And now from the level deep immense there heaves
A boiling mount of brine, and still it swells,
Rears wavelike foaming down on us and breaks
To belch a ravening monster at our feet
Whose threatening brow is broadened with huge horns,
Whose body, cased in golden glint of scales,   1540
Thrashes a train of sinuous writhing whorls.
Indomitable bull, malignant dragon,
Its long-drawn bellows rumble down the shore;
Heaven quails, earth shudders at the portent, air
Reeks with its pestilential breath. The wave
Withdraws again, aghast at what it bore.
We fly to the nearby temple; not one lingers
Or wraps himself in unavailing valour.
Hippolytus, honouring his hero blood,
Hippolytus alone checks, wheels his team,   1550
Snatches the spears, charges upon the creature,
Aims, and unerring flings. A gaping slash
Fair in the monster's flank drives it in bounds
Of pain and fury to the horses' feet
To roar and wallow and from flaming jaws
To spatter them with blood and cloud and fire.
Reckless, they plunge aside. They hear no more,
Answer no more to bridle or to voice.
The charioteer spends all his strength in vain
While they redden the bits with spume that is bright
        with blood.   1560
Even, men say, some more than mortal shape
Borne on the horrible confusion plied
Their dusty flanks with goads. Where terror leads
        them
Stand rocks. The axle screeches, snaps. The car
Crashes in fragments; and my fearless master
Drops tangled in the reins . . . — Forgive my weakness.
In that tormenting image lives a source
Of quenchless tears. — I watched, my lord, I watched
Your helpless son dragging behind the steeds
His hands had fed. He tried to call to them: 1570

Instead, his cries startle them. So they gallop
And make one wound of all his living flesh.
   Now as the plain is pealing with our grief
The violent fit is spent. They slacken speed,
And stop, where close at hand his father's tombs
And ancient sculptures hold the chill remains
And memories of Kings. I run, behind me
Run all his guard, reading the traces painted
By his gallant blood, past the empurpled crags,
Past dripping brambles hung about with spoils   1580
Of bloody hair. I reach him, I speak; he gives me
A hand and greets me with a dying gaze
That quickly closes. And I hear these words:
   'My guiltless days are forfeit to the Gods.
Do you after my death be watchful over
The sad Aricia; and, sweet friend, if ever
My father undeceived should come to mourn
The misadventure of a slandered son,
To lay in peace my blood and wailing shade
Bid him be gentle to the captive maiden,   1590
Render her . . . ' On the word the lifeless youth
Fell back into my arms a ravaged corpse,
The dreadful triumph of an angry Heaven,
Where not a father's eye could undertake
To know his child.
Theseus   O child! O dearest hope
I cast away! Gods, ye unswerving Gods,
Too faithfully ye served me! Now must life
Henceforward be a death of long-drawn sorrow.
Theramenes   And now in fear and haste Aricia,
Stealing, my lord, from your captivity   1600
To hear his nuptial vow before the Gods,
Approached. There are the red and steaming grasses,
And there — what welcome for a bride's regard! —
There is Hippolytus, but motionless,
Featureless, bloodless. First she seeks to question
Her misery, and, seeing, still demands
Hippolytus. Then, too pitifully assured,
After one glance reproachful to the skies
Cold, with one cry, lifeless upon the dead
She falls. Ismene, weeping, is beside her   1610
And draws her back to life and life's despair;
And I, still subject to the hostile daylight,
Return to speak a hero's last desires
And so fulfil the grievous ministry

His dying heart committed to my love.
— But here I see the deadliest of his foes.

Enter Phaedra, Panope *and* Guards

Theseus   Well, victory is yours: my son is gone.
Much, much I could suspect; deep rankling doubt
Acquits him in my heart and troubled mind —
But he is dead: your sacrifice, my lady;   1620
Take it, find satisfaction in the forfeit
Unmerited or just. It matters little
That evermore my eyes be blindfolded;
Let him be criminal if you accuse.
His loss alone is theme enough for sorrow,
No need to look for new and fearful knowledge
That, impotent to bring the dead again,
Could pile at most new suffering on the old.
Let me escape, leave you and leave these shores,
Flying the bloody image of a son   1630
Mangled — before that harrying memory
I could long for exile from the world of men.
All things upbraid me, all increase my anguish —
My very name (for nameless, I could hide),
The very honours that the Gods bestowed,
Whose murderous grace I'll mourn, and not again
Importune them with fruitless prayers of mine;
Do what they might, their fatal condescension
Could not console for what they took away.

Phaedra   Theseus, I have repented of my silence.   1640
Your son requires his innocence from my lips;
Yes, he was guiltless.

Theseus   This to me, his father!
And on your solemn faith I sentenced him.
Can any pretext for an act so vile —

Phaedra   My time is measured. Listen to me, Theseus.
I, on your dutiful and temperate son,
Looked with profaning and incestuous eyes —
The flame of Heaven lighted in my bosom
A fatal fire. Oenone did the rest;
She feared Hippolytus, my passion known,   1650
Would publish all the madness that he loathed;
Presuming on my feebleness, she came
With that base story of my victim's guilt.
Self-chosen, easy death among the waves
Punished her perfidy and foiled my anger,
And by now the knife would have cleft my destiny,
But goodness still cried out for vindication.

I chose the slower path. I chose to pour
Into your ears before I joined the dead
The chronicle of my remorse. I have drained   1660
And mingled with my burning blood a draught
Medea left in Athens. Now already
Her poison makes its progress toward my heart
Striking that heart with cold it never knew;
Faintly already I perceive the daylight
And you I wrong by my unworthy presence;
And death, blurring the sunbeams from these eyes
Whose glance polluted them, restores the light
To perfect purity.

Panope   My lord, she is dying.
Theseus   And would the dark remembrance too might
            die   1670
Of what she has done! Come, all is now too plain.
I must enfold what still remains to touch
Of my dear son, and expiate in tears
The blind curse I shall evermore bewail
With dear-bought honours rendered at his tomb;
And, better to placate his injured spirit,
I will forget the voice of ancient vengeance
And look upon his lover as my child.

ATHALIAH
(1691)

INTRODUCTION

In 1668 Racine was called upon by Mme de Maintenon, the King's morganatic wife, to provide some kind of dramatic script to be recited and sung by the pupils of the convent-school she had founded for daughters of the impoverished nobility at Saint-Cyr.

> Most of the finest verse in our language having been written on very worldly themes, and our most beautiful airs being made for languorous and effeminate words liable to produce a dangerous effect on young minds, the illustrious persons who have consented to take charge of that establishment ... did me the honour of ... asking if I could not write, on some subject of piety and morality, a sort of poem in which song could be mingled with narrative, and the whole linked together by an action to make it more lively and less tedious.
>
> I offered them the subject of Esther, which struck them at once [as suitable] ... And for my part I thought I should find it quite easy to treat, since without altering any scriptural circumstance of any importance — which to my mind would be a kind of sacrilege — I could fill my whole action with nothing but the scenes which God himself, if I may put it so, has set forth.
>
> So I undertook the task, and discovered that as I worked on the lines laid down, I was in some sort carrying out a plan which had often passed through my mind, which was to bring a chorus and singing into the dramatic action in the same way as in the ancient Greek tragedies, and use for chanting the praises of the true God that part of the activity of the chorus which the heathens used to sing the praise of their false divinities.
>
> (*Esther*, preface)

So that in these two respects, as has been pointed out above, Racine in turning from Greco-Roman tragedy was nearer to the Greek model than ever before.

The result, *Esther* (1689), was a brilliant social occasion, preserved for us by the pen of Mme de Sévigné; but the play was a religious melodrama in only three acts, more remarkable for its lyrics and its changes of scene than its dramatic qualities. *Athalie*, written two years later for a similar purpose, had the full length and stature of a tragedy, and a more carefully studied imitation of the Greek chorus: but unhappily, for reasons still uncertain, it never obtained a proper performance in Racine's lifetime. There were simply a few private 'rehearsals' at Versailles without costume or scenery. The Comédie Française took it up (without choruses) in 1716, and it became one of the poet's most admired works.

Free from the constraints of the commercial stage, from which his rediscovered Christian scruples alienated him, Racine could innovate, enlarging his former dramatic form in some ways, amputating it in others. The lyrical and musical element was something which theatres were forbidden to use, even had they wanted to, by the terms of the monopoly granted to Lully's opera. He made what for the time was a bold use of Old Testament poetic language — at this time he knew his Bible well, for a Catholic layman. He used a child actor, as he had not done in *Andromaque*. The strictly dramatic action, carried on by the spoken scenes, though no shorter than the complete text of several of his earlier plays, is shorn of the love-interest which the Paris public insisted on: but it is still the traditional kind of story based on a political coup, with admirable suspense and a well-engineered climax — not to mention the enormous added import, that the royal line which we see saved and restored is the line of David from which the Messiah is to come. The intensity of passion that characterises Racine's tragedy is not abated: to the rock-like conviction and prophetic gift of the High Priest and the cruel ambition of the usurping Queen is added a savagery for which the Old Testament narrative gives abundant warrant. The religious sentiments so vividly portrayed are those of the Old Testament interpreted by Christianity, but by the Christianity of Racine's age and country, with limitations (intolerance, Divine Right, a serenely providentialist reading of history) which are only too evident today.

The characters, all but Mattan, are more than pasteboard emblems of virtue or vice. Jehoiada shows a duplicity which has worried some commentators (and Racine himself, who prepared a list of precedents in biblical and church history in case he was challenged on the point). Athaliah shows dignity, wise statesmanship, courage, loyalty and gleams of mother-love and even kindliness, which have put certain modern readers on her side against the zealots.

This complexity adds life and depth; it is at the same time a

last reminder of Racine's devotion to the teaching of the
Poetics, and particularly to the precept we have seen him
quote so often, that the hero who falls in a tragedy must have
something we can pity. *Athaliah* was not to be a Sunday-
school pageant like *Esther*, but in this as in other respects a
tragedy in the fullest sense. We are invited to condemn the
victim of Jehovah far more strongly than the victim of Venus,
but both must arouse pity.

The triumph of good over evil in the denouement is not
itself unequivocal. For the pious Joash (himself a victim, as we
tend to see him, of a pitilessly strict upbringing) was to fall
from grace once the influence of Jehoida was removed, as we
are reminded by lines full of tragic irony in the play (1222,
where see note; 1500).

The reintegration of music with drama had made
seventeenth-century France think of the opera, which had
been created in its French form under Lully (now recently
dead). People had spoken of the *Esther* project as an opera.
But Racine's innovations were different — his chorus hardly
appeared on stage except to fill the intervals between acts, and
the action was still conveyed by spoken scenes. Musicologists
see *Athalie* rather as a bridge leading to the oratorios of
Handel, who was to use this subject among many others taken
from French tragedy.

In France, although tragedy (without music) continued in
popular favour, but without inner vitality, for another hundred and forty years, the genre produced its last masterpiece in
this play, which seemed to promise a new lease of life, but
could not give it.

PREFACE (EXTRACTS)
(1691)

[Racine begins by sketching the history of the kingdoms of Israel and Judah (with Benjamin), which divided after the death of Solomon; the privileged position of the Temple of Jerusalem (in Judah) as the only place where God accepted sacrifice; and the functions of the priests and Levites in the Temple worship.]

I thought it well to go into these details so that those who have not sufficient memory of Old Testament history should not find difficulty in reading this tragedy. It has for its subject the recognition and enthronement of Joash; and according to the rules I should have entitled it *Joash*. But most people having heard of it only under the name of *Athaliah*, I preferred not to present it under another title, since in any case Athaliah plays so considerable a part in it, and it is her death that ends the play. Here are some of the main events which preceded that great action.

[The history follows of Ahab king of Israel and his wife Jezebel, and their daughter Athaliah who married Jehoram king of Judah, and who, after his death and that of their son Ahaziah, killed all her grandsons in revenge for the extermination of Ahab's line in Israel by Jehu (II Kings 8.16—11.1 and II Chronicles 21.4—22.10).]

. . . But happily Josabeth, the sister of Ahaziah and daughter of Jehoram (but by a different mother from Athaliah), arrived during the slaughter of the princes her nephews and contrived to remove from among the dead bodies Joash, a baby still at the breast; she entrusted him with his nurse to the High Priest her husband, who hid both in the Temple, where the child was reared secretly until the day he was proclaimed king of Judah. The account in Kings says this was the seventh year afterwards; but the Greek text of Paralipomena [Chronicles], followed by Sulpicius Severus, says it was the eighth. This was my justification for showing him as a boy of nine to ten, so that he could be old enough to answer the questions put to him.

[The verisimilitude of this episode is defended. Authorities are quoted for attributing Jehoiada's rising to the priests

and Levites without the help of soldiery, as was fitting for
the preservation of the line from which was to come the
Messiah, 'the light promised to David'.]

History does not specify the day of Joash's proclamation.
Some commentators suggest that it was on a feast-day: I have
chosen the Feast of Pentecost, which was one of the great.
feasts of the Jews. It commemorated the giving of the Law on
Mount Sinai, and was also the time for offering to God the
first loaves made from the new harvest; for which reason it was
also called the Feast of the First-Fruits. I thought these circumstances would provide me with some variety for the songs
of the chorus.

This chorus is made up of maidens of the tribe of Levi, and
I make its leader a sister of Zechariah: it is she who leads the
chorus into her mother's presence. She sings with it, speaks on
its behalf, and acts like the figure in ancient choruses named
the coryphaeus. I have also tried to imitate from the ancients
that continuity of action in virtue of which their stage never
remains empty, the intervals between acts being marked simply
by hymns and moral reflections of the chorus, inspired by the
events taking place.

I may be considered somewhat bold for having dared to
show on the stage a prophet inspired by God, foretelling the
future. But I have taken the precaution of putting nothing into
his mouth but expressions taken from the prophets themselves.
Although Scripture does not say expressly that Jehoiada was
gifted with the spirit of prophecy, as it does of his son, it does
show him as being a man filled with the spirit of God. Moreover, does it not appear from the Gospel that he could have
prophesied simply in virtue of his high-priestly office? So I
picture him as seeing in the spirit the fatal falling-away of
Joash, who after thirty years of a very devout reign gave himself up to the evil counsels of flatterers and defiled himself
with the murder of Zechariah, the son and successor of the
great High Priest. That murder, committed inside the Temple,
was one of the main causes of the anger of God against the
Jews and all the misfortunes which came upon them afterwards. It is even stated that from that day the responses of
God entirely ceased to be delivered in the sanctuary. All this
has given me occasion to make Jehoiada go on at once to predict both the destruction of the Temple and the fall of Jerusalem. But as the prophets generally combine consolations
with their threats, and also because my action is concerned
with the crowning of one of the Messiah's ancestors, I have

taken the opportunity to allude to the coming of this consoler, whom all the righteous of old yearned to see.

This scene, which forms a kind of episode, calls for music quite naturally, because many prophets were accustomed to go into their inspired ecstasies to the sound of instruments. Witness the company of prophets who came out to meet Saul with harp and lyre before them, and Elisha himself who, consulted about the future by the kings of Judah and Israel, said, like Jehoiada here, 'Bring me a minstrel.' Add to this that the prophecy is very effective in augmenting the excitement in the play, by the consternation and the different emotions aroused in the chorus and the leading characters.

Genealogical table for *Athaliah*

DRAMATIS PERSONAE

Joash	King of Judah, son of Ahaziah
Athaliah	widow of Jehoram, grandmother of Joash
Jehoiada	High Priest
Josabeth	aunt of Joash, wife of the High Priest
Zechariah	son of Jehoiada and Josabeth
Salomith	sister of Zechariah
Abner	one of the chief captains of the Kings of Judah

Azariah, Ishmael, and the three other chiefs over the Priests and Levites

Mattan	apostate priest, now Chief Priest of Baal
Nabal	confidant of Mattan
Hagar	attendant on Athaliah

Company of Priests and Levites
Followers of Athaliah
Nurse of Joash
Chorus of girls from the Tribe of Levi

The scene is in the Temple at Jerusalem, in an outer room of the dwelling of the High Priest.

ACT I

JEHOIADA, ABNER

Abner   Yes, I have come today into the Temple
To worship God, and celebrate with you
After the usage of the earlier times
That day of days, when on Mount Sinai's height
The Law was given us. How all has changed!
No sooner had the priestly trumpet sounded
The feast's return, the holy people streamed
Into these courts hung round with splendid garlands
To pass, in ordered ranks, before the altar
Bearing the earliest increase of their fields,   10
Thank-offerings, to the Lord of all the earth.
Priests were too few to serve the sacrifices.
Now, one presumptuous woman in her violence
Has turned those happy days to days of gloom.
Only a handful of the faithful dare
Show some faint shadow of the ways of old;
The others have forgotten God, or even,
Initiates of the hideous mysteries
Of Baäl, throng his altars, and blaspheme
The sacred name their fathers called upon.   20
    I dread that Athaliah, to speak plainly,
Will tear you from your altar, and abandon
The last reluctant semblance of forbearance
To end the tale of her revenge with you.
Jehoiada   Why should these fears have come to you
        today?
Abner   Do you expect to walk in righteousness
Untroubled? That unflinching strength of purpose,
More glorious in Jehoiada than his mitre,
Is what she hates, and always has; and always
Your love for our religion has to her   30
Proved you a dangerous rebel. More than this,
Since every virtue is abhorrent to her,
She hates your faithful consort Josabeth.
While you, Jehoiada, sit in Aaron's seat
Josabeth's brother was our latest King.
Moreover Mattan, priest and renegade,

161

Far more malevolent than Athaliah,
Is always at her elbow, Mattan, traitor,
Deserter from our altars; enemy
Of all that is good. It is true, he was a Levite   40
Who now wears Baal's mitre and serves him;
That is a light thing — he will never rest
Until this Temple, which rebukes his conscience,
Has been destroyed, and with it — if he could —
The very God whose name he has denied.
He uses every perfidy to hurt you —
At times affects to pity you; and often
He praises you with an assumed affection
That hides his inward venom. He tells the Queen
That you are to be feared, or else he plays   50
On her unquenchable desire for gold
With tales of treasure long ago amassed
By David, and hidden in a secret place
Known to you only. Now, these two last days,
The arrogant Queen has seemed as if immersed
In black despair. Last night I watched her face
Turned towards the Holy Place with looks of fury
As if she saw that some avenger there
Lay hidden in the vastness of this pile
Armed by the Lord to bring her doom upon her.   60
Trust me, the more I think, the less I doubt
The anger of this bloody child of Jezebel
Is poised to strike you down, and she will come
To challenge God, even in his sanctuary.
Jehoiada   He that can still the raging of the waters
Can bring to naught the counsels of the ungodly.
I bow obedient, Abner, to his will,
And fearing God I have no other fear.
— Not that I am unthankful for the zeal
That brings you here to warn me of this danger.   70
I see your heart still hates unrighteousness
And you are still a son of Israel.
But secret indignation, unbreathed virtue,
Are they enough? Can it be called a faith,
The faith that never acts? Eight years and more
A godless alien usurps the rights
Of David's throne, butchers her own son's infants,
Spilling unpunished their most royal blood,
And lifts her arm against the Lord himself:
While you, a pillar of this tottering state,   80
You, reared in the armies of Jehoshaphat

Our godly King, you, captain of our host
Under his son Jehoram; the only bulwark
Of Judah's cities when the unlooked-for death
Of Ahaziah at the hands of Jehu
Scattered his men of war — do you now say
'I fear the Lord, I reverence his word'?
Hear his reply, Abner. Thus says the Lord:
'Why do you boast your zeal, who honour me
With your lips only? Can you think that I   90
Have need of anything you have to give?
Do I desire the blood of bulls and goats?
The blood of your Kings cries out, and no man hears.
Rise up, break off all covenant with evil;
Root out iniquity from among my people;
Then you may come and bring me offerings.'

Abner   What can I do, among a people broken,
Judah cast down, and nerveless Benjamin?
All the old courage of the ancient days
Died with the failing of the kingly line.   100
God has himself, they say, departed from us,
He, once so jealous for the Hebrew name,
Can see its honour in the dust, unmoved,
And his long-suffering is at an end.
For us those terrible hands no longer work
The countless wonders that dismayed mankind;
The holy Ark is dumb, and gives no answers.

Jehoiada   When did a time bring forth more miracles?
When did his arm more clearly show its might?
Ungrateful people, have you eyes to see   110
And see not? Mighty wonders all around you
Astound your ears, but not your stubborn hearts?
What, Abner, must I bring to memory
Each of the marvels that our time has known?
The downfall of the tyrants in Samaria,
And God found faithful in his lightest threat?
The wicked Ahab stricken, and his blood
Drenching the vineyard he had killed to gain;
Hard by, the horrible end of Jezebel
Trampled to death under the horses' hooves,   120
The mangled members of her hideous corpse
Left to the dogs that came to lap her blood?
The ranks of the false prophets put to rout;
The fire from heaven upon the sacrifice;
Elijah lording it over the elements,
The skies shut up and turned as if to brass

Three years, while earth saw neither dew nor rain;
The dead raised at the bidding of Elisha?
Do not these things declare, confess it, Abner,
A God, the same yesterday and today,   130
Able to show his glory when he wills,
Holding his people always in remembrance?

Abner   Yes, but the honours promised once to David,
Promised afresh to Solomon his son,
Where are they? We had hoped that from their race
A goodly line should rise, king after king,
Till over every tribe and every nation
One of them should establish his dominion,
Make war and discord cease, and at his feet
Behold the powers and princes of the world.   140

Jehoiada   Why question now the promises of God?

Abner   This son of David, where will he be found?
Can God himself bring back to leaf again
A tree dried up and withered to the roots?
That Prince was killed, an infant in his cradle;
And eight years after, shall the dead return?
If only Athaliah's stroke had missed,
If one drop only of the royal blood —

Jehoiada   What would you do?

Abner   Oh happy day for me!
How eagerly I'd kneel before my King,   150
While our two tribes in loyalty — But why
Deceive myself with hopes as vain as these?
No heirs of those triumphant kings remained
But the sad Ahaziah and his children:
By Jehu's spear I saw the father pierced;
You saw his mother massacre the sons.

Jehoiada   Press me no more. But when the lamp of day
Has made a third part of its heavenly round,
When the third hour assembles men for prayer,
Return, as resolute as I see you now.   160
God will perhaps by some great benefit
Show that his word is irremovable
And faithful. Go. I must prepare myself
For the great feast; and now already dawn
Touches the Temple pinnacles with light.

Abner   What is this benefit that I cannot guess?
— But Princess Josabeth has come to join you,
And I take leave, to mingle with the faithful
And share with them the splendours of this day.

Exit

Enter Josabeth

Jehoiada   This is the hour, Princess. For I must speak   170
  And your inspired deceit must be confessed.
  Too long unrighteousness exalts itself
  And points a mocking finger at our God,
  Saying, because of what we have to hide,
  That all his promises are nothing worth.
  Why, now success has whetted her ambition,
  Your father's wicked widow longs to burn
  Offerings to Baal even on our altar.
  We must reveal this King your hands conveyed
  Beneath the shadow of the wings of God   180
  And brought up in his Temple. He will show
  The high heart of the princes of his line.
  In understanding, now, he outstrips his age.
  Therefore, before I make the story known,
  I go to offer him before the Lord
  By whom kings reign. Then, having called together
  Our Levites and our priests, I shall proclaim him
  Heir and successor to the Kings they served.
Josabeth   Does he know yet his name and his high
      calling?
Jehoiada   He still thinks that he is Eliakim,   190
  A child abandoned by an unknown mother
  And taken up in pity by myself.
Josabeth   After the dangers that I saved him from
  How many other dangers wait for him!
Jehoiada   What, does your faith grow weak? Are you
      afraid?
Josabeth   My lord, I shall be guided by your wisdom:
  I left to you all care for his upbringing
  As soon as I had rescued him from death,
  And even fear the force of my own love
  And shun his sight as much as lies in me,   200
  For fear that some unguarded time of weakness
  Betray the secret that I had to keep.
  Still more, the last three days and nights have been
  A time of mourning and of prayer for me.
  But now, tell me at least what friends you have
  Who will be ready to support you. Abner,
  Brave Abner, will he be upon our side?
  Have you his oath to rally to the King?
Jehoiada   There is no doubt of Abner's loyalty;
  But he has yet to learn we have a King.   210
Josabeth   Then who will you appoint as guard to Joash?

Is it to Obed you reserve the honour,
Or Amnon? For my father favoured them.

Jehoiada Each one has sold himself to Athaliah.

Josabeth Then who will fight against her mercenaries?

Jehoiada Did I not say? Our Levites and our priests.

Josabeth I know that in secret, in redoubled strength,
They have been mustered by your watchful care,
Burning with love for you, with hate for her,
And bound beforehand by most solemn oaths   220
To David's son when he shall be revealed.
But noble as their ardour is, can they
Ensure, alone, the triumph of his rights?
Are they enough for such a work as this?
Certainly Athaliah will be swift,
Once she has heard the first and faintest rumour
That here is hidden a son of Ahaziah;
She will call up her savage soldiery
To ring our walls and batter down our gates.
Against such men, the ministers of God   230
Who only know how to lift up pure hands
In prayer and lamentation for our sins,
And only shed the blood of sacrifices,
What can they do but die, and let him die?

Jehoiada Have you forgotten God who fights for us?
God, who befriends the innocent and the orphan,
And chiefly shows his might where there is weakness?
God, who hates the oppressor, he who swore
To root out in Jezréël all the race
Of Jezebel and Ahab; God, who smote   240
Their son-in-law Jehoram, and his son,
To show his justice still pursues their seed;
God, whose avenging arm, though slow to fall,
For ever threatens all their sinful line?

Josabeth It is the dreadful judgement on those Kings
I fear for my unhappy brother's son.
Who knows if the contagion of their sin
Has not condemned him from his earliest years?
Can he be separated from their sentence?
Will God be merciful for David's sake?   250
Alas, the thought of how I saw him first
Returns each moment to dismay my soul.
The chamber was strewn deep with slaughtered
          princes,
And Athaliah, with unwearied hate,
Bore her own dagger and cheered on her men

To carry through the carnage. Suddenly
My eyes encountered Joash, left for dead;
I still remember how his desperate nurse
Had vainly tried to shield him with her body
And now, exhausted, clutched him to her breast,   260
Bloody and motionless. I took him up,
And as my tears fell thick upon his face
They brought back life; I felt his helpless arms
Clutch me, for fear perhaps, or to caress me.
But visit not my loving fears on him,
O Lord. He is the precious remnant of
Your servant David, brought up in your courts,
Nurtured in love of your most holy Law,
You are the only father that he knows.
And if, while now he braves a murderous Queen,   270
My faith is wanting, and if flesh and blood
Cannot restrain these tears I shed for him,
Preserve the heir of all your promises
And punish me alone for this my weakness.

Jehoiada   No, there is nothing sinful in these tears,
But God commands that we should trust in him,
Josabeth, and his anger will not blindly
Visit a father's sins upon the son.
Today the faithful remnant of our race
Will all be here to offer him allegiance.   280
For David's race is held in veneration
No less than Athaliah's is abhorred.
They will be moved to see the modest grace
That speaks in Joash of his kingly blood,
And God's own voice will speak to them, not mine,
And speak more clearly in his holy Temple.
Our last two kings have turned away from him:
Now we must have upon the throne a man
Who one day will remember that God's priests,
Out of the dark oblivion of the grave,   290
At God's command, restored him to his place
Lighting anew the vanished light of David.
All-seeing God, if it is known to you
That he will fall away from David's path,
Let him be as the fruit untimely plucked
Or withered by the frost within the bud.
But if this child will be obedient
And humbly serve your holy purposes,
Then put his rightful sceptre in his grasp;
Deliver over into my weak hands   300

His mighty enemies; confound their counsels;
Be pleased, O God, be pleased to pour upon
The Queen and her ungodly minister
That spirit of confusion and of blindness
That ever ushers in the fall of princes.
I must be gone. Farewell. Your son and daughter
Are at the doorway, leading in the maidens
Of the most holy of our families.   *Exit*

                    Enter Zechariah, Salomith *and* Chorus
Josabeth   Dear Zechariah, do not stay, but follow
To serve your father in his holy office.   310

                                    Exit Zechariah

Daughters of Levi, young and faithful band
Burning already with the love of God,
You who so often share my grief with me,
Children, the only solace of my sorrow,
The wreaths you bear, the coronets on your brows,
Used to fit well with these solemnities;
But in our day, alas, of scorn and pain,
What fitter offering than the tears we shed?
Hark: yes, I hear the priestly trumpet sound
Telling that soon the Temple courts will open.   320
While I prepare myself for our procession,
You, linger here and chant a hymn to god.   *Exit*

Chorus
    All heaven and earth declare
    The brightness of his glory.
Let the people bless God, let them praise him always;
For the Lord was the King before time had its being.
    Give thanks for his gift, for his grace.

Solo
    But even if a tyrant's will
      Should stamp our worship out
      And make our anthems still,
                                  330
His name shall never lack its praise.
    For one day tells the next,
    The nights repeat the story,
    All heaven and earth declare
    The brightness of his glory.
    Give thanks for his gifts, for his grace.

Chorus
    All heaven and earth declare

The brightness of his glory.
Give thanks for his gifts, for his grace.

Solo
He gives the flowers their lovely form and colour;   340
    He gives trees, and their fruits so sweet.
  He gives in turn the sun and showers,
    The cool of eventide
    After the high noon heat.
    The fields return his gifts
    With grain that man may eat.

Solo
        He has fashioned the sun
        To give life to creation,
        And light itself
        Is the work of his hands;   350
  But what are they beside the treasure
        Of his most perfect Law,
        Of his holy commands?

Solo
        O Sinai, tell again
        The ever-precious story
            Of that morning most solemn
        In eternal fame,
  When amid the roar of the flame
        Hid in the thundercloud
            The Omnipotent came,   360
            And men gazed from afar
            At a glint of his glory.
What meant the lightning flash, the whirling smoke
            And the earthquake and fire
            And the great voice that spoke,
        The sound of trumpets, the roll of thunder?
            Had he come to undo
            The world that he had made?
    And, on its ancient bases swayed,
        Would he tear its whole frame asunder?   370

Solo
        No, he came to reveal
        To the sons of his grace
        The splendour of his Law
        And he himself as Lawgiver;

To require of our favoured race
   To love the Lord our God
      And to love him for ever.

Chorus
  Oh how kind and how just his Law!
    Oh how sweet, how divine its beauty!
      It is most right,   380
  It is our happy duty
    That we worship our God
    With a love full of awe.

Solo
      From fear and bondage
      Our fathers he led;
      And he gave them to eat
      A celestial bread.
      He gives us himself,
      And our loving Lawgiver
      Requires only this,   390
      That we love him for ever.

Chorus
  Oh how kind and how just his Law!

Solo
      He cleft the waters
      Before their face,
      And the spring burst forth
      In a dry desert place.
      He gives us himself,
      And our loving Lawgiver
      Requires only this,
      That we love him for ever.   400

Chorus
  Oh how kind and how just his Law!
    It is most right,
  It is our happy duty
    That we worship our God
    With a love full of awe.

Solo
  You who have nothing more than the fear of a servant,
Hard hearts, can love itself never find a return?

Is it hateful to you, is it a bitter torment?
     Is love a law you cannot learn?
    Servants learn fear for the masters above them: 410
    Children learn love from the fathers that love them.
    Would you take from your God every gift that you use,
     And still your love refuse?

Chorus
    Oh how kind, oh how just his Law!
    Oh how sweet, how divine its beauty!
     It is most right,
    It is our happy duty,
     That we worship our God
     With a love full of awe.

ACT II

SALOMITH [CHORUS remains]

                            Enter Josabeth
Josabeth   Enough of singing, children; leave your
    hymns.   420
  Come now and join the prayers of our people.
  This is our time. Approach the festival
  And in our turn draw near before the Lord.
                             Enter Zechariah
  But what is this? What brings you back, my son?
  Why are you running, pale and out of breath?
Zechariah   Oh mother!
Josabeth   Well?
Zechariah   The Temple is profaned.
Josabeth   What happened?
Zechariah   And the altar is forsaken.
Josabeth   You make me tremble. Tell me all, my child.
Zechariah   When to the giver of our daily food
  Father, as High Priest, had presented loaves,   430
  First of the harvest, as the Law commands,
  And now was lifting up in bloody hands
  The steaming entrails of peace-offerings —
  Eliakim stood by him, he and I
  Ready to serve in our long linen robes —
  While the beasts' blood was sprinkled by the priests
  Against the altar and on the assembled people,

A sudden stir arose and filled the air
Dismaying us, and every head was turned.
A woman — is it lawful even to name her? ...   440
A woman — it was Athaliah ...
Josabeth   Heaven!
Zechariah   Into a court reserved for men alone
She strode with arrogant and defiant step;
She was advancing on the Holy Place
Where only Levites tread. At her approach
The people in amazement started back;
And then my father — Oh how stern his eye!
Not Moses was more terrible when he stood
And threatened Pharaoh — cried out 'Queen, go back.
This is a place of fear and reverence;   450
Your woman's sex, your wicked life, alike
Make you unworthy. Have you come to face
The awful majesty of the living God?'
The Queen glared back at him with looks of rage;
Her lips were ready with some blasphemy,
When it may be the angel of the Lord
Appeared before her with a glittering blade —
Certainly her speech froze, her frenzy fell,
Her eyes were fixed and dared not turn away.
The sight, above all, of Eliakim   460
Seemed to amaze her.
Josabeth   She saw Eliakim?
Zechariah   We both were staring at the evil Queen,
Both horror-stricken. Then the priests closed in
And we were led away. I know no more;
But I came to tell you of this dreadful thing.
Josabeth   Yes, she has come to snatch him from our
          arms
Even at the altar. And perhaps, this moment,
The precious object of so many tears ...
O God, remember David; pity us.
Salomith   Is there a reason why you fear so much?   470
Zechariah   Does someone want to kill Eliakim?
Salomith   Can he have roused the anger of the Queen?
Zechariah   Could anyone fear an orphan, unprotected?
Josabeth   The Queen is here! My children, come with me,
We must not meet her.   *Exeunt all*
                    Enter Athaliah, Hagar, Abner, attendants
Hagar   Why linger here, my lady,
Where all you see offends you? Come away
And leave the Temple to the priests that throng it

With all their hubbub. Come back to your palace
And give some peace to your distracted mind.
Athaliah   It is impossible. You see my weakness,   480
You see my wandering thoughts. Go, call for Mattan,
Tell him to come, and come without delay;
And would his ministrations could restore
That peace I long for and I never find!

                                        Exit Hagar
Abner   My Queen, forgive my boldness. If Jehoiada
Seemed over-zealous, it should not surprise you.
Such are the eternal statutes of our God;
Himself he planned his Temple and his altar,
And limited its service to the line
Of Aaron only; to the Levites gave   490
Their ranks and offices, with the stern command
That none of their posterity permit
Any approach to any other God.
Why, you, consort and mother of our kings,
Are you so much an alien in our midst
As not to know our laws? Then why, today . . .
Here is your Mattan. I will leave him with you.
Athaliah   No, Abner, do not go: I need you here.
Forget Jehoiada's seditious outburst,
Forget the foolish mass of superstitions   500
That bars your Temple to the rest of men.
I have a deeper reason for misgiving,
And I know that Abner, reared to arms from youth,
Is true of heart, and renders what is right
Equally to his God and to his princes.
Remain with me.

                                        Enter Mattan
Mattan   Great Queen, is this your place?
Why this distracted air, why this dismay?
What brings you here among your enemies
In this unholy Temple? Do you not
Still fear and loathe it as you always have?   510
Athaliah   Listen to me, both of you; hear my words.
I will not now bring back the past to mind
Nor justify to you the blood I have shed.
All I have done I thought it well to do,
Abner. I do not take as arbiters
Unruly subjects. Say they what they may,
My acts are justified by Heaven itself.
After the victories my reign has seen,
The name of Athaliah is revered

From sea to sea. Jerusalem has peace.   520
No more the Jordan fears, as it did of late
Under your Kings, to see its banks laid waste
By roving Arab or by Philistine.
The Syrian treats me as a Queen and sister;
And even that false enemy of my house
Who thought to make another prey of me,
Jehu, fell Jehu, quakes in Israël,
Hard pressed by mighty neighbours that my art
Raised up against that butcher, leaving me
Unchallenged and supreme, to taste the fruits   530
Of skill and prudence quietly in my kingdom.
But these last days, a care has come to ruffle
The even course of my prosperity:
A dream — that ever I should come to fear
A dream! — oppressed and devours my heart.
I flee it everywhere, it never leaves me.
    It was a night of horror and thick dark,
And Jezebel my mother stood before me,
Clad richly, as the day she met her death;
Nothing had dimmed her spirit, on her cheeks   540
Still glowed the borrowed beauty of the colour
That she had painted on them, to repair
The irreparable cruelty of time.
'Tremble,' she said, 'true daughter of your mother,
The terrible God of the Jews will conquer you
As he did me; and it is hard to fall
Into those hands, my child.' With this, the ghost
Seemed to bend forward to my bed; and I
Stretched out my arms to it, only to find
A mass of mangled flesh and bone, and slime,   550
And tatters rolled in blood, and ghastly limbs
Fought over by the dogs that fed on them.
Abner   Great God!
Athaliah   After these horrors, I perceived
A little child in linen, dazzling white,
Such as the priests about the Temple wear.
The sight revived me, and my anguish ceased;
But as I looked and marvelled at his air
Of gentleness and noble modesty,
Suddenly he whipped out a treacherous blade
And drove it in my breast. — Perhaps these visions   560
So disparate, so incongruous, seem to you
A trick of chance; and I was first ashamed
Of having feared a figment of sick fancy.

But it remains with me; and twice again
I have dreamed the self-same dream, and twice again
In slumber I have seen the self-same child
About to stab my body as at first.
Weary at length with horror, I resolved
To turn to Baäl, pray for his protection,
And seek for some relief before his altars.   570
But see how fear can act on mortal minds!
Some impulse drove me to the Jewish Temple,
Some fancy that I could appease their God,
By presents stay his anger, and dispose
This God I do not know to show me mercy. —
Chief Priest of Baäl, I confess my weakness. —
I come, the people scatter. Offerings cease.
The High Priest faces me in indignation;
And while he speaks — what terror, what amazement! —
I see that child again that threatened me,   580
That awful figure of my sleeping vision.
I knew that long white linen robe at once,
That bearing and that walk, those eyes, that face:
It was he, walking at the High Priest's side,
Until they quickly carried him away.
This was the reason that has made me stay here,
And why I called you to consult you both.
Mattan, what means this portent past belief?
Mattan   The vision, and the meeting, both alarm me.
Athaliah   This child I dread, Abner, you saw him too.   590
Who is he? Of what tribe, what family?
Abner   There were two children serving at the altar.
One is Jehoiada's and Josabeth's;
I did not know the other.
Mattan   Why debate?
You must lay your hands on both of them, my Queen.
You know I spare Jehoiada, humour him,
Without a thought of rancour or revenge,
And all my counsels are inspired by justice.
But after all, were it his own true son,
Would he spare a criminal one moment?   600
Abner   How can a child be called a criminal?
Mattan   Heaven has revealed him with a sword in hand,
And Heaven is just and wise, and all it shows
Is certain. That is enough.
Abner   But, for a dream,
Are you content to shed a young child's blood?
You have not yet found out who is his father

Or what he is.

Mattan   If he is dangerous
His case is judged. Suppose he is nobly born,
Then his high rank should make us fear him more;
But if his lot is common and obscure,   610
Who cares if a little worthless blood is spilt?
Are monarchs bound to show each such scrupulous
          justice?
Often their lives depend on sentences
Made and performed at once. How can we load them
With long and tedious examinations,
When to be suspect is offence enough?

Abner   Is this a language for a priest to use,
Mattan? What, I, a man inured to bloodshed,
Stern minister of royal vengeances,
Am I the advocate of the oppressed?   620
And you, who should be as a father to them,
You, minister of peace in days of wrath,
Do you cloak your grudge under a show of loyalty?
The swiftest bloodshed is for you the best?
You ordered me to speak without pretence,
Queen. So, what is this cause of fear? A dream,
And in the dream the likeness of a child
That you believed you saw again today.

Athaliah   You may be right, Abner, and I mistaken.
I may have made too much out of a dream.   630
So then, I must examine him again
And look more closely at his face and features.
Let the two children come before me now.

Abner   I fear . . .

Athaliah   Will they refuse to do my bidding?
What must I think of such a strange refusal?
It might suggest some thoughts I would not harbour.
Jehoiada shall bring them, or his wife.
I can speak as a monarch when I will.
Your priests, Abner, have cause, to put it plainly,
To thank the indulgence Athaliah shows them.   640
I know the liberty with which they speak
Against my actions and against my rule;
And still they live, and still their Temple stands.
Jehoiada must curb his uncouth fervour
And not provoke me more than once like this.
Go.   *Exit* Abner

Mattan   Now I can speak my mind without restraint.
There is a secret monster growing up

Here in the Temple, Queen. Do not delay
Until the storm bursts and the lightning strikes.
Abner saw the High Priest before the daybreak.   650
You know how loyally he served his Kings:
What if Jehoiada designs to foist
This threatening child into their vacant place?
His own son, or some other?
Athaliah   That might be.
I begin to understand the heavenly warning.
But I will clear up every cause of doubt —
A child can seldom hide his thoughts, and often
A single word will give away a plot.
So I will see the boy and question him;
And you, good Mattan, leave me, show no sign,   660
But put my Tyrians in readiness.
                              Enter Josabeth, Joash, Zechariah,
                                   Salomith, two Levites, Chorus
Josabeth (*to the two* Levites)
You servants of the Lord, watch over them,
These little ones so precious in my eyes.
Abner (*to* Josabeth)   Have no more fear, Princess; I
      answer for them.
Athaliah   Heaven! the more I look, the less I doubt
This was the child. It fills my heart with horror. —
Wife of Jehoiada, is this your son?
Josabeth   Which? this, my lady?
Athaliah   This.
Josabeth   I am not his mother.
That is my son.
Athaliah   Then, you, who is your father?
Answer me, child.
Josabeth   Till now, the hand of God —   670
Athaliah   What makes you so concerned to answer for
      him?
Leave him to speak.
Josabeth   At such a tender age,
What knowledge can you hope to learn from him?
Athaliah   His age is innocent, and has no guile,
As yet, to travesty the simple truth.
He shall tell me all about himself.
Josabeth (*aside*)   Give him, O God, your wisdom in
      his speech!
Athaliah   What is your name?
Joash   I am called Eliakim.
Athaliah   Your father?

Joash   They have told me I'm an orphan
   Left in the hands of God when I was born.   680
   I never knew my father or my mother.
Athaliah   You have no kinsfolk?
Joash   They have cast me off.
Athaliah   How? At what time?
Joash   As soon as I was born.
Athaliah   But someone knows what country you
      belong to?
Joash   Here in the Temple is my only country;
   I never knew another.
Athaliah   Where were you found?
Joash   Where there were fierce wolves waiting to
      devour me.
Athaliah   Who brought you here?
Joash   A woman no one knew,
   Who went away, and never said her name.
Athaliah   But who took care of you when you were
      little?   690
Joash   Could God forget his children in their need?
   He gives their food to birds and to their young,
   And all things in creation feel his goodness.
   I pray to him every day; and like a father
   He feeds me from the offerings at his altar.
Athaliah   Another marvel comes to trouble me:
   This gentle voice and childish air, this grace,
   Slowly drive out the enmity I felt,
   And something else . . . Could I be touched by pity?
Abner   You see the sort of enemy this is,   700
   My lady, and how false were your forebodings —
   Unless the stab that seemed so dire a portent
   Was just that pity that you seem to fear.
Athaliah (*to* Joash *and* Josabeth)   You want to go?
Josabeth   You have heard all his story;
   And he might weary you if he stayed too long.
Athaliah   No, no. Come back. — What do you do each
      day?
Joash   Worship the Lord, and listen to his Law.
   I learn to read it in the Book he gave us.
   I even write it out in my own hand.
Athaliah   What's in your Law?
Joash   It tells us to love God.   710
   It says that any word against his name
   Sooner or later brings its due reward;
   That he defends the weak and fatherless,

Brings down the proud, punishes murderers . . .
Athaliah   I see. But all the people living here,
   What do they do?
Joash   Pray God and bless his name.
Athaliah   Does God expect that we should spend our
      lives
   In prayer and contemplation?
Joash   In his Temple
   All worldly occupations are forbidden.
Athaliah   What pleasures have you then?
Joash   Sometimes at the altar   720
   The High Priest lets me hand him salt or incense.
   I hear the chants of God's exceeding greatness,
   And see the splendours of his ceremonies.
Athaliah   What an existence for a child like you!
   Have you no pastimes pleasanter than that?
   Come to my palace, see me in my glory.
Joash   Shall I forget the benefits of God?
Athaliah   No, I will not compel you to forget him.
Joash   You never pray to him at all.
Athaliah   But you may.
Joash   And watch the worship of another God?   730
Athaliah   I have my God, and him I serve. You too
   Can serve your own. They are both mighty Gods.
Joash   Mine is the one that all the earth should fear,
   My lady. He is God, and yours is nothing.
Athaliah   Come with me. Pleasures shall surround
      your path.
Joash   The joy of the wicked passes like a flood.
Athaliah   Who are these wicked?
Josabeth   My lady, pray excuse
   A child . . .
Athaliah   I like to see how you have taught him.
   Listen, Eliakim. I have taken to you.
   I think you seem no ordinary child.   740
   You see I am the Queen. I have no heir.
   Throw off that robe, and leave your low employment;
   I want to let you share in all my treasures —
   See if I do not mean it. Come this moment;
   You shall be near me, feast and sit with me;
   I'll treat you just as if you were my son.
Joash   As if I were your son?
Athaliah   Yes. What do you say?
Joash   To lose a father such as mine, and for . . .
Athaliah   Well? Speak.

Joash   And for a mother such as you!

Athaliah   His memory is good; I recognise   750
    The teaching of Jehoiada and his wife.
    So that is the return you make to me
    For the tranquility I let you live in —
    Poisoning the minds of simple children,
    Bringing them up in unreflecting hatred!
    You only speak my name with execration.

Josabeth   How could we keep our sorrows from their
      ears?
    The whole world knows. Yourself you glory in them.

Athaliah   Yes, I have taken vengeance on my progeny
    In just reprisal for my murdered kin;   760
    And it was just, and I am proud of it.
    Could I have seen father and brother butchered,
    My mother hurled down headlong from her palace,
    And in a single day, oh sight of horror!
    Slain with the sword, full fourscore royal princes?
    — For what? Because of some unruly prophets
    She punished for their ravings. — And could I,
    Disarmed by an absurd and craven pity,
    Unworthy Queen, unfeeling daughter, see this,
    And not at least, against these wild excesses,   770
    Take life for life, give outrage back for outrage,
    And mete out to the offspring of your David
    The sufferings of the rest of Ahab's line?
    Would I be here, had I not trampled on
    My woman's weakness, my maternal love,
    And checked your plotting at a single stroke
    With all that blood I shed of my own race?
    So now the pitiless vengeance of your God
    Has ended every pact between our houses.
    David I abhor; and his descendants,   780
    Though they be also mine, I know them not.

Josabeth   So you have conquered? Let God see, and
      judge.

Athaliah   This God of yours, so long your shield and
      refuge,
    What is he doing? What is his promise worth?
    When shall we see this King over the nations,
    This son of David that you dream about?
    — But we shall meet again. I leave well pleased.
    I came to see: I have.   *Exit*

Abner   Did I not promise?
    Here is the charge that I received from you.

Enter Jehoiada *and* Levites

Josabeth   Did you hear all the arrogance of the Queen,   790
　My lord?

Jehoiada   I heard it all, and suffered with you.
　These Levites with me were prepared at need
　To bring you help or perish by your side.
　(*To* Joash, *embracing him*)
　May God watch over you, courageous child,
　Who bore such noble witness to his name!
　— Abner, I thank you for this weighty service.
　Do not forget the hour when I expect you. —
　And we, whose eyes have been defiled, our prayer
　Disturbed by this ungodly murderess,
　Let us go back, and I will make an offering   800
　So that its blood may purify again
　Even the marble that her feet have touched.

Exeunt all but Chorus

Chorus   (*First part spoken by several voices*)
1.　Surely we see a new star rise.
　What manner of man one day shall this child be?
　　Already he defies
　The dangerous lure of power and dignity
　And will not let his spirit be beguiled
　　By all their vanity.

2.　　While all make haste to pray
　　To Athaliah's Baal,   810
　　　One child stands up to say
　That God eternal will prevail;
　And this Elijah of today
　Rebukes that second Jezebel.

3.　Who knows your secret
　Or who shall declare
　Your generation, child?
　Are you some prophet's heir?

4.　So the boy Samuël
　Grew hidden by the tabernacle's side.   820
He grew to be the Hebrews' oracle and guide;
　May you in turn bring hope to Israel!

(*Sung*) *Solo*
　Who is so favoured as he,
　The child that is loved by God

Who walks with him continually,
    Listens to him,
    And is led by his rod?
    Hid away from the world,
    The best of heaven's gifts
    Will from his birth attend him.   830
Evil example and the tempter's lures
    Cannot come near if God defend him.

Chorus
    Blessings, blessings will attend him,
For God is close to teach and to defend him.

Solo
    So in an untrodden glade
    By a river sweetly purling,
    Sheltered in tranquil air and shade
Opens and blooms a lily, nature's darling.
    Hid away from the world,
    The best of Heaven's gifts   840
    Will from his birth attend him.
Evil example and the tempter's lures
    Cannot come near if God defend him.

Solo
    Ah God, amid how many dangers
Lie the ways of a child that is loving and pure!
    If he would keep the faith
    And not betray the vision
    Many the fights he must endure.
    How many allies has the devil!
    And where can the righteous rest?   850
    For the earth lies under evil.

Solo
    Zion, city of David,
    His cherished abode,
    Holy mount that so long
    Was the dwelling of God,
    How have you earned instead
    The rebuke of your Lord?
O Zion, Zion, say, can you bear to behold
    A usurper abhorred
Set on the throne of all your Kings of old?   860

Chorus
     O Zion, Zion, say, can you bear to behold
        A usurper abhorred
  Set on the throne of all your Kings of old?

Solo
     Hushed now is the music of lays
        Which King David outpoured
     In ecstasies of praise
     Calling upon his God
        As his Father and Lord.
  O Zion, Zion, say, can you bear to behold
     An alien Queen, and her false god adored,   870
  Cast down the God revered by all your Kings of old?

Solo
     O God, stretch out your arm!
     How long, O Lord, how long
        Shall the wicked lift up
        Their reproach in your face —
     Vaunting themselves in pride
     Before your Holy Place,
     And mock the faithful few,
     The few whose faith is strong?
     O God, stretch out your arm!   880
     How long, O Lord, how long
        Shall the heathen lift up
        Their reproach in your face?
(Spoken)
  Why cling, they say, to virtue chill and cloistered?
        Why not pursue
     The pleasures of the days?
  Where is your God? What can he do?

(Sung)
Solo
  From bloom to bloom, from pleasure to new pleasure,
  Let fancy range, I hear the heathen say;
        Gather them while we may.   890
  Today is ours, we have no other leisure.
        The years pass, and are gone
        And their tale's known to none,
        But today we have song
        And a moment to treasure;
  We may not see another sun.

Chorus
>   Their part it is to weep
>   In confusion and mourning,
>   Unhappy souls
>   That will not see the dawning
> Of the new Zion in eternal light.
>   It is we who may sing,
>   We to whom God declares
>   The good he prepares,
>   It is we who may sing
>   Of his mercy and might.

Solo
>   Of joys they love so well
>   For their treacherous seeming
>   What is there that remains?
>   — What remains after dreaming
> When the day comes and minds are clear.
>   And when they wake —
>   Oh to wake to that fear! —
> And see the poor man take his place
> Where he tastes to the full God's ineffable grace,
>   They shall drink from his cup
>   Of wrath and indignation,
>   Shall drain it to the dregs,
>   That day when they shall hear
> The doom of their criminal race.

Chorus
>   Oh to wake to that fear!
>   Oh dread reward of dreaming!
>   Oh sleep that cost too dear!

ACT III

[*CHORUS remains*]

                                    Enter Mattan *and* Nabal
Mattan   Go in, you girls, and say to Josabeth
    That Mattan asks to speak to her in private.
One of the Chorus
    Mattan! O God of Heaven, punish him!   *Exit* Chorus
Nabal   What, scatter and disappear without an answer?
Mattan   Come in.   *Enter* Zechariah

Zechariah   Presumptuous man, where are you going?
    Advance no further than the spot you stand on.
    This is the house of God's appointed servants,   930
    Where heathens may not tread. Who do you want?
    My father on this festival avoids
    The impure approach of all idolaters;
    My mother is bowed in prayer before the Lord,
    And will not easily be called away.
Mattan   Then we will wait, my son; be reassured.
    My message is to the Princess your mother.
    I come to bring an order from the Queen.
                            Exit Zechariah
Nabal   The children have their parents' arrogance.
    But what is Athaliah's purpose now?   940
    Can she no longer hold to one intention?
    After Jehoiada's insolence this morning,
    After the child that stabbed her in her dreams,
    She meant to vent her anger on the priest
    And set up you and Baal in this Temple.
    We talked of it; you let me see your pleasure;
    I hoped for a portion of such splendid spoils.
    Why has she changed again?
Mattan   Friend, these last days
    She is not the Athaliah that I know,
    No longer the fearless and clear-headed Queen   950
    Who always took opponents unawares
    And knew the value of an instant lost.
    Some wretched scruple has made a coward of her,
    That lofty soul wavers and temporises
    And is, in short, a woman. I had worked
    To add my poison to an angered mind
    Already moved by portents from above;
    She had commissioned me to serve her vengeance
    By charging me to summon out her guard.
    But, whether this child that they produced for her,   960
    An orphan foundling, so they give it out,
    Had cured the terror of that fearful dream,
    Or whether something in him worked on her —
    I found her hesitant, irresolute,
    Already putting off the stroke of justice,
    Full of resolves conflicting each with each.
    I spoke, and said, 'I have sought out the truth
    About this child. They talk of his high birth;
    Jehoiada shows him to conspirators;
    He names him to the Jews as a new Moses,   970

And backs his claims with trumped-up prophecies.'
No lie was ever happier in effect:
My words produced an instant flush of anger.
'Why should I languish in uncertainty?'
She said, 'I will have done and end my doubts —
Take this decree yourself to Josabeth:
"The flame is kindled and the sword is drawn;
Nothing can save the Temple from destruction,
Except that child, as hostage for their conduct." '

Nabal   Why not? To save an unknown infant's life,   980
Perhaps by chance committed to their care,
Will they endure to see the weeds enwrap . . .

Mattan   Ah, but you do not know Jehoiada:
No man more arrogant. Sooner than yield a child
That he has dedicated to his God
You'd see him face torments unspeakable.
Moreover it is evident they prize him;
If I have understood the Queen's report,
Jehoiada has not said all he knows
About his birth. But be he what he may   990
I can predict that he will be their ruin:
They will defy the Queen. Then I can act,
And fire and sword at last will rid me of
This Temple that I loathe.

Nabal   You show great passion.
Is it the cause of Baal that inspires you?
An Ishmaelite myself, as you remember,
Baal and God are all alike to me.

Mattan   My friend, can you imagine me so foolish
As to be zealous for a useless idol,
A brittle block of wood that worms devour   1000
Over its altar daily, in my sight?
By birth a servant of this other God,
Mattan might still be serving him today,
If strong ambition and the thirst for power
Could be content with so severe a yoke.
To you, Nabal, I need not tell again
Of the famous struggle when I dared to stand
Against Jehoiada for the High Priest's censer,
Of my hidden stratagems, violent confrontations,
My tears, my hopeless rage. He came off best.   1010
I chose another course, studied the court,
By slow degrees I gained the ear of Kings
Until my word became an oracle.
I learned their secret leanings, flattered them,

Sprinkled each treacherous descent with flowers,
Held nothing sacred but their appetites,
Changed weights and measures at their lightest whim.
Jehoiada's rough words and rigid code
Were not more hateful to their pampered pride
Than I was welcome, with my sleight of hand,   1020
Cunning to cover all unseemly truth
And find fair pretexts for their raging lusts —
Shedding the poor man's blood without remorse.
Finally Athaliah brought her God
Into the land, and put him in a temple.
Jerusalem wept and wailed at her defilement,
The sons of Levi howled their consternation
Up to the skies above; and I alone,
I the apostate, seconded the plan
And set the example to the craven Jews.   1030
By this I earned the rank of Baal's priest,
And, dangerous to my rival once again,
Wore my own mitre and could walk his equal.
Yet, I confess it, in my lofty seat
I cannot lose the last remains of terror,
Cannot forget the God that I have left;
And this it is that makes me hate his Temple.
I long to prove, by laying it in dust,
That all his threats of vengeance cannot touch me;
And in the wreckage, deaths and desolation   1040
Strike till my felonies have stilled remorse.
— But here is Josabeth.

Enter Josabeth

Mattan   Sent by the Queen
To bring back peace and put an end to hatred,
Princess, with that forbearance Heaven lent you,
You will not marvel that I come to you. —
There is a rumour (not that I believe it)
Which, added to the warnings of her dream,
Would have brought down upon Jehoiada —
Already suspect of seditious plots —
The full effect of Athaliah's fury.   1050
I will not speak of my poor intervention:
Although I know what he has done to harm me,
It is well to answer injury with kindness.
So now you see me bearing terms of peace.
Live on unfettered, solemnise your feasts;
Only one proof she asks of your submission
Which is — I did my utmost to dissuade her —

That orphan boy she says she saw with you.
Josabeth   Eliakim!
Mattan   Regrettable, I know;
   She may give too much credence to a dream.   1060
   But you will make a mortal enemy
   If I do not receive that boy at once.
   The Queen expects your answer urgently.
Josabeth   Such are the terms of peace, then, that you
       spoke of!
Mattan   Could you one moment think of not accepting?
   Is peace not worth a gesture of compliance?
Josabeth   I should have marvelled if, even for once,
   Mattan had overcome his native bent,
   And after all the evil he has wrought
   Could bring about the slightest show of good.   1070
Mattan   How does this hurt you? Is there any threat
   To lay a hand on your son Zechariah?
   What is this other child you cherish so?
   To me the marvel is how well you shield him.
   Is he so rare, so exquisite a treasure?
   Some liberator promised you by Heaven?
   Take care: refusing him, you may confirm
   Dark rumours that are spreading in our city.
Josabeth   What rumours?
Mattan   That the child is nobly born,
   Picked by your husband for some grand design.   1080
Josabeth   A rumour fit to serve the spite of Mattan!
Mattan   Princess, if I am wrong you will correct me.
   I know that in her hatred for all falsehood
   Josabeth would prefer to give her life
   Sooner than let herself be guilty of
   The slightest word against the simple truth.
   Tell me, is nothing known about the child?
   Does utter darkness cover his descent?
   Do you not know yourself from whom he came,
   Fathered by whom, into Jehoiada's hands?   1090
   Tell me: I listen and I will believe you.
   Princess, give glory to the God you worship.
Josabeth   Is it for you to invoke, you son of evil,
   A God you make profession to blaspheme?
   Do you make bold to call upon his truth,
   You, priest of error, who sit upon a seat
   Infested and polluted with imposture?
   You, nurtured in malice and in treachery?
                 Enter Jehoiada

Jehoiada   What, in this place, is this the priest of Baal?
  And you, daughter of David, talk with him,   1100
  And let him talk with you, and never fear
  That from the abyss that yawns beneath his feet
  Flames may erupt and catch you even now,
  Or walls collapse on him, and crush you too?
  Why is he here? How dare God's enemy
  Defile the air we breathe, who labour here?
Mattan   Such violence befits Jehoiada.
  He would however have been more discreet
  To show a Queen respect, and not insult
  The messenger that she has deigned to send.   1110
Jehoiada   Tell me then, what disaster she foretells,
  What order such a messenger has brought?
Mattan   I have conveyed her will to Josabeth.
Jehoiada   Then leave my sight, monster of wickedness.
  Go and fill up the tale of your misdeeds.
  God has a place for you beside Abiram
  And Dathan, Doeg and Ahithophel.
  The dogs that made a meal of Jezebel
  Foresee the day his fury falls on you;
  They cluster round your door, and watch their prey.   1120
Mattan   Wait till the day is out — and we shall see —
  Which — . Nabal, let us go.
Nabal   Where are you going?
  What strange distraction has come over you?
  This is the way.   *Exeunt* Mattan *and* Nabal
Josabeth   The storm is about to break.
  The Queen in rage demands Eliakim.
  The secret of his birth and your design,
  My lord, will be no secret for much longer.
  Mattan as good as gave his father's name.
Jehoiada   Who can have told that traitor? You do not
      think
  That your confusion spoke too openly?   1130
Josabeth   I mastered it in every way I could.
  But trust me, now the danger is very near.
  Let us keep the child and wait for better days,
  And while the enemy deliberates,
  Before they seize him here and drag him from us,
  Let me conceal him for a second time.
  The highways and the gates are not yet closed.
  Shall I convey him to some wilderness?
  I can go now. I know a secret way
  By which unseen myself, with him unseen,   1140

Over the brook of Kidron he and I
Can pass into that wilderness where David
Trusting like us for safety to his speed,
Weeping, escaped a son that sought his life.
For him, I shall fear less the bears and lions . . .
But, Jehu — why refuse his helpful arm?
Perhaps this counsel is a way of safety:
Let us entrust our treasure to his hands.
Today we can convey it to his realm.
The road is not long. Jehu is not unfeeling,   1150
And David's name finds favour in his eyes.
Alas, but how could any King endure —
Unless another Jezebel had borne him —
Not to take pity on such a suppliant?
Is not his cause the common cause of Kings?

Jehoiada   How can you talk to me of fear and flight?
Can you hope anything from Jehu's help?

Josabeth   Does God forbid all thought and all
        precaution?
Do we not wrong him if we trust, and wait?
Do not his purposes depend on men,   1160
And did he not employ this Jehu's hand?

Jehoiada   Jehu, though chosen in his deep designs,
Jehu, on whom I see you place your hopes,
Has been forgetful of those many mercies.
Jehu has spared Ahab's accursed daughter,
Walks in the faithless way of Israel's kings
And spares the shrines of Egypt's hideous god.
Jehu, that on high places dares to burn
Unlawful incense that the Lord forbids,
Is too unworthy to uphold his cause: 1170
His heart's not upright, and his hands not clean.
No, no, our help is in the name of God.
I will not hide Eliakim. I'll show him
Wearing the crown of David on his head.
I'll do it even earlier than I meant,
To be beforehand with the plots of Mattan.

                    Enter Azariah *with* Chorus *and* Levites

Jehoiada   So, Azariah, is the Temple shut?
Azariah   Each of the gates was bolted in my sight.
Jehoiada   You only and your priestly band remain?
Azariah   Twice I have walked around the sacred courts. 1180
No one is left. None have returned that fled. —
A scattered flock, and helpless in its fear.
Only the sons of Levi cleave to God;

For, since our nation came from under Pharaoh,
It has not known a terror such as this.
Jehoiada   A craven people, ay, born to be slaves,
Brave against God alone! — Come, our work waits.
But why have we these children in our midst?
A Member of Chorus
My lord, how could we separate from you?
Surely we are no strangers in the Temple;   1190
Here with you are our fathers and our brothers.
Another   If we have not the strength, like Jael* once,
To drive a nail into a tyrant's head
And so avenge the shame of Israël,
At least we can pour out our lives for God:
While you resist the charge of the attackers,
We will at least call on his name with tears.
Jehoiada   So these are they that arm themselves for
        thee—
Priests, and children, O Wisdom everlasting!
But who can move them if thou hold them up?   1200
Thou, when thou wilt, canst bring us from the grave;
Thou woundest, healest; killest, givest life.
They come as trusting, not in their own merits,
But in thy name, so often called upon them,
Thy oaths, sworn to the holiest of their kings,
This Temple, where thy majesty abideth,
Which shall not fall until the sun go cold.
— But my heart thrills with an ecstasy, whence I
        know not.
Is it the Spirit of God that falls upon me?
It is. He burns in my breast. He speaks. He opens   1210
My eyes to read into the hidden ages.
— Levites, bring music; let your harmonies
Assist the influence that works in me.
Chorus (*sings*)   Be still and hear the oracle of God.
And let the comfort that falls from his voice
        Drop like the dew at morning
On tender herbs, that our hearts may rejoice.
Jehoiada   Hark, heavens, to my word; and earth, give
        ear.
Jacob, say no more that thy Lord sleepeth.
The Lord ariseth: sinners, hide in fear.   1220
                    Music, then Jehoiada speaks again

---

*Judges chap. 4. [Racine's note]

Has gold, fine gold, been turned to lead?*
What is this priest left dead in the Holy Place?†
Weep, adulterous city, weep and hide thy head;
   Jerusalem, that killest all thy prophets,
   Thy God hath cast away the love he bore thee,
   Thy incense is an outrage in his face.
   — Where are you taking those women and babies?‡
The Lord hath cast to the ground the Queen of cities,
Put down her kings, made prisoner her priests,
God hath cancelled his own appointed feasts.   1230
   Temple, fall down; cedars, spit flame.
   Jerusalem, my treasure and my woe,
How hast thou lost thy glory in a day?
Oh for two founts of tears instead of eyes
     To weep thy overthrow!

Azariah   The Temple!
Josabeth   David's throne!
Chorus   O God of Zion,
   Remember yet thy mercies of old time!
              Music, then Jehoiada *speaks again*
Jehoiada   What new Jerusalem §
Out of the old waste places cometh forth
Shining with light, sealed with immortal splendour?   1240
   Sing, nations of the earth!
She is reborn, lovelier and more fair.
   Why do these children flock to her,
   More children than she ever bare?‖
   Lift up, Jerusalem, lift up thy head.
   Kings are here, wondering at thy glory
   Kings of all nations fall before thee,
   Kissing the ground where thou dost tread.
All peoples press to follow where thy light is shed.
Blessed the heart aflame with love for Zion,   1250
   Burning in zeal and adoration!
   Heavens above, pour down your dew
   And from the earth come forth salvation!
Josabeth   But how, alas, how shall these great things
     be?
How can the promised Saviour come to us
If all the lineage . . .

---

* Joash.
† Zechariah.
‡ Captivity in Babylon.
§ The Church.
‖ The Gentiles. [Racine's notes]

Jehoiada   Go, Josabeth,
    Bring out the royal crown that David wore
    On his anointed brow. (*To the* Levites)
                    You, come with me
    Into that store, hidden from eyes profane,
    Where David laid those countless swords and spears   1260
    Once reddened with the blood of Philistines,
    And, full of years and honours, hallowed them
    For ever to the God that gave him victory.
    These shall be your arms. How could they serve
    A nobler cause? Come, I will give them out.
                    Exeunt all but Salomith *and the* Chorus

(*The first part of this scene is spoken*)
Salomith
            Peril and terror, sisters!
    What of the gifts we thought to lay
            First-fruits, sheaves, sweet incense,
    On the altar of God today?

Chorus
1.   Swords will clash in this quiet air,   1270
            — How can we bear to see them? —
    Yes, and the spears of deadly battle
            Flash, in the house of prayer.

2.   Why is Jerusalem silent,
    Thoughtless of God, and hard of heart?
    Why does Abner at least, brave Abner,
            Not speak to take our part?

Salomith
            Ah, sister, in those courts whose only law
    Favours the bold, condemns the weak;
    Nothing but flattery and fawning   1280
    Will buy the things that courtiers seek.
    Then who for friendless innocence
            Will find the heart to speak?

Chorus
3.   In all the turmoil of this day of doom
    They bring the royal crown — but why? for whom?

Salomith
            The Lord himself has spoken;

But what his prophet's words betoken
Who knows, for who can read their hidden sense?
Will he stretch out his hand for our defence?
      Or leave us broken?   1290

(The rest of the scene is sung)
Chorus
    Promises, menaces, unsearchable predictions!
How can we reconcile such maledictions,
      With so much tender care?
Words of dread, words of joy, words of hope and
    despair.

Solo 1
    Shall Zion be no more
    Than a ruin, forsaken?
Shall fire lay all her beauties waste?

Solo 2
    Zion trusts in her God;
    Her walls are surely based
    On his promise unshaken.   1300

1.   Her glory is departed
    Before my sad eyes.

2.   I see her light go forth
    To give light to all nations.

1.   Zion lies in the pit
    Of her humiliations.

2.   But Zion's face is in the skies.

1.   Oh fall that all must weep!

2.   Oh destiny most glorious!

1.   Hear the wailings of pain!   1310

2.   Hear the paeans victorious!

3.   Fear no more: for our God
    Every secret will remove.
One day will see the shadow vanish.

Trio   Though his justice will punish.
        He will save us in his love.

Solo   Unmoved for ever
  Stands he alone who loves his Lord.
The will of God only is his endeavour,
      And not his own reward.   1320
    Earth or Heaven can offer never
Joy like the quietude of him who loves his Lord
        Unmoved for ever.

ACT IV

JOASH, JOSABETH, ZECHARIAH,
a LEVITE [CHORUS remains]

Salomith   Beside my mother and my brother comes
    Eliakim marching with solemn tread.
    What are they bearing muffled up in cloths?
    What is that sword, sisters, that goes before them?
Josabeth (to Zechariah)   Lay on this board with
        reverence, my son,
    The hallowed volume of our sacred Law.
    And you, Eliakim, the august crown;   1330
    Set it down here, beside the Word of God.
    And near his diadem lay the sword of David
    Here, Levite, as Jehoiada commands.
Joash   What is this unaccustomed sight, Princess?
    Why have we brought the book, the sword, the crown?
    Since the Lord brought me here, never have I
    Seen such things brought together in the Temple.
Josabeth   Soon you shall know all that you ask, my son.
Joash   But do you want to try the crown on me?
    Ah no, Princess: it is too glorious;   1340
    Respect the memory of the king that wore it.
    A nameless child abandoned to the bears . . . !
Josabeth   Let be, my son; I do what is ordained.
                    (Tries the crown on him)
Joash   But I can hear you sobbing. Those are tears,
    Princess. Who are you crying for? Must I,
    Today, like Jephtha's daughter long ago,
    Be offered up as a burnt-sacrifice
    To turn away the anger of the Lord?
    Why then, what can a child refuse his father?

Enter Jehoiada

Josabeth   Ask him about the purposes of God,   1350
    And have no fear. We others, let us go.

      Exit, with Zechariah, Salomith, Levite *and* Chorus

Joash (*throws himself into the High Priest's arms*)
    Father!

Jehoiada   Well, son?

Joash   What are these preparations?

Jehoiada   It is your right, my son, that I should tell
    you.
    For you must hear, and hear before the rest,
    What God has willed for you and for his people.
    Call up new courage and redoubled faith:
    Now is the time to prove the ardent zeal
    My lessons fostered in your infant heart;
    Time to repay the debt you owe to God.
    Have you indeed this high, this noble will?   1360

Joash   I'll readily give my life if he requires it.

Jehoiada   You have listened to the story of our Kings.
    Do you remember, son, what strict commands
    A King must keep if he deserves to reign?

Joash   A good King, God himself has set it down,*
    Will set no store on riches or on gold;
    Will fear the Lord his God, and ever keep
    All the words of his Law, and all his statutes;
    And lay no grievous burdens on his brothers.

Jehoiada   So, if you had to choose a King for model,   1370
    Which is the one, my son, that you would follow?

Joash   David seems the most perfect King to me,
    For he was full of a great love for God.

Jehoiada   You would not walk after the wicked ways
    Of false Jehoram or of Ahaziah?

Joash   Oh, father!

Jehoiada   Yes, go on: what is in your thoughts?

Joash   May they all perish that would follow those!
    — But father, what is this that you are doing?

Jehoiada (*falls at his feet*)   I do you reverence as to my
    King.
    Joash, be worthy of your father David.   1380

Joash   I, Joash?

Jehoiada   You shall hear how in his mercy
    God foiled the haste of an unnatural mother
    And, even as her blade was at your breast,

---

*Deuteronomy 17. [Racine's note]

Made choice of you to save you from the carnage.
Her fury still pursues you; just as then
She sought her son's last child to take his life,
Now, not less earnestly, although your name
Is hidden from her, still she plans your death.
But I have soldiers loyal and prepared
Under your banners to defend your right.   1390
    Come forth, brave leaders of the holy houses
That share the honour of our ministry.

                        Enter Azariah, Ishmael
               and the three other Levite leaders

Jehoiada   King, these are they who will uphold your
    cause.
    Priests, now you see the King I promised you.
Azariah   Is it Eliakim?
Ishmael   This child we love . . . ?
Jehoiada   Is true successor to the kings of Judah,
    The last of hapless Ahaziah's sons,
    Known, you remember, by the name of Joash.
    The tender blossom plucked before its time
    Was mourned by Judah, and by you, as if   1400
    He had died among his brothers. He was struck
    With the same dagger; but God turned the blow,
    Preserved a spark of life within his breast;
    And by his grace the killers were outwitted
    While Josabeth smuggled her nephew out
    Bleeding, and muffled in her robe, and here
    Brought back and hid the infant and his nurse
    With me as sole accomplice of her theft.
Joash   How can I thank you, or repay you ever,
    Father, for so much love and so much care?   1410
Jehoiada   Store up your gratitude for later times.
    So here's your King, in whom alone you hope.
    Thus far his safety has been my concern;
    Now, servants of the Lord, complete my work.
    For soon the murderous child of Jezebel
    Will know that Joash sees the light of day
    And try to thrust him back into the grave.
    She wants to kill him now, before she knows him.
    You, priests of God, you must strike before she
        strikes,
    To end the shameful bondage of the Jews,   1420
    Avenge your princes' deaths, bring back your Law,
    And both our tribes must know and own their King.
    It is an enterprise of weight and danger,

I know. I face a Queen of headstrong courage
Set on her throne, commander of a host
Of mercenaries and idolatrous Jews.
But my strength is in the Lord, whose work I do.
Think how all Israel hangs on this young life.
God's vengeance is at work: her mind is troubled;
I have assembled you despite her vigilance;   1430
She thinks us here unarmed, without defence.
We must crown Joash quickly and proclaim him,
And then march out unflinching, as his soldiers,
Calling upon the Arbiter of Battles,
Stirring up faith again in hearts asleep,
March to her very gates, and strike her there.
    What heart, however sunk in sin and sloth,
Could fail to follow us as we advance
Armed with the arms of God, and in his cause?
A King that God has reared in his own house;   1440
Aaron's successor followed by his priests,
Leading the sons of Levi into battle,
And in their hands that every man respects
The arms that David offered to the Lord?
God will pour out his terror on his foes.
Shrink not, dip your arms deep in godless blood;
Strike down the Tyrians, strike Hebrews too.
Are you not sons of Levites famed of old,
Who, after Israel in the wilderness
Gave sinful worship to the God of Nile,   1450
Smote their own kin, and in that faithless blood
Consecrated their hands, to earn for you
The noble privilege that you for ever
Alone may serve the altars of the Lord?
    I see you all are burning to be gone.
But first of all, here on this holy Book,
Swear to the King that Heaven restores to you
That you will live and fight and die for him.

Azariah   We will. We swear for us and all our brethren
To put back Joash on his fathers' throne,   1460
Nor to lay down the weapons we were given
Till we avenge him of his enemies.
Should any break his word, and fall away,
Great God, then let thy anger visit him;
Let him and his be parted from thy grace
Among the dead that thou rememberest not.

Jehoiada   King, do you take this Law to be your rule
And swear to keep it everlastingly?

Joash   How could I ever fail to live by it?
Jehoiada   Ah, son — for thus I dare address you still;   1470
  Allow that word of love, forgive these tears
  Wrung from me by the pain I needs must feel —
  You never knew the court, you never saw
  The deadly fascination of a throne.
  There is a madness in absolute power,
  A magic in the voice of flatterers.
  Soon they will tell you that the holiest laws
  Command the common crowd but bow to Kings;
  That Kings are bound only by their own wills;
  That all else yields before their majesty;   1480
  That toil and hardship are the people's lot,
  Which must be governed with an iron rod
  And, if not mastered, will itself be master.
  And thus with lie on lie and crime on crime
  That innocence we love will be defiled
  And they will make you loathe the truth at last,
  And paint all virtue with a hideous face.
  The sagest of all Kings they led astray.
      Promise upon this Book, before these present,
  To keep the Lord ever before your eyes,   1490
  To punish wickedness, protect the good,
  Take God for judge between the poor and you,
  Knowing that in your linen robe you were
  As poor as they, and fatherless as they.
Joash   I promise to observe the Law's commands.
  If I forget thee, Lord, then punish me.
        Enter Josabeth, Zechariah, Salomith *and* Chorus
Josabeth (*embracing* Joash)   O King! O son of David!
Joash   O my true mother!
  Dear Zechariah, come, embrace your brother.
Josabeth   Fall to the ground before your King, my son.
  (*While they embrace*)
Jehoiada   Such union never cease between you,
          children!   1500
Josabeth   You know then from what source your life
          began?
Joash   I know what death your hands have saved me
          from.
Josabeth   Then I can call you, Joash, by your name.
Joash   Joash will love you like Eliakim.
Chorus   Then this is . . .
Josabeth   This is Joash!
Jehoiada   Listen all.

This Levite brings us news.

                          Enter a Levite

Levite   Something is afoot,
What, I know not, against the house of God;
But trumpets everywhere blare out their threats.
I saw the gleam of fires, the shapes of banners:
The Queen is drawing up her men in battle.   1510
By now, all ways to safety have been cut,
Defiant Tyrians have compassed round
This holy mountain where the Temple stands.
One of them shouted, between blasphemies,
That Abner is in bonds and cannot help us.
Josabeth (*to* Joash)   Dear child, I thought that God
        had let me save you.
Alas! I did whatever lay with me;
God is forgetful of your father David.
Jehoiada   How dare you speak such words, and draw
        his anger
On you, and on the King you love so well?   1520
What if he snatched him from your arms for ever
And with him all the hope of David's house?
Are we not here upon the holy mount
Where once, in faith, the Father of our race
Lifted his hand against a blameless child,
Bound, on the logs, the fruit of his old age,
Leaving to God to carry out his promise,
While he surrendered, with his well-loved son,
His only hope of seed to follow him?

    Friends, we disperse. Let Ishmael take charge   1530
Over the walls that front the rising sun;
You, those toward the Bear; and you the west,
And you the south. Let no one, priest or Levite,
Be rash enough to appear before the time
And so betray my plans; but let each man
Die fighting in the post where he was placed.
Our enemy is blind, and looks on us
As frightened sheep fit only for the slaughter,
Displaying only disarray and panic.
Let Azariah cleave to the King's side.   1540
(*To* Joash)
Come you, dear scion of a valiant line,
To warm the spirits of our men, and first
Come and assume the crown before their eyes,
Then, if you perish, perish as a King.
Go with him, Josabeth. (*To a* Levite)

                              Go, fetch our weapons.
          Children, stay here and offer God your tears.
                              Exeunt all but Salomith *and* Chorus

(Sung)
Chorus
    Go, sons of Aaron, go your way:
        Your fathers before you had never
    A higher cause for their endeavour.
    Go, sons of Aaron, go your way: 1550
        Defend your King, your God,
        Quit you like men today.

Solo
        Where are the shafts of your anger,
        Great God, and the gleam of your sword?
    Are you not a jealous Lord?
    Are you not the Lord, the Avenger?

Solo
    Oh forget not the love that was ever of old,
        God of Jacob; turn, and deliver.
    Will you only recall our transgressions untold?
        Are you not the Lord, the Forgiver?   1560

Chorus
    Oh forget not the love that was ever of old!

Solo
    It is God that they seek to banish,
    They aim their blows at him;
        Blindly infatuate
    They cry against us in their hate:
    'The feasts of your God shall all vanish.
        Take the weight of his yoke
        From the shoulders of all.
        Let his saints die the death,
        And the last altar fall.   1570
    Let not his name, let not his glory
        Find any place in our story.
        No more he nor his Christ
        Shall be served or adored.'

Chorus
    Where are the shafts of your anger,

      Great God, and the gleam of your sword?
   Are you not a jealous Lord?
     Are you not the Lord, the Avenger?

Solo
1. Dearest hope of this our land;
     You, of a glorious tree   1580
    Latest, tenderest flower;
     O child, then must we see
    You cut off in an hour,
    Plucked for a second time
    By an unnatural hand?

2.   Did an angel stand over
     Your cradle to save?
     From the point of the knife
  Was he your one protection?
  Or, laid in the night of the grave,   1590
  Was it the voice of God
  Called you to resurrection?

3. His father's father sinned,
     And his father rebelled;
  So, from this child, O God,
     Is your mercy withheld?
  And must he bear the load
  Of their misdeeds for ever?

Chorus
Oh forget not the love that was ever of old!
   Are you not the Lord, the Forgiver?   1600

(Spoken)
One of the Chorus
   Sisters, I can hear
The savage Tyrian trumpet speak.

Salomith
Even the soldiers' shouts are clear.
   The dreadful hour is near.
Quick, come away and let us seek
   Our shelter unafraid
Under the sanctuary's awful shade.

ACT V

[*CHORUS remains*]

Enter Zechariah

Salomith   What news, dear Zechariah? What has happened?
Zechariah   Pray now as you have never prayed before.
This hour may be our last. The order's given,   1610
Sister, the dreadful battle is upon us.
Salomith   And what of Joash?
Zechariah   Joash has been crowned.
The holy oil was poured over his head,
And oh, the joy that gleamed in every eye
To see our King delivered from the dead!
Sister, we saw the scar where he was pierced,
And we were shown too the devoted nurse
Who in some secret corner of this building
Watched over him, unseen herself by all
Except my mother, and the eye of God.   1620
Our Levites wept and cheered for joy and love,
While he, courteous and humble in the tumult,
Greeted them with a handshake or a smile,
Promised to take account of all their counsel,
And hailed them as his fathers or his brothers.
Salomith   And are the tidings known outside?
Zechariah   Not yet;
Only within the Temple. Soundlessly,
Formed in four troops, the sons of Levi have taken
Their stations at the gates, to wait the moment
When all will charge together with the cry   1630
'God save King Joash!' But my father's prudence
Holds back the King and keeps him out of danger
With Azariah for his guard. The Queen
Mocks at the weakness of our gates of brass,
And till her engines come and break them down,
Waves a bare blade and cries for blood and ruin.
There were some priests, sister, who would have had
Our precious Ark at least conveyed away
Into a cavern dug in times of old.
But father cried, 'Your fear dishonours God!   1640
This Ark, that dashed to earth so many towers,
Turned Jordan back, so many times subdued
The false gods of the heathen, shall it now
Give way before the railings of a woman?'
All this time mother, almost dead for fear

Stands near the King, speechless, turning her eyes
Now towards him, and now towards the altar.
She would draw pity from a heart of stone.
At times the King embraces her and tries
To reassure her. — Sisters, follow me,   1650
Come, and if our King must meet his death,
Let us all die with him.

Salomith   Who dares to knock
With these repeated strokes, and sends our Levites
Running this way and that, hiding their arms?
Are our defences breached?

Zechariah   Dismiss your fears:
God has sent Abner to us.

              Enter Jehoiada, Abner, Ishmael *and two* Levites

Jehoiada   Can I trust
My eyes, good Abner? How have you avoided
The troops that hem us in on every side?
We thought that the blaspheming child of Ahab
Had sent you where you could not foil her purpose   1660
And chained those generous hands.

Abner   It's true, my lord.
She knew my courage and she knew my zeal;
But that was not the worst. Cramped in my cell
I sat expecting, first, to hear the Temple
Had sunk in ashes; then, to see her come,
Fiercer than ever after all the carnage,
To rid me of a life unbearable —
For would that sorrow long ago had closed it
When I outlived the last of Judah's kings!

Jehoiada   What miracle has rescued you at last?   1670
Abner   God knows what works in that cruel heart of
                        hers.
She sent for me, and spoke as one distraught:
'You can see your Temple is surrounded,'
She said, 'My fires will turn it all to ashes.
I do not think your God can rescue it.
Yet still its priests — but they must act at once —
May buy their lives if they will do two things:
They must give up, firstly Eliakim,
But also something that I know they hold —
A treasure long ago by your King David   1680
Hoarded, and passed into the High Priest's hands
Under the seal of secrecy. Yield me these,
Tell them, and they may live.'

Jehoiada   Well, my dear Abner,

Give me your counsel: what are we to do?
Abner   All David's gold — if it be really true
That here you guard a secret hoard of David —
And all besides, whatever rich or rare
You may have saved from her rapacious grasp,
Give it. Or would you let those murderers
Break down the altar, burn the Cherubim,   1690
Lay their unhallowed hands upon the Ark,
And spill your blood within the sanctuary?
Jehoiada   But Abner, can a generous heart consent
To send a helpless child to execution,
A child I hold in trust from God himself,
And sell that life to purchase our deliverance?
Abner   Alas, God sees my heart; and would to God
She might forget an unoffending child
And think the sacrifice of Abner's blood
Sufficient to avert the wrath of Heaven!   1700
But what avails to struggle? You will all die,
But he will die as well. Does God demand
That we attempt the impossible for him?
Moses was doomed to perish in his cradle
Adrift upon the waters of the Nile
Because his mother feared a tyrant's law;
But God, against all human hope, preserved him;
The tyrant brought him up. And who knows now
What he will do for your Eliakim?
Whether he will not do as much today,   1710
And has not planted now a germ of pity
In the breast of the butcher of our kings?
At least, and Josabeth will bear me out,
I saw her shaken as she looked at him.
Her anger dropped. Princess, you have not spoken.
This child means nothing to you. Shall Jehoiada,
For nothing, have you killed, your son, all these,
And leave to burn the only place on earth
Where God accepts the worship of his name?
What more could you have done if this young boy   1720
Were the last remnant of the Kings your forebears?
Josabeth (*aside to* Jehoiada)   You see how much he
        loves the royal house.
Speak to him now. Why not?
Jehoiada   Too soon, Princess.
Abner   Time is more precious than you think, my lord.
While you stand here and ponder your reply,
Over there Mattan, glittering with fury,

Calls for the word to charge, the hour of bloodshed.
Must I fall down and clasp your reverend knees?
Ah, by that holiest place that only you
May tread, where dwells the majesty of God,   1730
Consider not the price they make you pay,
Let us think only how to meet this blow.
A moment's respite, then at dawn — this night —
I'll put the Temple in a state of war,
Secure, and ready to defy attack.
But I perceive my pleadings, like my tears,
Will never move you; and your rigid virtue
Cannot be shaken. Then give me a sword,
A weapon, any weapon, so that Abner
Down at the Temple gates, where she expects me,   1740
At least may find his death as fits a soldier.
Jehoiada   You have won me over. I accept your
            counsel.
We must avert this multitude of threats.
Yes, Abner, it is true: I guard a treasure
As the last hope left of our afflicted people
From David's time committed to my trust.
I had preserved it in the darkest secret;
But since your Queen requires me to reveal it
She shall be satisfied. Our gates will open.
Let her come, with her chosen men of war.   1750
But make her save our altars from defilement
By that outlandish rabble of her soldiers;
Save me the horror of the Temple sacked.
Priests and children — can they threaten her?
Settle with her the number of her escort;
And, for that child she dreads, Abner — I know
How upright is your heart — you shall be there;
You shall hear all I tell her of his birth.
You shall be judge between the Queen and him,
And you shall say if I should give him up.   1760
Abner   Enough, my lord. Already I proclaim
    Myself his guardian. I will take your message.   *Exit*
Jehoiada   Great God, now is your hour. Your prey
            draws near.
    Ishmaël, a word. (*Whispers to him*)
Josabeth   Almighty Lord of Heaven,
    Blind her eyes now, as once upon that day
    When you frustrated all her wicked plan
    And laid her tender victim in my breast!
Jehoiada   Be quick, wise Ishmaël. The time is short.

Do all I said, follow it point by point.
Most of all, at the gate, and on her way,   1770
Let her find nothing but profoundest calm.
                                        Exit Ishmael
    You children, get a throne for Joash ready;
Bring him in, followed by his priestly warriors.
    Go out and fetch here his devoted nurse,
Princess, and let your tears forbear to flow.
(*To a* Levite)   You, once the Queen in her fool-
        hardiness
Has crossed the threshold of the Temple doors,
Once she can change her mind no more, and turn,
See that our martial trumpets on the instant
Throw panic fear into the opposing ranks.   1780
Summon the people to the King's defence;
Cry, until every ear has heard the tale,
The miracle of Joash, saved and crowned.
Here he comes.   *Exit* Levite
      Enter Joash *attended by* priests *and* Levites
Jehoiada (*continues speaking*)
          Holy Levites, priests of God,
Conceal yourselves, and ring this place around.
Leave me to guide the impulse of your zeal:
Come forth, but only when you hear my voice.
    (*They all hide*)
    King, for this hope I think is in your grasp,
Come, see your enemies cast down at your feet.
The persecutor of your younger days   1790
Advances now in haste to bring you death.
But fear her not. For here in your defence
Amongst us stands God's Angel of Destruction.
Assume your throne, and . . . But the door has
        opened.
Suffer this hanging for a space to hide you. (*Draws it*)
Princess, your cheeks grow pale?
Josabeth   Ah, can I see
The Temple fill with murderous men at arms
And not lose colour? See, how many soldiers . . .
Jehoiada   I see that they have shut the Temple door,
And all is well.
      Enter Athaliah *and her attendants*
Athaliah   I have you now, deceiver,   1800
Brewer of factions and conspiracies,
Trusting sedition to secure your aims,
Sworn enemy of high authority.

So you were trusting in the help of your God;
Do you still trust him now? For he has left
His Temple, and your life, in my two hands.
What hinders me from using your own altar
To . . . ? No, the bargain that I've made, I'll keep;
And you, prepare to make your promise good.
The child, the treasure that you have to give me,   1810
Where are they?
Jehoiada   You can have your wish at once.
Here you can see them both.
                           (The hanging is drawn back)
                  Appear, dear child,
Worthy descendant of our royal line.
This heir of the most holy of our kings,
You know him, Queen? At least this scar you know,
From your own dagger. This is your King, your
        grandson,
The son of Ahaziah. Bow before him,
You people, you too, Abner: this is Joash!
Abner   Heaven!
Athaliah   Betrayer!
Jehoiada   Do you recognise
This most devoted daughter of the Jews   1820
Who nursed him at her breast? Josabeth snatched her
Out of your hands, the Temple took her in,
And God has saved her. These are what I hold
Of David's hidden treasure.
Athaliah   This invention
Of your malignity will cost him dear.
Soldiers, away with him, this hateful puppet!
Jehoiada   You soldiers of the living God, defend
    Your King!   *(Here the backcloth opens, the interior*
                   of the Temple is seen, and the Levites,
                   arms in hand, come out from all sides on
                             to the stage)
Athaliah   What is this? Treachery! I am lost.
Weapons and enemies are all around me.
Jehoiada   Look where you will, nothing can save you
    now.   1830
God has encompassed you on every side;
The God you mocked has left you in our hands,
So think of the account you have to render.
Athaliah   What, my unworthy soldiers terror-stricken?
You traitor, Abner, what a trap is this?
Abner   God is my witness, Queen, . . .

Athaliah   Let be your God,
    Draw sword. Avenge me.
Abner (*prostrating himself before* Joash)
                      On my rightful lord?
    On Joash?
Athaliah   Joash, that? Your king! Think, villains,
    Think, all my men are all around you still.
    Do you not hear them shouting for their Queen?   1840
    They are advancing. Rebels, you should tremble.
                          Enter Ishmael
Ishmael (*to* Jehoiada)   The Temple is freed, my lord,
        and out of danger.
    The heathen is in flight, the Jew submits.
    That army, like a smoke before the wind,
    Vanished before the voice of the Almighty.
    Our Levites shouted down over the ramparts
    Proclaiming Ahaziah's son alive,
    Telling how he was saved, how he is King,
    And Ahab's daughter taken in the trap.
    At that the trumpet sounds on every hand   1850
    And strikes into the host, mixed with our cries,
    That sudden terror and that wild confusion
    That Gideon sent upon the Midianite.
    The Tyrians flung their shields and spears away
    And fled the first, by any path they could;
    With them some frightened Jews; but all the rest
    Acclaim aloud the wonderful ways of God,
    Declare themselves for Joash, and rejoicing,
    With women, children and old men, embrace,
    And bless the Lord and him the Lord has sent.   1860
    All sing the resurrected son of David.
    The holy city has rejected Baäl,
    His evil temple has been broken open;
    Mattan is killed.
Athaliah   God of the Jews, you win!
    Yes, that is Joash; how can I deny it?
    That is the very place where he was pierced;
    He looks, he moves, as Ahaziah moved;
    He has all the marks of that detested blood.
    David wins, David! Only Ahab falls.
    This is your handiwork and yours alone,   1870
    Unpitying God! With dreams of easy vengeance
    You led me on, you filled my baffled mind
    With thoughts that veered a hundred times a day,
    Now working on my pity for a child,

Now blinding me with visions of those treasures
I feared to venture in the flame and pillage.
So, let him reign, this monarch you have made,
Let him inaugurate his dawning rule
By driving in the knife into my breast.
Hear now the dying wishes of his mother —   1880
Far more than wishes: I believe, I hope
That David's heir will earn the hate of all,
Break from your yoke and weary of your Law,
Hark back to Ahab's blood received from me,
Follow his father and his father's father,
Dash down your honours, desecrate your altar,
And bring about at last a day of vengeance
For Ahab, Jezebel and Athaliah!
Jehoiada   Take her away outside the Holy Place
Without delay. It must not be defiled.   1890
You, ministers of God, avenge your Princes
Whose blood cried out until her death shall still it.
Any man bold enough to take her part,
Let him too feel the fury of the sword.
                    Exeunt Ishmael *and* Levites *with* Athaliah
Joash   Look on my horror and affliction, Lord,
And turn away from me her curse; forbid
That ever it should be fulfilled in me.
May Joash die before he shall forget you!
Jehoiada   Call all the people in to see the King
And swear allegiance on their knees before him.   1900
Then all of us, the King, the priests, the people,
We will renew the covenant with God
That Jacob made, and full of thankfulness
And holy penitence for our transgressions
Swear to remain his people and his flock.
— Abner, your place is by the King once more.
                                        Enter a Levite
So she has paid the price of her defiance?
Levite   The steel has wiped the hideous record clean.
And now Jerusalem, so long her victim,
At last delivered from her hateful yoke,   1910
Exults to see her lying in her blood.
Jehoiada   King of the Jews, learn, by this dreadful
            end
Fit for her crimes, learn, and remember always
That there is one above that judges kings;
He is the friend of all the innocent,
He is the father of the fatherless.

NOTES

GENERAL INTRODUCTION

1   There is an orchestral and vocal 'realisation' of this score (with that of *Esther*) by Charles Bordes, published in Paris (L'Eglantier collection) in 1899. The Cambridge University Press possesses a revision of this *Athalie* by Mrs Walker-Morecroft, with Racine's French and my English words, and can supply a copy for a small fee to choirs and others interested.

ANDROMACHE

p. 3 [Preface of 1668]

Virgil: Neither preface of *Andromache* uses the title 'preface' (as do all Racine's other plays). Racine quotes Virgil in Latin (Aeneid III 292–3, 301, 303–5, 320–8, 330–2). I have borrowed Christopher Pitt's version of 1740; that of Racine's contemporary, Dryden (1697), is unfortunately rather free and does not bring out the points which are important for comparison with the tragedy.

p. 3, l. 11   *Polyxena*. See below, on l. 1373.

p. 3, l. 13   *Pelides*. Achilles.

p. 3, l. 30–p. 4, l. 7   Racine, like his predecessor Corneille, is always pleased to quote good classical authority when he can. When he makes changes in his plots he defends them by theoretical reasons, and, if possible, by resorting to different sources (cf. later in this preface, and *Phaedra*, preface, p. 106). The 'softening' of Pyrrhus (the word is typical of Racine's period) includes his whole behaviour as a lover. He had in fact been criticised for two opposite reasons — for showing too much of the submissiveness of the conventional modern lover, and for showing too little. Racine adroitly chooses the attack which is easier to rebut. Céladon was the principal male character in *Astrée*, the immensely popular pastoral novel by H. d'Urfé (1608).

p. 4, l. 2   Racine passes lightly over the fact (clearly indicated in Virgil's account) that the classical Andromache, as a prisoner after the fall of Troy, was a slave and in no position to resist Pyrrhus when he took her as a concubine (not a wife).

p. 4, ll. 14–16   Horace, *Ars Poetica* 120f. Aristotle, *Poetics* XIII; the theory of the tragic hero was well-known in Racine's time, and the paraphrase here is quite faithful. There is still argument about the real sense of the word here rendered 'fault'. Racine is disingenuous to the extent that he makes the theory cover any characteristic of a hero to which any critic may object. The argument reappears in the prefaces to *Iphigenia*, p. 54, and *Phaedra*, p. 105.

211

p. 8 Dramatis personae

confidant: a character, male or female (French *confident*, *confidente*), attached to a principal character of the same sex, sometimes as friend (as Pylades) or more often as a member of the household, but always addressed as *tu* and replying *vous*, who is by definition entirely loyal to that person's interests but has no other interest in the action. His or her function is to elicit information from the principal character for the benefit of the audience, and sometimes to offer advice (representing then one side in the conflict of motives, and commonly the baser or more materialistic way of looking at the situation). Playwrights used confidants to avoid soliloquies, which were considered contrary to verisimilitude; but they usually tried to reduce the number of these neutral figures. This is the only play of Racine to have as many confidants as leading roles.

Pylades appears in four Greek tragedies as the faithful companion of Orestes.

Cleone and *Cephissa* are invented characters; but their names are Greek.

Phoenix is seen with Achilles in the *Iliad* (Bk IX).

Buthrotum is opposite the island of Corfu on the Adriatic Sea.

The scene: 'Stage is a palace with columns, and in the background a sea with ships' (Notebook of Michel Laurent, stage-manager of the Hôtel de Bourgogne, where the play was produced).

11–12   It appears from this scene, and 494ff., that Orestes has followed Hermione's ship almost to Epirus, and after the storm wandered aimlessly, reaching Scythia (north of the Black Sea). The adventure alluded to there is probably meant to recall the *Iphigenia in Tauris* of Euripides. He soon returned to 'Greece' (57, cf. 10), by which Racine means the regions south of Epirus. All this is hardly consistent with 42–7.

96   Many critics have pointed out that until the last edition revised by Racine (1697) this line read ' . . . where passion drives me' (*Je me livre en aveugle au transport* – instead of *au destin – qui m'entraîne*). It is clear that in Orestes' mouth the two statements amount to the same thing.

153   Here, 207ff., and 266ff., there are echoes of the scene where Hector's son is killed by the Greeks immediately after the sack of Troy (Euripides, *Trojan Women*; Seneca, *Trojan Women*).

219   This substitution of another victim for Astyanax appears in an epic poem, *Clovis* by Desmarets de Saint-Sorlin (1657), Bk II. In the age of the divine right of kings it must have seemed less shocking.

231   'The wrath of Achilles' which caused him to withdraw for a time from the Trojan war, was caused by a slight from Agamemnon (*Iliad* I).

312   Terms like 'anger', 'hatred', 'punishment' are often used of the resistance of a lady and the patient suffering of her suitor in the seventeenth-century convention derived from Petrarch and pastoral. Pyrrhus knows they do not apply to this situation: I think he is offering

Andromache a face-saving way of yielding, as he intends to force her to do.

419   Hermione appeals to the conception often (as here) called *gloire* in seventeenth-century French literature. It corresponds usually to what Shakespeare's Hotspur and Falstaff (*Henry IV pt I*) call 'honour', and ranges in meaning according to the speaker from mere success and prestige (or chastity, in women) to self-respect and the voice of conscience. It had been a potent motive in the tragedies of Corneille and his contemporaries. But in *Andromache* Hermione violates it by failing to react properly to the neglect of Pyrrhus; Andromache, by refusing the offer of a royal marriage and kingship for her son; Orestes, by betraying his allies and by treachery and regicide; Pyrrhus, by mental cruelty to Andromache and by breaking his word to everybody in turn. Such faults, presented as pardonable if due to love, had begun to be shown in the tragedies of Philippe Quinault (from 1659). *Gloire* reappears in the French text corresponding to lines 60, 642, 866, 1217, 1406.

428   The first of several echoes of Dido, abandoned by Aeneas (in Virgil, *Aeneid* IV); cf. 1104, 1436ff.

448   The 'deliberation' (usually a soliloquy) had been much used in Corneille's tragedies (1635–74). This is the first of three in *Andromache* which betray the speaker's irresolution by failing to conclude or concluding against logic. Cf. 998ff., 1430ff.

463ff.   Pyrrhus seems to contradict this when he implies, 1322ff., that he saw Hermione for the first time in Buthrotum, when he had already fallen in love with Andromache.

887   In the *Iliad* (XXIV 765ff.) Helen speaks gratefully over Hector's pyre of having been defended by him against the reproaches of his kin.

1040   Racine gives his own different version here of Hector's words in the famous farewell scene from Homer (*Iliad* VI 394ff.), which he once praised in a manuscript note for 'mingling laughter, tears, gravity, tenderness, courage, fear and every kind of appeal' (Pléiade edition, II 714).

1215   Regicide for the seventeenth century was the murder of the father of his people, the vicegerent of God. It counted as parricide, the most heinous of crimes.

1307   Why does Pyrrhus come to Hermione at this point? (Simply because Racine has never yet shown the two together?) It is not in his nature to show gratuitous cruelty. Perhaps we should remember that, as Hermione is supposed to be leaving, she must in etiquette take leave of the King her host (cf. Hippolytus in *Phaedra* 141ff.). Unity of Place obliges him to come to her, not vice-versa, as it obliged him to come to Orestes in Acts I and II.

1359   Hermione supposes that Andromache will be pleased by any injury done to the Greek cause.

1368ff.   The killing of Priam by Pyrrhus is described, Seneca, *Trojan*

Women 44ff., Ovid, *Metamorphoses* XIII 409ff. Cf. the player's speech in *Hamlet* (II 2).

1373   The killing of Polyxena by Pyrrhus, after the sack of Troy, to appease the spirit of his father Achilles, is described in Euripides, *Hecuba* 98ff.; Seneca, *Trojan Women* 1132ff.

1379ff.   This groundless assumption that Hermione never loved him may be mere 'irony', or an attempt by Pyrrhus to salve his own conscience, or (as I think) a pretence which will save Hermione's face if she accepts it (cf. above, note on 312). There is a partial parallel in Corneille, *Sophonisbe* (1663), III 2.

1405   Hermione returns from the *tu* of furious passion to the formal *vous* in these lines (cf. Introduction, p. xiv). They seem to represent a change of mood caused by her own words in the previous line (cf. 1461, and *Phaedra* 1174ff.). The delay of a day gives Pyrrhus a last chance to show at least pity; it may also be the only chance to countermand his assassination. At 1411 the *tu* returns.

1532   In the first edition Orestes brings Andromache with him as prisoner, and Hermione later sets her free. The climax of the denunciation of Orestes is thus delayed by 24 lines, and this must be why the episode was cut out at the earliest opportunity. But we have lost the only appearance of the titular heroine in Act V, and a strange speech in which she says that her greatest sorrow is that she must be false to her love for Hector by mourning Pyrrhus. This is no admission of a repressed passion, as some have thought; only the recognition that her marriage has imposed on her the obligations of a widow (the counterpart of the obligations he had accepted, 1114). There is a parallel in Quinault's *Mort de Cyrus* (1658—9). Cf. below 1630ff.

1665ff.   Fits of delirium accompanied by visions of the Furies (who pursued murderers within the blood-tie − but regicide would have been included, see note on 1215) assail Orestes because of the killing of his mother, in two plays by Euripides (*Iphigenia in Tauris*, *Orestes*). Visions of punishment in the underworld accompany moments of remorse in several tragedies of Seneca (*Hippolytus*, *Hercules on Oeta*, *Medea*). Orestes is not guilty, here, of the crime of his Greek prototype.

IPHIGENIA

p. 53 Preface
p. 53, l. 7   Lucretius, *De natura rerum*, I 84ff. Racine quotes in Latin: the translation here is that of Thomas Creech (1714). The other references to the sacrifice are: Aeschylus, *Agamemnon* 184ff. (and later 1555ff.); Sophocles, *Electra* 530ff., 566ff.; Horace, *Satires* II iii 119f.; Ovid, *Metamorphoses* XII 23ff.

p. 53, l. 29   Pausanias, *Corinthiaca* XXII. Racine gives prominence to the most ancient authority and to his reputation, even though not a line of Stesichorus has survived; the same is true for Euphorion (below, p. 54, l. 27). No source before Racine ever spoke of two Iphigenias, only of a different parentage for the one usually described as daughter of Agamemnon and Clytemnestra.

p. 54, l. 7   *my denouement.* 'The denouement should arise out of
the plot itself, and not depend on a stage artifice [Greek *mechane*,
Latin *machina*; cf. the phrase *deux ex machina*]' – *Poetics* XV. Cf.
below, l. 17.

p. 54, l. 16   *deserves her punishment.* A reference to the *Poetics*
XIII; cf. *Andromache*, preface, l. 14ff. and note, p. 211.

p. 54, l. 28   Virgil, *Eclogue* X 50f.; Quintilian, *Institutio oratoria*
X i 56. Racine supplies these two references in footnotes.

p. 54, l. 30   Parthenius, *On the passions of love* XXI. It will be
obvious that there is no connection between the Lesbian princess and
any tradition concerning Iphigenia, except through the ingenuity of
Racine. He will attach Aricia in the same way to two different tra-
ditions; cf. the notes on her name, p. 217.

p. 55, l. 4   '*tragikotatos*'. *Poetics* XIII. '*compassion and terror*'.
ibid., VI, XIII–XIV.

p. 55, l. 20   Quintilian, *Institutio oratoria* X i 26.

p. 56 Dramatis personae

All the principal characters appear in the genealogical table before
Andromache, p. 7.

Agamemnon, *Achilles*, *Ulysses*, characters of Homer for whom Racine
thinks it necessary to give no description. The first two are sufficiently
described in the first scene; Ulysses, hero of the *Odyssey*, was renowned
for his cunning.

Eriphile learns her parentage only in the last scene. She is an invention
of Racine, cf. preface, p. 54.

Eurybates is a herald in the *Iliad.* The other minor characters are
fictitious, but have Greek names.

Chloris is called Doris by Racine; but the name has become so acclimat-
ised in English that it seemed incongruous here, and I have taken the
liberty of changing it. *confidant*, see p. 212.

Aulis, a port in Boeotia on the NE coast of mainland Greece, shielded
from the Aegean by the long island of Euboea.

'Stage is tents, and in the background a sea and ships.' (M. Laurent, cf.
p. 212). Agamemnon's tent must have been downstage centre, and
opened so that characters in it could be seen, but could behave as if in
the same privacy as was afforded in other tragedies by the conventional
room in a palace. We must presumably imagine a rear compartment
(unless it is a separate tent) to which the women can retire.

48ff.   This prodigy is said to have worried V. Hugo, on the ground
that oars are most useful when the wind drops. Euripides simply says
there was a calm. Racine probably never saw the sea (though he had
travelled down the Rhône); a recent critic has wondered if he fully
understood the use of oars and sails.

57   *Calchas* the seer appears in the *Iliad* and in Euripides' *Iphigenia in*

Aulis. He prophesies, but is neither a priest nor a sacrificer in the Greek poets.

131   *Mycenae* in the Peloponnese is only a few miles from Argos (159); Agamemnon ruled over both. Racine appears to consider the two names as interchangeable to denote the capital of the king.

164   Ulysses' role is taken by Menelaus in Euripides. Racine may have preferred not to show Menelaus demanding the death of his own niece.

271   *Patroclus* was Achilles' close friend and comrade in arms in the *Iliad*. This boast echoes *Iliad* IX 46ff. and XVI 97ff.

715   Everyone in the play thinks Eriphile must be of Trojan birth, no doubt because her guardian had told her she would learn her parentage in Troy (443ff.). (Her mother Helen was there.) The audience or reader would be no wiser until the denouement, unless they had read the preface, though Racine has provided several 'clues', notably Clytemnestra's words (1290ff.).

1262   After his brother Thyestes had seduced his wife, Atreus killed Thyestes' children and served their flesh to their father in a feast, supposedly of reconciliation; the sun moved backward in the sky in horror (cf. 1710). Seneca has a tragedy on the theme.

1336   The confrontation of Achilles with Agamemnon (IV 6), and all that follows from it, have no counterpart in the sources. The speeches of this scene draw inspiration, not from Euripides (where the two never meet), but from their dispute, over a different woman, Briseis, in the *Iliad*, Bk I.

1559   *harvests of renown*. Achilles loves *gloire* in its most elementary sense (cf. note on *Andromache* 419), and he sees no obstacle in his love (1590). But here, to check him and save her father from his violence, Iphigenia tries to show that love for her is indeed an obstacle (cf. 1586), and throws in a mention of her own *gloire* (1607, 1623), which for her consists in obedience and self-sacrifice. *Gloire* is the French word used in all these passages.

1671   Iphigenia says in French, 'if you love me, by this mother-love, . . .' (*si vous m'aimez, par cet amour de mère*, . . .). She never calls Clytemnestra 'mother', though Agamemnon is '*mon père*' slightly more often than '*Seigneur*' — perhaps a significant detail.

1710   *Sun*. See note on 1262 above.

1814   *Come now, and take her* . . . Racine does not follow the prevailing theatrical tradition by which any play with a happy ending brought all the surviving characters together on the stage for a triumphant finale. Iphigenia is safe: but too much has been said and done for us to want to see this tragic family together again. When Agamemnon returned to Argos after the fall of Troy, it was to be murdered by his wife and her lover.

PHAEDRA

p. 105 Preface

p. 105, l. 5   *The most reasonable thing.* The statement has been diversely interpreted. I suggest that it is explained by the reference below to Aristotle (the embodiment of reason).

p. 105, l. 15   *when forced to reveal it.* This analysis goes no further than the end of the first act: it is here that the plot parts company with that of Euripides, who includes no interview of Phaedra with Hippolytus.

p. 105, l. 36   *Euripides was blamed* . . . The only known source for this remark is not classical, but an edition of the *Poetics* by P. Vettori (1560). Vettori goes on however to explain that Hippolytus is in fact guilty of *hubris* (commentary on chap. XIII).

p. 106, l. 6   *Virgil relates* . . . *Aeneid* VII 761ff. *Aesculapius.* See Ovid, *Metamorphoses* XV; but only sixteenth-century authorities have been found for the statement that Aricia was Athenian, not Italian.

p. 106, l. 14   *Plutarch. Life of Theseus* XXX—XXXI, XXV. This to Racine is history rather than legend.

p. 106, l. 41   *Socrates.* According to Diogenes Laertius, *Life of Socrates*, II 5.

p. 107, l. 5   *The true purpose of tragedy.* This was an almost universal tenet of the Renaissance and the seventeenth century, but will not be found in antiquity.

p. 110 Dramatis personae

Aricia. Her connection with Pallas (cf. ll. 53, 424) is Racine's invention.

Theramenes, Oenone, Ismene, Panope. Fictitious names bestowed by Racine on utility characters, but taken from Greek legend or history.

confidant. Cf. p. 212.

Trozen, a Greek by-form of the more usual *Troezen.* Gilbert Murray preferred it in his edition of Euripides (Oxford Classical Texts, 1902) and in his translation of *Hippolytus,* where, according to his principles of pronunciation, it rhymes with 'serene'. According to the principles I adopt (cf. p. xiv) it rhymes with 'frozen'. I use it because 'Troezen' would be indistinguishable from 'treason'. The town, which was the birthplace of Theseus, is to be inherited by Hippolytus (ll. 480ff.). It lies opposite Athens on the Saronic Gulf. Euripides (alone of Racine's sources) set his tragedy there.

'Stage is a palace with arches. A chair at the beginning.' (M. Laurent, cf. p. 212.)

p. 111 Act I   Euripides (after a prologue) and Seneca both open their plays with Hippolytus, who dwells on his love of hunting and shows his hate for love. Here that impression is given, then corrected. The modern note is compensated by a wealth of mythological allusions.

12ff.   The river *Acheron* is in Epirus (cf. preface, p. 106 and ll. 743, 980); *Elis* and *Taenarum* (Cape Matapan), in the Peloponnese; the Icarian Sea, off Asia Minor (*Icarus*, son of Daedalus, has associations through the latter with Cnossos and Pasiphaë).

155   This scene follows Euripides fairly closely as far as line 269.

204   *that Barbarian's child.* The argument comes from Euripides; the nurse thinks Hippolytus will be tempted to usurp the throne. The son of an Athenian by a non-Athenian woman was considered a bastard.

255   *Ariadne.* A tragedy on the abandonment of Ariadne by Theseus on Naxos (cf. ll. 91, 657, and Plutarch) had been produced in Racine's theatre in 1672 (*Ariane*, by Corneille's younger brother Thomas).

270   For Phaedra's first sight of Hippolytus, and the shrine she built, Racine has drawn on the prologue spoken by Aphrodite in Euripides.

283   *I searched the entrails.* She inspected the victims' entrails (like Dido, *Aeneid* IV 64; cf. *Iphigenia* 203, 1317) to see whether the Gods were favourable to her prayers for composure of mind.

296   *I banished him.* Racine's invention.

351   Oenone is wrong — Phaedra's love remains incestuous, according to the morality of Racine's day, which he would neither have wished nor dared to flout. Athenian law in Euripides' time permitted marriage with a stepson (and his play never mentions incest, only adultery; his Theseus is never presumed dead); but not Christian canon law nor French civil law. Phaedra never believes Oenone, cf. l. 714.

363   *ramparts that Minerva reared.* Athens.

453   *To waken pain.* There is less cruelty here than modern readers have thought (and certainly no sadism). All love, in the post-Petrarchan convention, is pain until it is rewarded by the beloved's favours (cf. Theseus' 'sighs' above, 449); Aricia's ambition is to awaken a response in the 'cold' Hippolytus. The thought of such a victory, which would not be worth winning in the case of Theseus (448), introduces in French the word *gloire* (cf. note on *Andromache* 419); she is using the language of the day to say how proud she would be to win the love of such a man.

473   *Alcides.* Hercules.

498ff.   Aricia, as daughter (according to Racine) of Pallas, belongs to the direct royal line, by-passed when Pandion II adopted Aegeus. Theseus was son of Aegeus: Hippolytus dutifully justifies his father's kingship by his exceptional services. See genealogical table, p. 109.

573   *incensed my Goddess.* Hippolytus has not had an answer to his declaration of love, and asks for one in seventeenth-century terms (his 'uncouthness' is only relative). A first declaration was an act of disrespect to a 'goddess': commonly the suitor, as Molière's Magdelon admits, 'finds ways of appeasing us later on' (*Précieuses ridicules* sc. 4).

639   *Yes, Prince.* Racine follows Seneca fairly closely from here to *the thread of life and death* (659). From that point the Roman heroine descends to direct entreaty, and Racine goes his own way.

723   *Give it me.* She snatches it from the scabbard. In Seneca Hippolytus himself draws, but seeing Phaedra eager to die at his hands, flings the sword away.

751   This is the offer of the crown of Athens (for Phaedra's son, cf. above, ll. 738f.). The word 'honours', in English and French, can = 'regalia'.

936ff.   Words appropriate equally to the true situation and the false accusation which Phaedra has already authorised. It is uncertain whether we should take them as a conscious equivocation.

1030   The use of the sword as evidence (cf. ll. 909ff.) is found in Seneca.

1057   The confrontation with Hippolytus is freely adapted from Euripides.

1086   *Neptune.* Cf. l. 621. Euripides and Seneca both adopt the legend making the God Theseus' father.

1157   *Pillars of Hercules.* Straits of Gibraltar.

1176   The Homeric Gods swear by the Styx.

1295   The *urn* comes from the *Aeneid*, VI 432. Minos did become judge of the dead; but Seneca refers to him as still alive and king of Crete. The Roman Phaedra expects punishment after death — this form of hyperbolical self-denunciation is fairly common in his characters. It is doubtful whether an ancient Greek would have thought she deserved it. Virgil shows her after death in company with others who died for love, in the *lugentes campi* — sad but free from torment (*Aeneid* VI 445ff.).

1310   *never reaped the sweets.* Critics interpret these words as an impenitent hankering after the sweets of sin; but the context makes it natural to read them as a plea in extenuation of that sin, which was never committed in act.

1383   Hippolytus plans nothing less than war against his father, on the ground that Phaedra's falsehoods have made Theseus act unjustly. It is surprising that he expects aid from other Greek states: but some might be expected to give shelter to Aricia as a legitimate claimant to the throne (as France did to the Stuarts).

1412   This miraculous temple (to which Hippolytus failed to appeal in defending himself before his father) looks like a hasty expedient by Racine to solve Aricia's dilemma. It has been suggested that his audience would have thought of a French form of marriage, irregular but valid, consisting of an exchange of promises in a church before witnesses, but without a priest. In ancient Greece or Rome marriage did involve torches, but not vows nor temples; seventeenth-century dramatists base their descriptions on the type of (Catholic) ceremony familiar to their public.

1521ff.   The narrative of Hippolytus' death comes of course in all the versions of the story; but only in Racine's does the hero attack and wound the monster.

1617ff.   The brief finale is Racine's own. The suffering of Theseus is brought out far more than in the ancient sources; and Phaedra's death, with the word purity on her lips — in which several critics have seen an aspiration which is almost a redemption — is poles apart from her hysterical suicide over Hippolytus' mangled remains in Seneca.

1662   *Medea*. The magician had come to Athens as wife of Aegeus after being abandoned by Jason in Corinth. She had tried to poison Theseus when he arrived to claim his birthright. An opera on that subject, *Thésée*, by Quinault and Lully, had been played in Paris in 1675.

ATHALIAH

p. 156 Preface
p. 156, l. 33   *a boy of nine or ten*. Racine does not mention that both Old Testament accounts (II Kings 11.21, II Chronicles 24.1) say that Joash was seven years old 'when he began to reign'.

p. 157, l. 6   *Pentecost* appears in our Old Testament as the Feast of Weeks, Leviticus 23.15—21 and Deuteronomy 16.9—11.

p. 157, l. 10   *these circumstances* are in particular the themes of the first chorus, 322—419.

p. 157, l. 18   *continuity of action*. This, like the use of a coryphaeus, shows closer imitation of the Greek model than in *Esther*. (It may not have been a very popular innovation, since it abolished intervals.) In *Esther* the chorus sometimes sings in the middle of acts, and ends the action with a long song of thanksgiving — both departures from Greek practice which Racine does not repeat here.

p. 157, l. 29   *from the Gospel*. See John 11.51.

p. 157, l. 34   *Zechariah*. See II Chron. 24.15—23 (cf. Matthew 23.35) and ll. 1221—2 below, with note.

p. 158, l. 3   *This scene*, III 7, i.e. ll. 1177—1265. *episode*, in the sense of added incident, cf. *Poetics* XVII, end.

p. 158, l. 6   *prophets*, I Samuel 10.5.

p. 158, l. 9   *a minstrel*. II Kings 3.15. The French text quotes from the Vulgate, *Adducite mihi psaltem*.

p. 160 Dramatis personae

The characters from Joash to Zechariah are biblical; so are Azariah,

Ishmael and Mattan. The other characters are fictitious, and the names, including Eliakim, come from other parts of the Old Testament.

I have said that the forms of the names are taken from the Authorised Version (except that of Josabeth, which comes from II Paralipomena (Chronicles) in the Vulgate: Jehosheba or Jehoshebeath was too unwieldy). Racine used the Vulgate forms except for 'Joad', which he says in his preface comes from Josephus.

confidant, see p. 212.

The *scene* is transferred from the normal room in a royal palace to one in the Temple precincts, which are the centre of the action and to which all the characters have occasion to come (except Athaliah, whose two entries are explained by special motives). For the scene-change in Act V, see note on l. 1828.

85   *Ahaziah.* II Kings 9.21—7, II Chron. 22.7—9.

117f.   *Ahab.* I Kings 21.17—19, II Kings 9.24—6.

119ff.   *Jezebel.* II Kings 9.30—7.

123f.   Elijah's triumph over the priests of Baal, I Kings 18.19—40.

126ff.   Elijah announces a drought, I Kings 17.1ff.

128   Elisha brings a dead child to life, II Kings 4.32—7.

216   Racine chooses to follow II Chron. 23 rather than the version of II Kings 11.4ff. which suggests that Jehoiada brought in soldiers. Cf. preface.

534   The dream of evil portent is familiar in modern and even ancient tragedy. The content of this one must go back to Aeneas' dream vision of his dead brother Hector, *Aeneid* II. There is no dream in any of the biblical accounts of Athaliah.

537   Racine wrote, literally, 'It was during the horror of a deep night' (*C'était pendant l'horreur d'une profonde nuit*). *Horreur* could in his time still suggest the original Latin sense – the emotion that causes the hair to stand on end. He had noted a line of Aeschylus' *Libation-Bearers* in his copy, where the chorus speaks of the horrible cry of Clytemnestra in a midnight dream, which has caused her to send offerings to the tomb of the husband she murdered. It contains the expression *phobos orthothrix* (l. 32); Racine translates, 'Fear that makes the hair stand up . . . ' and adds 'Terrible dream'.

662ff.   This scene contains unexpected reminiscences of the opening episode of Euripides' *Ion* (308—23), where Ion, brought up an orphan in Apollo's temple at Delphi, meets Creusa (his mother, though neither of them knows it) and answers her questions.

765   For the killing of Ahab's sons (seventy, not eighty; but *soixante-dix fils de rois* is metrically impossible), see II Kings 10.1—7.

1092   To a Jew this expression was equivalent to 'Tell the truth' (Joshua 7.19, John 9.24), as Racine must have discovered.

1116f.   *Abiram and Dathan.* Numbers 16.1—35; *Doeg*, I Samuel 22.18; *Ahithopel*, II Samuel 15.12; 16.23; 17.1, 23.

1167   The golden calf, of which the worship was revived in Israel (II Kings 10.29), was identified in Racine's time with the Egyptian bull-god Apis. Cf. 1449 below.

1204   A Hebraism, cf. II Chron. 7.14: My people, which are called by my name (but see Authorised Version, margin: 'Heb., upon whom my name is called'). The Vulgate, which Racine must have followed, trans-lates literally, *super quos invocatum est nomen meum.*

1221   On Jehoida's prophecy, see preface, p. 157. The borrowings are mainly from Deuteronomy, Jeremiah, Isaiah and the Psalms.

1221—2   Note the footnote, and see preface, ibid. Only Racine's comments make the allusion to Zechariah explicit: the characters in the tragedy cannot understand, and it seems unlikely that Jehoiada does. If so, the knowledge would throw a new light on his perseverance in his plans; but it has been shown that St Thomas Aquinas and some other authorities laid it down that a prophet, though inspired, might not understand his own message.

1323   Moreau's score ends the act with a setting, half solo, half for full choir, of the last four lines of Jehoiada's prophecy (1250—4).

1346   *Jephtha's daughter.* Judges 11.30—40.

1448ff.   Cf. Exodus 32.25—9.

1523ff.   Abraham was commanded by God to sacrifice Isaac in Moriah, Genesis 22. Racine mentions in the preface that the site was traditionally identified with that of the Temple.

1828   Stage-direction. The curtain behind the throne, which has formed the backcloth up to now, is drawn aside to reveal (presumably) another backcloth with a view of the Temple interior, imagined as something like the nave of a cathedral, which is what the frontispiece of the first edition shows. It will be remembered that this play was never in fact produced in Racine's lifetime, only 'rehearsed' without costumes or scenery (cf. Introduction p. 154). The convention whereby the drawing of a curtain opens up the interior of a building, common early in the seventeenth century, was continued in some comedies (cf. Molière's *Dom Juan* III 5), and complete changes of elaborate scenery were a feature of French opera, and of the 'machine-plays' that had preceded them — so called precisely because of their free use of mech-anical devices for 'flying' scenery and showing aerial flights or descents of deities. Tragedy, however, had avoided all this.

1853   *Gideon.* Judges 7.15—23.

PRONUNCIATION OF PROPER NAMES

(See p. xiv)
The symbols used are those of *The Concise Oxford Dictionary*.

Abī'ram
A'chĕron (-k-)
Achill'ēs (-kill'-)
Āe'gēus (2 syllables)
Āegī'na (-ji-)
Agamem'non
Ăhăzī'ah
Ahĭ'thophel
Alcī'des (-sĭ-, not -sē-)
Andrŏ'măchē (-kē)
Antī'ŏpē
Ariad'nē
Arī'cĭa (or like 'Patricia')
Astȳ'ănax
Ăthălī'ah
Ā'trēus (2 syllables)
Atrī'dāē
Āu'lis (aw-, not ow-)
Ăzărī'ah
Cēphis'sa (sē-)
Cer'cȳon (ser'syon)
Clĕŏ'nē
Clytemnes'tra
Cŏcȳ'tus (kŏsī'-)
Dā'than
Elī'ăkim
Ē'lis
Epī'rus
Erech'thēus (-k-, 3 syllables)
Erĭ'phĭlē
Eurȳ'bătēs
Hĕ'cŭba
Hermī'ŏnē
Hippŏ'lȳtus
Hȳ'men
Ī'cărus
I'lĭum
I'phĭgĕnī'a
Ismē'nē
Jĕhŏ'ram
Jĕhŏī'ada
Jŏ'săbeth
Mēdē'a
Megāē'ra (-jē-)
Mĕnĕlā'us (4 syllables)
Mī'nos
Mī'nŏtaur

Mycē'nāē (mĭsē'nē)
Ōenŏ'nē
Ores'tēs
Pasĭ'phăē (4 syllables)
Pan'ŏpē
Patroc'lus
Pē'lēus (2 syllables)
Pĕrĭbōē'a (-ē-)
Phāē'dra (-ē-)
Phōē'nix (fē-)
Pīrĭ'thŏus (4 syllables)
Pit'thēus (or like 'Matthew')
Pŏlȳ'xĕna (-ix-)
Procrus'tēs
Pȳ'lădes
Pȳr'rhus
Să'lămis
Scăman'der
Scī'ro (sī-)
Scȳ'thĭans (sĭ'-, 'th' as in 'the')
Sī'nāī (2 syllables)
Sin'nis
Tāe'nărum
Tēlĕ'măchus (-k-)
Thĕră'mĕnēs
Thē'sēus (2 syllables)
Thȳes'tēs
Tȳn'dărus
Zĕchărī'ah (-k-)